Intricate Thicket

I0879560

Modern and Contemporary Poetics

Intricate Thicket

Reading Late Modernist Poetries

MARK SCROGGINS

THE UNIVERSITY OF ALABAMA PRESS

Tuscaloosa

The University of Alabama Press
Tuscaloosa, Alabama 35487–0380
uapress.ua.edu

Typeface: Caslon and Museo Sans

Manufactured in the United States of America

Cover image: *Entanglement* (detail) © 2009 by Carol Prusa; silverpoint, graphite, titanium white with acrylic binder on acrylic hemisphere with metal leaf, fiber optics and video, 60 x 60 x 30 inches; courtesy of the artist
Cover design: Michele Myatt Quinn

∞

The paper on which this book is printed meets the minimum requirements of American National Standard for Information Sciences—Permanence of Paper for Printed Library Materials, ANSI Z39.48–1984.

Cataloging-in-Publication data is available from the Library of Congress.
ISBN: 978-0-8173-5804-4
E-ISBN: 978-0-8173-8806-5

for
Eric Murphy Selinger
and
Norman Finkelstein

Contents

III. POETICS

Acknowledgments

Whatever the myths might say about the solitude of the writer, I've found that writing about poetry is an eminently social process. Most of these pieces owe their first publication, or their very existence, to editors of periodicals, books, or websites: Zach Barocas, Dan Beachy-Quick, Joel Bettridge, Joseph Donahue, the *FlashPoint* editorial collective, Ed Foster, C. S. Giscombe, Eric Hoffman, Paul Naylor, Lou Rowan, Eric Murphy Selinger, and John Tranter. Some of them began life as talks given at various conferences, including the Modern Language Association's annual meeting, the University of Louisville Conference on Literature and Culture since 1900, "Eye, Ear, & Mind: A Conference on the Poetry of Ronald Johnson" at the University of Buffalo in 2000, and "To Gather Us In: A Conference on Poetry and Poetics in Honor of John Taggart" at Shippensburg University in 2001. "Queen Victoria's Birthday Present" was delivered at Boise State University in 2010, at the gracious invitation of Janet Holmes. Perhaps half of the pages here were written for Herbert Leibowitz's *Parnassus: Poetry in Review*, and the ruthless blue-pencilling to which they were subjected at Herb's and Ben Downing's hands has taught me more about writing prose than any number of graduate degrees.

Many of the ideas here, such as they are, were talked out over the years in electronic, telephonic, and even face-to-face exchanges with poets, writers, and critics much sharper than myself, whose insights I have mercilessly pillaged and refunctioned: Robert Archambeau, Joel Bettridge, William Bradley, Robert Creeley, Joseph Donahue, Rachel Blau DuPlessis, Norman Finkelstein, Benjamin Friedlander, C. S. Giscombe, Alan Golding, Richard Greene, John Latta, John Matthias, Paul Naylor, Peter O'Leary, Ted Pearson, Marjorie Perloff, Peter Quartermain, Susan Schultz, Eric Murphy Selinger, Jessica Smith, John Taggart, Barrett Watten, and Robert Zamsky. I owe a lot to the keen-eyed students in various seminars and workshops I've taught on poetry, poetics, and biography over the years, among them P. Jill Anderson, Su Carlson, Laura Quinlan DeJong, Jeanne Genis, A. J. Ferguson, Raymond Gibson,

Peggy Hamilton, Shannon O'Brien, Michael J. Pagán, Simone Puleo, and Liz Rodrigues. The English Department of Florida Atlantic University has always warmly supported my work. When I began writing the pieces collected here, I was a new assistant professor; now, as one of the aging silverbacks of the department, I still find talking to my colleagues a perpetually stimulating experience. Among them, Eric Berlatsky, Adam Bradford, Ayşe Papatya Bucak, Oliver Buckton, Andrew Furman, Taylor Hagood, and Lisa Swanstrom are especially valued interlocutors.

Of course, my closest interlocutor remains my colleague, friend, and partner, Jennifer A. Low, who sacrificed many hours more profitably devoted to her own writing in deflating my balloon-like sentences and wrestling my syntax into something resembling English. I thank her with much love, as I thank our daughters, Philippa and Daphne, for not (too much) minding their father's frequent absence in the land of laptop, notebook, and legal pad.

* * *

"Coming Down from Black Mountain," "The Palace of Wisdom and the Six-Minute Poem," "Truth, Beauty, and the Remote Control," "Dark Matters," "Marrow-Bones and Turkish Delight," and "One Last Modernist" appeared in *Parnassus: Poetry in Review*; "Still Diving the Mauberley Trench" appeared first in *Parnassus*, then in different forms in *The Salt Companion to John Matthias* and as an afterword to Matthias's *Collected Longer Poems*; "Z-Sited Path: Late Zukofsky and His Tradition" appeared in *The World in Time and Space: Towards a History of Innovative American Poetry in Our Time*; "Notes and Numbers" first appeared in part in *Facture*, and was reprinted in *Ronald Johnson: Life and Works*; "Johnson's American England" appeared in *Ronald Johnson: Life and Works*; "A Note on Johnson's Anagrams" appeared in *Golden Handcuffs Review*; "The Piety of Terror" appeared first in *FlashPoint*, and was reprinted in *Jacket*; "Mules and Drugs and R&B" appeared in *American Book Review*; "Woodpaths, Obscure" appeared in *Jacket*; part of "A New Negative Capability" appeared in *Talisman: A Journal of Contemporary Poetry and Poetics*, and another part in *Colorado Review*; "The Lighthouses" appeared in *Big Bridge*; "Sound and Vision" appeared first in *FlashPoint*, and was reprinted in *Jacket2*; "A Fragmentary Poetics" was published on *The Cultural Society* website.

Introduction

> I saw the sweet-briar & bon-fire & strawberry wire now
> relaxed into intricate thicket.
>
> Ronald Johnson, "Upon First Opening a Cuckoo"

These nineteen pieces are a selection from what I've written over the past decade and a half about late twentieth- and early twenty-first-century poetry and closely related matters. The vast majority of them are occasional: they were called into existence by an editor's invitation, or were concocted as talks to be delivered at some gathering, scholarly or otherwise. Most of them directly address particular books of poetry or the careers of particular poets. I've never been particularly comfortable writing about "schools" of poetry or overall "tendencies," and as I've grown older I've become increasingly aware of how very little any one reader can know of a poetic landscape that seems richer, more densely populated, and more multifarious with each passing year. Every time I hear some savvy commentator writing about the "state of contemporary poetry," I think of Walt Whitman's wonderfully daffy line about containing multitudes, and I think of Charles Bernstein's variation: "I contain no multitudes; I can't even contain myself."[1]

For a number of years, I was fascinated by the concept of "postmodernism." I threw it around in my writing. I read scores of books on the subject. I even used the term in the title of several of the courses I taught. More and more, however, I've grown weary of the entire conversation around the subject. David Harvey has done brilliant work in describing our contemporary economic and geopolitical era as one of "postmodernity," and Fredric Jameson, building on the work of the Marxist economist Ernest Mandel, has made a compelling case for postmodernism as the cultural condition of "late capitalism."[2] But neither of them—even Jameson, who writes (if in passing) about Bob Perelman, a poet I very much admire—has much to say that seems to me of use in reading and describing contemporary poetry. And I am no more convinced by anyone else's explanation of contemporary poetry's postmodernism. Whenever I read a book or article that attempts to define the "postmodern" in poetry, I end up discovering that whatever *differentium* this latest writer has come up with was already present—back in modernism itself.

If there is any term that speaks to what interests me in contemporary poetry, it's a phrase that one is more likely to hear in British than in American circles: "late modernism." The "high" modernist poets—Ezra Pound, T. S. Eliot, Gertrude Stein, William Carlos Williams, Mina Loy, Marianne Moore, and so forth—were a fearless bunch. It was not merely in their break with the forms and meters of English verse since Chaucer—Moore's syllabic stanzas, Pound's experiments in seat-of-the-pants quantitative verse, the jagged, abruptly lineated speech prosodies of Williams and Loy—that the modernists distinguished themselves. They dealt in fragments: splintered shards of speech, broken-off narratives and conversations, unfinished gestures. They brought into question the notion of the poet's "voice"—that singular organ so vaunted by the Romantics, but really subtending English poetry from its earliest days. They alluded, incessantly, to previous cultural artifacts. They refused to "say," straightforwardly, what they meant, in ways that hearkened back to the Metaphysicals and the *trobar clus*. And some of them knit their fragments, their allusions, and their opacities into redoubtably complex and fiercely resonant wholes—"intricate thickets," in a phrase I've borrowed from Ronald Johnson.

My sense of the presence of modernism in the contemporary moment is close to that of Marjorie Perloff, who argues in her *21st-Century Modernism* that "the aesthetic of early modernism has provided the seed of the materialist poetic which is increasingly our own."[3] If I were to attempt to trace the genealogy of the "materialist poetic" of the writing I find most compelling and congenial, I'd reach back to that first generation of English-language "high" modernist poets, and to the poets of the generation that followed them—especially Louis Zukofsky, Lorine Niedecker, and George Oppen. But this collection in no way intended to be a systematic history of late modernist poetry, or even of the late modernist poetry that I value: rather, it's a series of snapshots, of individual and small group portraits of poets at particular moments in their careers. Nor is it intended to be an exhaustive critical analysis, but a series of forays in the spirit of *Here: these are some poems, some books that have caught my attention—perhaps they deserve yours as well; you decide.*

I'm slightly ambivalent about the term "poetries" in my title; as one friend remarks, you don't find biochemists and inorganic chemists calling their shared discipline "chemistries," though what they do is surely further apart than what Susan Howe and, say, Billy Collins do. But I think the plural, as awkward as it may sound, gets at something crucial. The poets I write about here are indeed all working in roughly the same verbal medium (though Ian Hamilton Finlay certainly pushes the envelope), but their approaches, their goals, their overall *ethoi* are different enough to call for some marker of plurality, some recognition of the sometimes radically diverse paths they have taken.

These essays bear the marks of their moments. Having completed his enormous *The Alphabet*, Ron Silliman has gone on to an even more ambitious project, *The Universe*. Anne Carson has published a number of books since *The Beauty of the Husband*, all of them of interest, none of them recapturing (to my mind) the shattering impact of *Eros the Bittersweet*. Ted Enslin's stream of books came to a close, alas, with his death in 2011, and Ian Hamilton Finlay's forty-year experiment in garden poetics ended when he died in 2006. (Happily, his garden Little Sparta is now maintained by a trust.) But John Matthias remains as strong a poet as ever, as evidenced by *Kedging* and *Trigons*, and the shoal of new work in his most recent *Collected Short Poems*.

Any attempt to capture an inclusive picture of contemporary poetry—even of a particular corner of contemporary poetry—in a given moment is doomed to incompletion and partiality. I have opted to present these pieces largely as they were first published (though I have removed some infelicities, revised some judgments, eliminated some moments of repetition from essay to essay, and replaced citations to reflect the most recently available texts). Generally speaking, I have refrained from attempting to update them, to make them all exercises in criticism of the second decade of our millennium.

Three pieces here might seem anomalous. In "One Last Modernist," I write about the career of Guy Davenport, a writer better known for his essays, translations, and fiction than for his poems. Davenport was, however, a poet of great gifts, even if he tended to dismiss his own work in verse as youthful dabblings, and in general I've found that his work speaks as much or more to contemporary poets as to any other readership. "Queen Victoria's Birthday Present" is a series of thoughts about the problems of literary biography, largely prompted by my work on *The Poem of a Life: A Biography of Louis Zukofsky*, and attempts to tie the practice of biography-writing to some principles articulated in Zukofsky's own statements of poetics. "A Fragmentary Poetics" is perhaps an exercise in self-indulgence, an attempt to examine and define some aspects of my own practice as a poet.

Notes

Epigraph: Ronald Johnson, *The Book of the Green Man* (New York: Norton, 1967) 51.

1. Charles Bernstein, *My Way: Speeches and Poems* (Chicago: U of Chicago P, 1999) 97.

2. David Harvey, *The Condition of Postmodernity: An Enquiry into the Origins of Cultural Change* (Oxford, Eng.: Blackwell, 1990); Fredric Jameson, *Postmodernism; or, The Cultural Logic of Late Capitalism* (Durham, NC: Duke UP, 1991).

3. Marjorie Perloff, *21st Century Modernism: The "New" Poetics* (Oxford, Eng.: Blackwell, 2002) 3.

Intricate Thicket

I

Longer Views

Coming Down from Black Mountain

Charles Olson, Robert Duncan, Robert Creeley

Five and a half decades ago, as the summer of 1957 wore into fall, the poet Charles Olson—who stood six foot six in his stockings, who had been in his day a champion high school orator, John F. Kennedy's freshman writing instructor at Harvard, the discoverer of Melville's marginalia, an organizer on FDR's 1944 reelection campaign, and an amateur archaeologist in the Yucatán, and who was now the rector of tiny Black Mountain College in the western wilds of North Carolina—locked the college's doors for the last time and handed the keys to its new owners. Classes having ended in late 1956, Olson had been selling the campus off piecemeal, building by building, field by field. Now the final assets had been liquidated, and Black Mountain was no more.

Opinions would differ on Olson's few years at the helm of Black Mountain: some would argue that he had driven the college—always on shaky financial ground—over the edge into bankruptcy, while others insisted that he'd done the best he could with an untenable situation, and managed to produce a remarkable efflorescence of art and writing on a very frayed shoestring.[1]

Established in 1933 by the Classicist John Andrew Rice, Black Mountain had always put the arts at the heart of its curriculum, and under the direction of the Bauhaus veteran Josef Albers, it had become a center of experimentation like no other. There were no set curricula or courses of study: the students designed their own education, and students and faculty lived in a communal setting that over the years fostered numerous collaborative endeavors. The artists and musicians who served on the faculty, or who visited for the summer sessions, represent a cross-section of creative thought in mid-century America: Albers and his wife, the fabric artist Anni Albers, Walter Gropius, John Cage, Merce Cunningham, Willem de Kooning, Franz Kline, David Tudor, Stefan Wolpe, the photographers Aaron Siskind and Harry Callahan. And many of the students who worked with them went on to become at least as famous: Robert Rauschenberg, Kenneth Noland, and Cy Twombly are only the best known. Buckminster Fuller raised his first geodesic dome at Black Mountain; John Cage staged his first multimedia "happening" there.

While Olson was a trained dancer and had well-developed interests in contemporary music and visual art, one of the effects of his rectorship was to turn the college into a free-form writing workshop, a hive of literary activity that gave rise to the so-called Black Mountain poets. Previously, Black Mountain had been known for its visual arts teaching. In its waning days, as most of its artists and musicians were packing their bags, Olson called in his poet friends Robert Creeley and Robert Duncan to teach the dwindling student body. Their teaching styles could not have been more different, and were emblematic of the differences in their poetry. Olson himself would lecture in bravura four- or five-hour sessions, the classroom's air growing blue and acrid with the smoke from his cigarettes, its chalkboards overflowing with names, dates, quotations, and diagrams; it was an endless, authoritarian, oceanic monologue.[2] The shy Creeley, who sometimes had to be physically forced into the classroom, would read aloud, talk about poets he loved—William Carlos Williams, Hart Crane—and discuss the jazz musicians whose works had so influenced his own.[3]

Duncan's seminars were exercises in the most basic building blocks of poetry: they began with vowel sounds, then moved on to consonants and whole syllables (eventually, one assumes, they arrived at lines and stanzas). Like Albers, Duncan saw himself as exploring the foundational materials of his art. Given that he usually began his seminars at 8 A.M. and that Olson's lectures often ran past midnight, their students must have been seriously sleep deprived.[4]

Literary historians love "movements": the Imagists, the Symbolists, the Objectivists, the Language poets. Movements—along with schools and groups—are like file folders: they give scholars a pigeonhole in which to stow poets, allowing future generations to pluck out the major ones—"See, he never fit into that category in the first place!"—while leaving the minor ones to gather dust. It's true that Olson and Creeley influenced each other profoundly, and that Duncan looked to both of them as "fire-sources" of the contemporary. The three dropped each others' names frequently in print and conversation, and to some degree logrolled for each other. But what really got people thinking of them—along with their students Ed Dorn, Joel Oppenheimer, Jonathan Williams, John Wieners, Michael Rumaker, and Fielding Dawson, and a penumbral crowd of others who'd never set foot at Black Mountain, including Larry Eigner, Denise Levertov, Cid Corman, and Paul Blackburn—as a *movement* was Donald Allen's 1960 anthology, *The New American Poetry 1945–1960*.[5]

The New American Poetry was the countercultural backpacker's volume of choice for at least two decades, a veritable scripture of hipsterdom: a well-thumbed copy of the anthology, with its familiar cover of flag-evoking red and white stripes, was to the young person of the 1960s, weary of the polished, formal ironies of Richard Wilbur and the Boston Brahmin angst of Robert Lowell, what a copy of *Atlas Shrugged* was to the adolescent neoconservative of the 1980s.

Critics have carped at Allen's selections for a half-century now—such is the fate of the anthologist. Allen, an editor at Grove Press with a good eye for what was up-and-coming in poetry, did his best to make sense of a vast sea of poetry that was largely invisible to the readers of the literary journals of the 1950s, and that had entirely failed to register with the editors (Donald Hall, Robert Pack, and Louis Simpson) of *New Poets of England and America* three years before.[6] Rather than present his unfamiliar poets alphabetically or by date of birth, he sorted them by geography and aesthetic school. The results are almost too well known to bear repeating: Beat poets, New York School poets, the San Francisco Renaissance, and—leading off the book, with Olson at their head—the Black Mountain poets.

The New American Poetry is, in fact, a rather Olson-centric affair: not only does he lead off the book, but also Allen gives him more space than any of his forty-three other poets. And the first of the prose manifestos appended to the end of the anthology is by Olson as well. "Projective Verse," as the essay is titled, was first published in *Poetry New York* in 1950, the year before Olson went down to North Carolina. If there is a single theoretical text central to the Black Mountain poets, this is it. "Projective Verse" is one of those turning-point documents in poetics, like Wordsworth's Preface to the 1800 *Lyrical Ballads*, Mallarmé's "Crise de vers," or Pound's "A Few Don'ts by an Imagiste." Olson wrote it, of course, for the usual reason: to defend and explain his own work. It argues for what Olson called "composition by field," as opposed to "closed" verse, which is to say the formal poetry fostered by New Criticism. But "Projective Verse" is more than just another manifesto on behalf of free verse. Rather, it advocates a principle of movement. The poem, according to Olson, is not emotion recollected in tranquility, but rather a "high energy-construct [sic] and, at all points, an energy discharge."[7] As such, it is not an artifact, not a well-wrought urn, but a process.

In Olson's earlier work, "projectivism" operates largely at the level of syntax. "The Kingfishers" (1949), a mid-length poem that opens *The New American Poetry*, makes itself a "high energy-construct" by means of its hailstorm of quotation (Rimbaud, Chairman Mao, Plutarch, Francis Parkman on Cortez and the Aztecs, Norbert Wiener on cybernetics) and speculation. Nevertheless, it also makes a rather clear and coherent assertion: the West has reached a cultural and spiritual dead-end, and we must look for new sources of vitality, whether in the Chairman's East or the cultural traces of prehistoric eras.

Much of what makes Olson's poetry so exciting—and, at times, so frustrating—can be seen in the first lines of the poem's second section:

I thought of the E on the stone, and of what Mao said
la lumiere"
                    but the kingfisher
de l'aurore"
                    but the kingfisher flew west
est devant nous!
                    he got the color of his breast
                    from the heat of the setting sun![8]

First, and most obviously, there's good old-fashioned modernist allusiveness here, in this case to Plutarch's essay "On the E at Delphi," to a 1948 speech of Mao (as related to Olson by a French correspondent), and to a folktale about the kingfisher and Noah's ark. Olson cross-cuts his sources, so that Mao's words intersect with the kingfisher story. That the poem was composed in the age of the typewriter is evident from the spacing of its lines, achieved by tab-stop. ("It is the advantage of the typewriter," Olson writes in "Projective Verse," "that, due to its rigidity and its space precisions, it can, for a poet, indicate exactly the breath, the pauses, the suspensions even of syllables, the juxtapositions even of parts of phrases, which he intends" [OP 245].) And those closing but unopened quotation marks? Like Olson's unclosed parentheses, they're part and parcel of his idiom, of a stammering lyricism in which the syntax constantly stumbles over itself and changes course. "Get on with it," he urges in "Projective Verse," "keep moving, keep in, speed, the nerves, their speed, the perceptions, theirs, the acts, the split second acts, the whole business, keep it moving as fast as you can, citizen" (OP 240).

Pound is of course on Olson's mind (in the late forties he had regularly visited the poet at St. Elizabeths), and if he doesn't entirely commit himself to Pound's collagist method, he emulates Pound in adopting a moral stance:

But I have my kin, if for no other reason than
(as he said, next of kin) I commit myself, and,
given my freedom, I'd be a cad
if I didn't. Which is most true. (CO 92)

There are lessons to be learned from the fall of the Mesoamerican empires and the cessation of the Kampuchean trade in kingfisher feathers, and these, Olson is convinced, are of great value to the West in 1949. "I pose you your question," he ends the poem. "Shall you uncover honey / where maggots are? // I hunt among stones" (CO 93).

Those "stones"—think "stony rubbish," handfuls of dust, fragments shored against ruins—should alert us to the poem's most important antecedent. For "The Kingfishers" is, of course—like Crane's *The Bridge*, Williams's *Spring and All*, and Hugh MacDiarmid's *A Drunk Man Looks at the Thistle*—a response to *The Waste Land*. In 1922, readers could take *The Waste Land* as a formally innovative expression of the impasse Western culture had reached with the Great War. By 1949, however, Eliot looked like the archbishop of an all-too-familiar aesthetic and social conformity. Rimbaud had grown up—as Rimbauds are too apt to do—into Matthew Arnold. The cure for what ails the West, "The Kingfishers" suggests, can be found not by evoking the wisdom of an Anglo-Catholic "thunder," but by digging down to the deepest sources of Western thought.

Everything you might possibly want to know about "The Kingfishers"—the circumstances of its composition, its evolution through various drafts, the sources of its allusions—can be found in Ralph Maud's exhaustive *What Does Not Change: The Significance of Charles Olson's "The Kingfishers."* There's nothing unusual about this kind of study (how many books have been published on *The Waste Land*?), but there's a touch of the obsessive in Maud's systematic hunting-down of Olson's sources. The whole book, it would seem, is designed to set straight the "errancies" in Guy Davenport's 1974 article "Scholia and Conjectures for Olson's 'The Kingfishers.'"[9] Maud's pedantry is even more evident in his most recent venture into Olsoniana, *Charles Olson at the Harbor*, subtitled *A Biography*. "This is a reactive biography" are Maud's first words. What he reacts against is Tom Clark's 1990 *Charles Olson: The Allegory of a Poet's Life*, a book so flawed, in Maud's view, that "my complaints can now with honor be put into a book-length format where, having grown from righteous nitpicking through glorious indignation, they can be a castle of perseverence against the spread of Clark's misinformation."[10] Maud cites Boswell's desire to correct the errors of Sir John Hawkins's and Mrs. Piozzi's lives of Johnson; but Boswell was never so Miltonic in his rhetoric.

Clark's biography, while solid in certain ways, reeks of disillusioned discipleship, most evidently in his relentless negative psychologizing and his tendency to put the worst possible spin on Olson's every action. But Clark's shortcomings hardly justify the existence of *Charles Olson at the Harbor*. Far better is Maud's earlier *Charles Olson's Reading*, also subtitled *A Biography*.[11] Olson was nothing if not bookish, and Maud's year-by-year tracing of the books Olson read, bought, and borrowed amounts to a unique record of a life lived largely among books.

Olson had been trained as a scholar at Harvard and Wesleyan, but he brought to his scholarship a passion and intensity not often found among the library-carrel crowd. Rarest of all was his synthesizing vision, his ability to step outside the normal paths of the critic and literary historian. In *Call Me Ishmael* (1947), a study of Herman Melville that rode the crest of the Melville revival of the 1930s, Olson demonstrated not only how Melville's reading of Shakespeare's tragedies shaped *Moby-Dick* but also the complex dependence of his imagination on the whaling industry and on America's spatial imagination of itself.

Olson certainly believed in the value of research. It was by dint of sheer tenacious spadework that he discovered the remnants of Melville's personal library, and through hard reading of Melville's marginalia that he discovered the extent of the links between *King Lear* and *Moby-Dick*. In *A Bibliography on America for Ed Dorn* (based on a letter he wrote to Dorn when he was a student at Black Mountain), he stresses the value of "*PRIMARY DOCUMENTS*":

> And to hook on here is a lifetime of assiduity. Best thing to do is *to dig one thing or place or man* until you yourself know more abt that than is possible to any other man. It doesn't matter whether it's Barbed Wire or Pemmican or Paterson or Iowa. But *exhaust* it. Saturate it. Beat it.
>
> And then U KNOW everything else very fast: one saturation job (it might take 14 years). And you're in, forever. (OP 306–07)

Many of Olson's shorter poems evince, if not "a lifetime of assiduity," at least some hard and concentrated reading. "There Was a Youth Whose Name Was Thomas Granger" (1946 or 1947) recounts, from trial transcripts and historical narrative, a grim incident of bestiality in colonial New England (CO 43–45). "Anecdotes of the Late War" (1955, CO 334–40) is a breathless, narrative-sprinkled analysis of the relationship between the Industrial Revolution and the American Civil War. Parts of it read, as do many of Olson's poems, like transcriptions of a graduate seminar. He was always a teacher at heart.

But Olson's own "saturation job," which is to say his major subject, was his hometown of Gloucester, Massachusetts, a fishing village to which he retreated after Black Mountain dissolved and where he based himself for the rest of his life. Just as Williams took Paterson, New Jersey, as the kernel for his long poem, Olson initially addressed his *Maximus Poems*, the vast project he began in 1950 and worked on until his death in 1970, to Gloucester. More specifically, the first poems are addressed to Gloucester native Vincent Ferrini, who had solicited Olson for his new literary magazine.

The first poem, "I, Maximus of Gloucester, to You," opens with one of the bravura passages in American letters:

> Off-shore, by islands hidden in the blood
> jewels & miracles, I, Maximus
> a metal hot from boiling water, tell you
> what is a lance, who obeys the figures of
> the present dance[12]

The outsized Olson has assumed an outsized persona, that of *homo maximus*, the "biggest man." Olson-Maximus, in these early poems, is rather a scold, berating townspeople for their materialism ("all is become billboards"), their passive submission to a regime of "pejorocracy" (the rule of the worse—a Poundian word). What Olson is proposing as an alternative is unclear, but he clearly wants his fellow citizens to somehow revitalize their relationship to their environment, their vocations, their community. Maximus calls it simply "form," and his first figure for it is the bird's nest:

> one loves only form,
> and form only comes
> into existence when
> the thing is born
>   born of yourself, born
>   of hay and cotton struts,
>   of street-pickings, wharves, weeds
>   you carry in, my bird
>   of a bone of a fish
>   of a straw, or will
>   of a color, of a bell
>   of yourself, torn

Another figure is the ever-moving, phallically uplifted "mast":

> in! in! the bow-sprit, bird, the beak
> in, the bend is, in, goes in, the form
> that which you make, what holds, which is

the law of object, strut after strut, what you are, what you must be, what
the force and throw up, can, right now hereinafter erect,
the mast, the mast, the tender
mast! (MO 6–8)

The *polis* is at the heart of Olson's concerns. But Gloucester's problems are more than just those of a fishing center in decline, more than the postwar anomie of a New England town. Olson wants to reassert the sense of a "human universe," which, in his view, had been lost around 450 BC, when Greek philosophy brought in the chilling instruments of "logic and classification" (OP 156).

In the letters he wrote Creeley from Mexico in 1951 (later published as *Mayan Letters*), Olson marvels at the way the contemporary natives of the Yucatán inhabit their bodies: "the flesh is worn as a daily thing, like the sun is . . . the individual peering out from that flesh is precisely himself, is, a curiously wandering animal . . . I come on, here, what seems to me the real, live clue to the results of what I keep gabbing about, *another* humanism."[13] This humanism Olson relates to Mayan glyphs, and these glyphs (like Chinese ideograms, according to Pound) have implications for contemporary poetics: "A Sumer poem or Maya glyph is more pertinent to our purposes than anything else, because each of these people & their workers had forms which unfolded directly from content (sd content itself a disposition toward reality which understood man as only force in field of force containing multiple other expressions."[14]

To get beyond the impasse of classificatory reason, the "archaeologist of morning" (as Olson called himself) felt he had to dig beyond the colonial history of Gloucester. *Maximus Poems IV, V, VI* (1968) has a cover depicting Gondwanaland, the southern continent of Pangaea (MO 167). To say the least, Olson's historical scope has broadened: "my memory is / the history of time" (MO 256). The latter two-thirds of *The Maximus Poems* take as their subject the whole of human history and myth. (I suspect Olson considered Milton something of a piker, in that he settled for retelling a single origin-story.)

The Maximus Poems is a problematic proposition at best for the reader, not least because of is its endless allusiveness. For help, one might turn to George Butterick's enormous *Guide to The Maximus Poems of Charles Olson*.[15] Butterick is quite good at clarifying Olson's obscurities, but he rarely ventures a guess at what Olson *means* by them. I have no particular beef with allusiveness, or with "difficult" poetry in general. But one gets the sense, as one plunges deeper into the swamps of *Maximus*—its scope expanding from Gloucester and the Atlantic cod trade to encompass pre-Hellenic mythology, the Neolithic Era, even the beginnings of continental drift—that Olson himself doesn't know where he's going and has only the foggiest idea of how his materials relate to one another. Hayden Carruth calls *The Maximus Poems* "a huge and truly angelic effort" (MO dust jacket). I'm inclined to see it as a Herculean effort—specifically, as resembling that hero's battle against the Hydra, which grew two heads for every one he chopped off.

Yet *The Maximus Poems* does have moments of remarkable, if awkward, lyricism, as in "Got me home, the light / snow gives the air, falling":

> how my own hills
> and how Gloucester Harbor suddenly
> coming in on 127 is hewn out
> all perfect in one sight
>
> look as though
> and, on the right as you pass Lookout
> or what was Hammond's
> Castle the straight to England
>
> which was true, Endicott
> sighted the Winthrop fleet's
> top-mast from Salem as
>
> they sat here just where 127 shows
> a brand new deck of cards ready
> in your hand put there
> as though Creation itself dropped
> and,
>
> with the cellophane off the
> full American continent going
> North by the Pole and
>
> West (MO 504)

History and geography ("SPACE") come together here in the poet's fond view, the New World open to its early settlers (Endicott, Winthrop) like a newly opened pack of cards, "ready / in your hand."

The effect is rather spoiled by the "dateline" at the bottom of the page: "written the day I returned from / —Magnolia—and read The Binnacle again as / printed by Robt Creeley in / the Albuquerque Review December 28 1961." That was, one might assume, typed or written at the foot of the page containing "Got me home," but ought it be part of the poem? And what, more troublingly, are we to make of the two lines that occupy an entire page a bit later in the work: "This living hand, now warm, now capable / of earnest grasping" (MO 506)? Butterick explains that these lines—which everyone will recognize as a slight misquote of the opening of Keats's "This living hand, now warm and capable"—were found written on an envelope in Olson's hand and, after his death, incorporated by Butterick (as editor) into *The Maximus Poems, Volume Three*. Butterick quotes a letter from Olson arguing that the passage isn't by Keats but by some unidentified Jacobean, perhaps Webster or Philip Massinger, then cites earlier passages of *Maximus* in which Olson uses the phrase "living hand" to refer to that of the Norse god Tyr, bitten off by the wolf Fenris.[16] It's easy to accept that "living hand" evoked a particular Norse myth for Olson; it's less easy to understand why Olson's jotting down of Keats's lines has become a page in *The Maximus Poems*.

Butterick is forthright about the challenges involved in editing the last volume of *Maximus*. When Olson died, he left few clues about what shape he wanted the volume to take. It fell to Butterick and Charles Boer, Olson's literary executor, to sort through his papers (so numerous that at one point Olson rented an adjacent apartment to house them), identifying which were "Maximus poems" and deciding how to order them. Butterick makes the best of an impossible job—one that would have been, he convincingly argues, almost as impossible for Olson himself, had he lived.[17] But the result is a farrago rather than a coherent sequence, and much has gotten in that is indistinguishable from raw research or "notes to self."

Perhaps that's just as well; perhaps that's precisely what Olson wanted. At the heart of his poetic is the notion of the poem as a verb rather than a noun, and he seems to have felt that the research process was itself poetic. *The Maximus Poems* is unbounded, unfinishable, for there will always be more for Olson to squeeze in. Nonetheless, the poem Olson designated as the last of *The Maximus Poems*—the stark "my wife my car my color and myself " (MO 635)—provides a kind of grim closure, enumerating a series of losses that will end with his own extinction. Duncan visited him in the New York hospital where he lay dying of liver cancer in 1970, and marveled at the big man's frame, his fat wasted away: "His skeleton was much more appropriate to his size than his flesh had ever been. He really looked like his Oceanus."[18] Of course Duncan would find a mythological parallel. But there truly was something oceanic about Olson's career.

* * *

When Olson wrote of the poem as a "high energy-construct," he was extending the modernist view of the poet as a kind of superior technician—even hygienicist—of language. The poem, Pound argued (thinking of Flaubert and James), ought to be at least as well written as prose. The poet's task, said Eliot (echoing Mallarmé's "*Donner un sens plus pur aux mots de la tribu*"), was "To purify the dialect of the tribe."[19] But what space does that leave for those who prefer to take inspiration from Blake's "Hear the voice of the Bard! / Who Present, Past, & Future sees"?[20] Among twentieth-century poets, Robert Duncan was unique in the extent to which he unabashedly wrapped himself in vatic singing robes.

Olson first met Duncan on a trip to San Francisco in 1947. They talked about ecology and California history, but Duncan, almost a decade Olson's junior (he was born in 1919), did not engage him as a *poet*. Indeed, he didn't seem aware that Olson *was* a poet.[21] Then in his late twenties, Duncan had frequented literary circles in New York, counting Henry Miller, Anaïs Nin, and Kenneth Patchen as friends, and he was now near the center of a nascent Berkeley cultural scene that included Kenneth Rexroth (as elder statesman), Jack Spicer, the poet-playwright-filmmaker James Broughton, and the film critic Pauline Kael (a close friend of Duncan). Duncan had published widely and had edited his own magazine, *Experimental Review*. He had caused a stir when his eloquent plea for gay rights, "The Homosexual in Society," was published in Dwight Macdonald's *Politics* in 1944. (A nervous John Crowe Ransom, who a year earlier had accepted Duncan's "An African Elegy" for *The Kenyon Review*, hastily pulled the poem—already set in type—from the magazine.)

We already know many of the details of Duncan's early life thanks to Ekbert Faas's *Young Robert Duncan: Portrait of the Poet as Homosexual in Society* (1983), but that book stops in 1950, when Duncan had yet to write any of the works for which he's now remembered.[22] Lisa Jarnot's long-awaited *Robert Duncan, The Ambassador from Venus* aims to give us the full Duncan, from his infant adoption into a theosophical household to his twilight years as the reigning poet-mage of San Francisco. Jarnot's is a deeply researched and well-written biography, though its barrage of quotidian detail grows relentless in the later chapters. One thing she makes clear is that Duncan, despite the brevity of his time at Black Mountain, had a strong affinity with Olson, Creeley, and Denise Levertov, and that he cherished the notion of a "Black Mountain community" even after he moved on to other poetic circles.

By the time Olson enticed the younger poet to come to Black Mountain College—for about half of its last year, 1956—Duncan had been writing poems for twenty years, trying out various lyric voices and emulating various masters: Cocteau, the Surrealists, Joyce, Stein, Edith Sitwell. Especially striking, given his later repudiation of *The Waste Land*, is how saturated his early verse is with echoes of Eliot. "From such clay our roots writhe" ("Persephone") echoes "What are the roots that clutch, what branches grow / Out of this stony rubbish," while "A third walks with us. Wounded splendor . . . He bears our wounds, tears that are blood" ("The Adoration of the Virgin") reminds us of "Who is that third who walks always beside you?" and passages of the *Four Quartets*.[23] "Their minds are vacant corridors / where winds may come from distances / and howl" ("Huon of Bourdeaux," CEP 194) combines three short passages from "Gerontion": "A dull head among windy spaces," "Vacant shuttles / Weave the wind," and "An old man in a draughty house / Under a windy knob" (with history's "contrived corridors" thrown in for good measure).[24]

Let's not mince words: Duncan's early verse is an echo chamber of earlier poets, and there are few lines that don't have precursors in his compulsive reading. What's striking is the sheer *range* of echoes—not merely of Eliot, Pound, H. D., Joyce, and Lawrence, but also of Milton, Keats, Shelley, Blake, and a host of others. Duncan always acknowledged his debts, and in this he resembled the modernists: Eliot genuflected to Dante and the Metaphysicals; Pound abased himself before Ovid, the troubadours, and Robert Browning; and even the fiercely self-confident Joyce admitted to having learned a thing or two from Édouard Dujardin. At the heart of modernism's avowal of sources, however, was a principle of rigid selectivity: you couldn't admire both the hard intellectual clarities of Donne and Dante *and* the high-flown rhetoric of Milton or the beautiful emotional vagaries of Shelley. Duncan, by contrast, was an omnivore, glorying equally in the Romantics and the modernists.

Of course, a pinch of every ingredient in the kitchen does not a coherent cuisine make. Once upon a time, as a callow would-be grad student, I was granted an hour's interview with Donald Davie, and proceeded to enthuse over Duncan: "I'm fascinated that he's so *eclectic*," I gushed. Between puffs on his recalcitrant pipe, Davie harrumphed, "Eclectic indeed. I'd say an eclectic *fudge*." It's true that in his early books Duncan can be fudgy, if not downright gooey. He doesn't really hit his stride until the mid-fifties, with *Writing Writing: A Composition Book (Stein Imitations)* and *Letters: Poems 1953–1956*. *Letters*, reissued in 2003 by Flood Editions in a beautiful new guise,[25] begins with "For a Muse Meant," part joke and part *ars poetica* addressed to Duncan's new correspondent, Denise Levertov. Duncan toggles between what he calls the "lyrick strain" and a Dadaistic assemblage that includes a laundry list of his current and abiding influences:

the addition of the un
plannd for interruption:
a flavor stinking coffee
(how to brew another cup
in that Marianne Moore—
E.P.—Williams / H. D.—Stein—
Zukofsky—Stevens—Perse—
surrealist—dada—staind
pot) by yrs R.D. (CEP 642)

With *Letters*, Duncan begins to find his mature idiom, in which all of his early experimental influences and all that he has learned of "open form" come together with his egocentric, neo-Romantic lyricism, a wildly eclectic, post-rational gathering of the whole. Duncan would call the vast design within which he saw himself writing the "grand collage," and he explores its workings in *The H. D. Book*, published by the University of California Press as the first hefty volume in *The Collected Writings of Robert Duncan*.[26] A rambling prose opus on which Duncan worked most intensely during the early sixties, *The H. D. Book* was published piecemeal over many years. For a time, there was a complete digital edition available on the web, but it's still a bit of a shock to see the almost seven-hundred-page print edition.

The H. D. Book begins with an account of the sixteen-year-old Duncan's "calling" to poetry, as he listened to his high school teacher Miss Keogh reading H. D.'s poem "Heat": "Unconscious of the content that made for that imprint and awakened in me the sense of a self-revelation or life-revelation in the pursuit of Poetry, I was conscious only of my excitement in the inspiration—the new breath in Language—and of a vocation. Whatever my abilities, it was here that I had been called to work."[27] The book starts as a personal essay, and if anything becomes even more Duncan-centered in its vast second section, "Nights and Days," which consists of a series of daybooks. But its long opening section includes a well-considered historical account of Imagism and a close examination of what one might call the *Da Vinci Code* side of early modernism: the strain of modernist thought, evident most clearly in Pound's *The Spirit of Romance*, that took quite seriously the notion that ancient Greek mystery cults and gnostic heresies survived into the Middle Ages among the Cathars, who supposedly transmitted them to the troubadours.

For his part, Duncan adds Freud to this gallery of occultists, of masters who specialize in looking beneath the surface. Where Yeats went to séances and H. D. went for analysis, Duncan takes theosophy and psychoanalysis equally seriously. (His parents were theosophists who consulted the stars before making important decisions and who discussed their previous lives in Atlantis.) Olson, for all his own esoteric learning, was skeptical. As early as 1954, he worried in *Against Wisdom as Such* that Duncan's Bay Area circle "seems to have become an école des Sages ou Mages as ominous as Ojai, L. A." (OP 260; Ojai, California, was best known at the time as the home of Jiddu Krishnamurti). The remark still bugged Duncan seven years later, when he quoted it in an *H. D. Book* chapter dated March 1961, commenting, "There is something about looking behind things. There is the fact that I am not an occultist or a mystic but a poet, a maker-up-of things."[28]

It's grand to see the whole of *The H. D. Book* in print. For a long while, the only real overview of Duncan's poetry was Robert Bertholf's erratic edition of the *Selected Poems*.[29] Duncan's later work—from 1960 on—was largely in print, in individual collections, but early Duncan—from his juvenilia through *Letters*—could only be sampled in Bertholf's idiosyncratic and textually suspect selection. All that has been changed, changed utterly, by two more volumes from California: the stout *Collected Early Poems and Plays,* and the even more massive *Collected Later Poems and Plays*, both painstakingly edited by the fine scholar Peter Quartermain.[30] No longer will one have to scour libraries or used bookstores to find the eccentrically printed originals: we are at last in a position to see Duncan, or at least Duncan's poetry, whole.

Duncan's mature period can be said to begin with *The Opening of the Field* (1960) and its bravura first poem, "Often I Am Permitted to Return to a Meadow." The poem, inspired by a repeated dream Duncan had, roots his poetry in "an eternal pasture folded in all thought / so that there is a hall therein // that is a made place, created by light / wherefrom the shadows that are forms fall" (CLP 3). Starting out from this dream-meadow, he ventured further and further over the next two and a half decades, winding his way through labyrinths of knowledge and experience, seizing upon connections ("rimes," he calls them) between centuries, continents, and cultures, tracing what he reads as the pulses of unseen spiritual forms and energies moving beneath the surface of everyday life.

"A Poem Beginning with a Line by Pindar" is perhaps the masterpiece of Duncan's early mature period. After describing Goya's painting *Allegory of Love, Cupid, and Psyche*, Duncan turns to Psyche's first task, the sorting of seeds. In that task, Psyche was aided by ants, an image that reminds Duncan of Pound in the military detention center near Pisa ("a lone ant from a broken hill"). The "man upon whom the sun has gone down" then merges with Duncan's figure of the poet as "the boundary walker," policing the threshold between creation and chaos (CLP 59–61). He also touches on the uncertainties associated with the occult "mystery of love":

There the children turn the ring to the left.
There the children turn the ring to the right.
        Dancing . . . Dancing . . .

And the lonely psyche goes up thru the boy to the king
        that in the caves of history dreams.
Round and round the children turn.
        London bridge that is a kingdom falls.

We have come so far that all the old stories
whisper once more.
Mount Segur, Mount Victoire, Mount Tamalpais . . .
        rise to adore the mystery of Love! (CLP 63)

What jars in the kaleidoscopic progression of "A Line by Pindar," and what Duncan surely meant to be jarring, is the second section, in which a reminiscence about "the old poets"—"their faltering / their unaltering wrongness that has style / their variable truths"—is broken by a ringing denunciation of political power:

Harding, Wilson, Taft, Roosevelt,
idiots fumbling at the bride's door,
hear the cries of men in meaningless debt and war.
Where among them did the spirit reside
that restores the land to productive order? (CLP 57–58)

If these lines allude to Whitman's "When Lilacs Last in the Dooryard Bloom'd," the idiom recalls Pound's Confucian, order-making voice. But as the sixties wore on, a less attractive, and far less measured, Poundian idiom infects Duncan's poetry: the obscene invective of the "Hell Cantos." Consider this passage from *Bending the Bow*:

                                Satan looks forth from
men's faces:
            Eisenhower's idiot grin, Nixon's
  black jaw, the sly glare in Goldwater's eye, or
  the look of Stevenson lying in the U.N. that our
  Nation save face . . . (CLP 334)

Duncan was at heart an anarchist, unable to bear authority, and also a communitarian, cherishing the ideal of a cooperative society of equals. His ideal of democracy had been betrayed again and again, but never so blatantly as during the Vietnam War, to which all of "Up Rising, *Passages* 25" is devoted:

> Now Johnson would go up to join the great simulacra of men,
> Hitler and Stalin, to work his fame
> with planes roaring out from Guam over Asia,
> all America become a sea of toiling men
> stirrd at his will, which would be a bloated thing,
> drawing from the underbelly of the nation
> such blood and dreams as swell the idiot psyche
> out of its course into an elemental thing
> until his name stinks with burning meat and heapt honors
> (CLP 366)

And on and on, for two and a half pages. Here, and in numerous similar passages, Duncan's emotion overmasters his art: this is mere rant.

In *The Opening of the Field,* Duncan began his series "The Structure of Rime," which mingles poetry with prose meditations on poetics. In *Bending the Bow* (1968), he presented the first thirty sections of *Passages*, which promised to be a project as big as *The Maximus Poems*. Yet he was uncomfortable with even the highly elastic form of *Maximus*. "*Maximus* was a poem which wasn't open," he told Ekbert Faas in 1973. "I mean, in my sense of open. Because Olson had never observed that open would mean that you couldn't begin or end."[31] And so, after "O!, *Passages* 37" (*Ground Work: Before the War*), he stopped numbering the sections of *Passages*. It's a gesture toward indeterminacy, but little more. Duncan expects too much in insisting on the openness of *Passages*, in the face of the reader's natural tendency to read a book from beginning to end, and to read a numbered sequence from 1 to 37.

Despite passages of invective, *Bending the Bow* is a magnificent book. In 1972, however, Duncan announced that he would offer no new collections until fifteen years had elapsed after *Bending the Bow*. In the event, he waited sixteen, publishing *Ground Work: Before the War* in 1984.[32] That book, a bulky collection of disparate poems—first-person lyrics, a dramatic monologue in the voice of Achilles, "Dante Etudes," "Seventeenth Century Suite" (a series of responses to Metaphysical poems), new installments of "The Structure of Rime" and *Passages*—disappointed only in its typography. But there it disappointed cruelly.

Duncan's concern with the oral performance of his poems and their visual appearance as "scores" thereof here reaches an almost insane pitch. In his preface, "Some Notes on Notation," he specifies that "a space of one and a half lines counts as one verse of arrest," that a double space after a comma "designates a caesura," and so forth (CLP 432–33). Frustrated by what he saw as the botch New Directions's typesetters had made of *Bending the Bow*, Duncan insisted that the book exactly reproduce *his IBM Selectric typescript*. The effect is ghastly. A typescript is a trial to read at best, and the typefaces Duncan used are particularly ugly. Printers have worked for centuries to achieve balances of line, space, and character that the eye finds attractive. Duncan, with his monospaced type, threw all that out the window, forcing the reader's eye to labor over lines that should pirouette and flow. After two decades of reading Duncan's poems in this crunky typescript, one finds it an immense relief to see that Peter Quartermain, in a prodigy of sensitive editing, has presented the poems of *Ground Work: Before the War* in a proper typesetting in this new California collection—with all of their fastidious spacings preserved.

The sequel, *Ground Work II: In the Dark,* is a truncated volume, for Duncan suffered almost total kidney failure in the midst of it, and was afterward able to eke out only a couple of poems. But what we have is strong, if at times very strange. There is a series of poems dedicated to "Master Baudelaire," experiments in word- and syllable-counts and vowel distributions, and poems largely in French—a halting French as strange to a native speaker as it is to a monoglot American.

"After a Long Illness," one of Duncan's last poems, concludes *In the Dark* on a heart-rending, intimations-of-mortality note. Duncan addresses his longtime partner, the painter and collagist Jess:

> Yes, I was afraid
> of not seeing you again,   of being
>   taken away, not
> of dying, the specter I have long
>   known as my Death is the
> Lord of a Passage that unites us;
>   but of
>   never having come to you that other
> specter of my actually living is.
>   Adamant.

Before the poem concludes, Duncan hears, characteristically, a voice from beyond, assuring him that his work has a place within a larger ensemble:

> "I have given you a cat in the dark," the voice said.
> Everything changed in what has always been there
> at work in the Ground: the two titles
> "Before the War", and now, "In the Dark"

underwrite the grand design.   The magic
has always been there,   the magnetic purr
run over me, the feel as of cat's fur
charging the refusal to feel.   That black stone,
now I see, has its electric familiar. (CLP 732)

The invective, the sentimentality, the whole complex of cosmic and occult paraphernalia, are part and parcel of the "magic" of Duncan's poetry. If Olson sought to be a universal, polymath professor, a kind of Arnold Toynbee in verse, Duncan aimed to be the high priest of a new gnosticism, revealing hitherto occluded spiritual forms. It's easy enough to dismiss it all as sheer dottiness—especially when Duncan assumes his most iridescent singing robes and levitates into the empyrean—but there are moments, many moments, when I find myself gripped by his lyrical voice and willing to be transported into "faery lands forlorn." As Samuel Johnson remarked, recalling how his friend Christopher Smart used to fall on his knees in ecstatic prayer in the middle of the street, "I'd as lief pray with Kit Smart as any one else."[33]

* * *

Even as we savor the great mass of the collected Duncan (and anticipate further volumes), we already have the two fat volumes of Robert Creeley's *Collected Poems*, which total thirteen hundred pages between them.[34] In the preface to the first volume, Creeley speaks of the "sense of increment, of accumulation, in these poems" (CP1 ix), and it's evident, when one regards these two doorstoppers, that sixty years of mostly small poems have added up to a rather substantial career. While Olson gathered young poets around him like graduate students, and Duncan—both before and after Black Mountain—presided over his "école des mages," Creeley was the real pop star of this troika. Like Olson's and Duncan's, his early chapbooks were published in scrappy, small-print-run editions. But in 1962, Scribner's, sensing something in the air, collected the bulk of seven fugitive publications in *For Love*. By 1972, there were thirty-nine thousand copies in print, and Creeley was a bona fide celebrity.[35]

The early Creeley poem is a deft, tightly bound, tentative variation on living speech, more often than not tense with the uncertainties of erotic desire. Creeley is the laureate of awkwardness, as in "The Lover":

What should the young
man say, because he is buying
Modess? Should he

blush or not. Or
turn coyly, his head, to
one side, as if in

the exactitude of his emotion he
were not offended? Were
proud? Of what? To buy

A thing like that. (CP1 135)

Here the enjambments, cutting against the grain of the syntax and forcing the reader into a kind of embarrassed stutter, mime the young man's mixture of embarrassment and pride—he has, after all, been sent on something of a knightly errand for his lady fair. (Modess, more mature readers might recall, was a brand of sanitary napkins.)

At other times, as in the all-too-famous "I Know a Man" ("As I sd to my / friend, because I am / always talking," CP1 132), Creeley uses his brittle enjambments to wrest a jittery energy from his lines, perhaps analogous to the frustrated urge to speak that he and his peers felt in the gray-flannel 1950s. These are literate poems, nodding and winking to Catullus, Cavalcanti, the troubadours, and the Cavalier wits (at times they achieve a kind of weightless lyricism reminiscent of Herrick), but they are always rooted in the rhythms of the spoken voice. A run of airy lyrics is inevitably broken by a poem in Creeley's patented hesitant stammer, his voice fumbling among words, trying and failing to say precisely what his heart holds. Take "For Love," the closing poem of the collection of that name:

Yesterday I wanted to
speak of it, that sense above
the others to me
important because all

that I know derives
from what it teaches me.
Today, what is it that
is finally so helpless,

different, despairs of its own
statement, wants to
turn away, endlessly
to turn away.

. . . .
Love, what do I think

to say. I cannot say it.
What have you become to ask,
what have I made you into,

companion, good company,
crossed legs with skirt, or
soft body under
the bones of the bed. (CP1 257–58)

Creeley's early poems often despair of their own statement—but statement, the stating of what is already known, is not their point. They exist, rather, in the search for expression and connection, the desire to come to rest in some momentary formulation as unexpectedly lovely as "soft body under / the bones of the bed."

After *Words* (1967), the follow-up to *For Love*, Creeley embarked on what Benjamin Friedlander calls, in his extraordinarily useful introduction to Creeley's latest selected, "a decade of sustained experiment."[36] It's here that the influence of Black Mountain is most evident, even if Creeley remained a poet far less flamboyant than Duncan and far less noisy than Olson. In *Pieces* (1969), he confronts the notion of "composition by field." For Olson, the "field" is above all a matter of space, most literally the space of the page. The "field" for Duncan is the "place of first permission," where the poet discovers himself in words, but also, as for Olson, the space of the page, where he can dispose words on a six-by-six grid, as in "The Fire, *Passages* 13," or let his lines spill toward infinity, as in *Ground Work: Before the War*. By contrast, Creeley is (aside from a few eccentric tab stops in his earliest verse) strictly a left-justified guy: His poems hug the margin, like a timid hiker on an alpine footpath. For him, the "field" takes on a temporal dimension.

However it might dispose itself on the page—and that disposition, mind you, is central to the reader's experience—the poem of necessity unfolds in time, one word following another. Olson touted the "stave and the bar" ("Projective Verse," OP 245) made available to the performing poet by the precise scoring of the typewriter, and Duncan in his readings took pains to indicate by pauses the spaces in his text, but the primary experience of the poem remains what it's been since Homer or Sappho: a single voice, speaking words one after another. That's so obvious it may seem banal to state it. But one must keep in mind the extent to which Olson, Duncan, and many others saw the poem as not merely a spatial field, but a vortex-like locus concentrating the voices of history, of tradition, of a spiritual "otherness." We may read their words one after another, but we're meant to be always aware of the enormous field around them.

It's precisely that one-after-anotherness that Creeley explores in *Pieces* and his other mid-period work. The poem doesn't strive to be a "vortex" or an "ideogram" or part of a "grand collage," but is satisfied to be the thumbnail tracings of unfolding experience, in all its inconsequence:

Kids walking beach,
minnow pools—
who knows which.
•
No thing grand—
The scale is neither
big nor small.
•
Want to get the sense of "I" into Zukofsky's "eye"—a locus of
experience, not a presumption of expected value.
•
Here now—
begin. (CP1 435)

Pieces is largely an experiment in emptying the first-person singular of its "expected value" (think "I wandered lonely as a cloud") and reframing it as a screen upon which whatever happens, whatever the poet thinks or perceives, can be cast in rapid-fire sequence, with no expectation of a higher "meaning" emerging.

Sometimes, these "little boxes," as Creeley called them, constitute intense examinations of the working of language itself:

One thing
done, the
rest follows.
•
Not from not
but in in.
•
Here here
here. Here. (CP1 388)

At other times, they seem little more than lineated shirt-cuff notes.

Creeley's diaristic tendency becomes especially predominant in *A Day Book* (1972) and *Hello: A Journal, February 29–May 3, 1976* (1978). With *Later* (1979), he mostly retreats from his sequential mode and instead writes separate poems, as in his early books. By this point he was no longer a countercultural pop star but a professor at SUNY Buffalo, and his publisher was New Directions, home of the quasi-institutionalized avant-garde. The very titles of his later books smack of retrospection and aging: *Later*, *Memory Gardens* (1986), *Echoes* (1994), *Life & Death* (1998). Far too many of these poems, for my taste, linger on the discomforts and indignities of encroaching age:

> Oh stay awhile,
> sad, sagging flesh
> and bones gone brittle.
>
> Stay in place,
> agèd face, teeth,
> don't go. . . .
>
> Lift to the vacant air
> some sigh, some sign
> I'm still inside. ("Oh," CP2 346)

Evident as well in Creeley's late work is his resurgent love for the New England poets of his childhood, the comforting rhymes of Longfellow, Lowell, and Whittier. He aspired to write immediately apprehensible, popular verse like theirs, and it led to passages of mawkish, almost simple-minded sentimentality:

> One's here
> and there is still somewhere
> along some road to hell
> where all is well—
>
> or heaven
> even
> where all the saints still wait
> and guard the golden gate. ("On Earth," CP2 627)

But Creeley was a poet who never hid his own emotions, who was never ashamed to weep. I remember him speaking at a Zukofsky celebration in Buffalo in 1997. After rambling through a few prepared remarks, he read—apropos of what I can't recall—the opening of Keats's "Ode to a Nightingale." Tears overcame him after a few lines, and in an anguished voice he choked out, "My God! He knew he was about to die, and he was only—only *twenty-five!*"

For Creeley, the poem's principal "field" was always made up of his own perceptions, thoughts, and emotions—love, desire, regret, fear, nostalgia. If his long odyssey among the twentieth-century avant-garde landed him back in his ancestral New England (at the time of his death in 2005, he was teaching at Brown), it was as much the New England of the extravagant Thoreau and the antinomian Dickinson as that of the Fireside Poets. Here, in its entirety, is "Generous Life," from *If I were writing this*:

Do you remember the way we used to sing
in church when we were young
and it was fun to bring your toys with you
and play with them while all the others sung?

My mind goes on its own particular way
and leaves my apparent body on its knees
to get up and walk as far as it can
if it still wants to and still proves able.

Sit down, says generous life, *and stay awhile!*
although it's irony that sets the table
and puts the meager food on broken dishes,
pours out the rancid wine and walks away. (CP2 601)

* * *

My own copy of *The New American Poetry* (nineteenth printing) had clearly been around a good deal before it found its way to me a quarter-century ago: its edges were stained, its pages were yellow and brittle, and one corner seemed to have been chewed by a dog. I like to imagine it as some young person's countercultural knick-knack, and I like to speculate on its inscription: "Vic—What better way to celebrate my new found freedom. Hope you enjoy this one, it's quite a collection, all our favorites. / Happy Spring Time / Love / A Friend . . ." What was that "new found freedom"? Release from prison? Graduation from high school? A divorce? And who were "our favorites"?

The New American Poetry retains, even in its shiny reprint by California, an air of companionate insurgency; you feel, in settling down with it, that you're in the company of Vic, Vic's friend, and everyone else over the last fifty years who's opened the book and been arrested by the first lines of "The Kingfishers." Of course, that company seems rather less select, less in-the-know, when you note that over a hundred thousand copies of the anthology have been printed since 1960, and that California's primary market for the latest reprint is the college classroom.

At the start of their careers, Creeley, Olson, and Duncan were publishing their own broadsides, chapbooks, and books, or else being published by the upstart and irrepressible Jargon Society. Their volumes were characterized by bold designs, shaky typography, and the occasional typo. But now, with collected editions of Olson and Creeley in print, and a complete Duncan well underway, these three poets have descended from their bastion of experimentation in the Blue Ridge Mountains, and settled in one of the largest and dreariest of the Cities of the Plain: Literaturesville. At least, that's what the bindings of their books—solid, serious, official—imply. I suspect that what lives within those bindings, the radical reformulations of sound and line, the challenges to orthodoxies political, sexual, and intellectual, the revaluations of time, space, and history, will never entirely be tamed and assimilated to whatever has come to replace the polite salon, nor to whatever electronic community will replace the classroom.

Notes

1. Of the many books about Black Mountain, the best remains Vincent Katz, *Black Mountain: Experiment in Art* (2003; Cambridge: MIT P, 2013). Martin Duberman, *Black Mountain: An Exploration in Community* (New York: Dutton, 1972) is a detailed personal history, though Duberman's impressions have been debated by some of the college's veterans. See also Mary Emma Harris, *The Arts at Black Mountain* (Cambridge: MIT P, 1987) and Michael Rumaker, *Black Mountain Days: A Memoir* (Black Mountain, NC: Black Mountain College Museum and Arts Center, 2003).

2. Tom Clark, *Charles Olson: The Allegory of a Poet's Life* (New York: Norton, 1991) 203–04.

3. Duberman, *Black Mountain* 395, 394.

4. Lisa Jarnot, *Robert Duncan, The Ambassador from Venus: A Biography* (Berkeley: U of California P, 2012) 153–55.

5. Donald Allen, ed., *The New American Poetry 1945–1960* (1960; Berkeley: U of California P, 1999).

6. Donald Hall, Robert Pack, and Louis Simpson, eds., *New Poets of England and America* (New York: Meridian, 1957).

7. Charles Olson, *Collected Prose*, ed. Donald Allen and Benjamin Friedlander (Berkeley: U of California P, 1997) 240; hereafter cited parenthetically in text as OP.

8. Charles Olson, *The Collected Poems of Charles Olson (Excluding the Maximus Poems)*, ed. George F. Butterick (Berkeley: U of California P, 1987) 87; hereafter cited parenthetically in text as CO.

9. Ralph Maud, *What Does Not Change: The Significance of Charles Olson's "The Kingfishers"* (Madison, NJ: Fairleigh Dickinson UP, 1997) 18; Guy Davenport, "Scholia and Conjectures for 'The Kingfishers,'" *The Geography of the Imagination: Forty Essays* (San Francisco: North Point P, 1981) 87–99.

10. Ralph Maud, *Charles Olson at the Harbor* (Vancouver: Talonbooks, 2008) 7–8.

11. Ralph Maud, *Charles Olson's Reading: A Biography* (Carbondale: Southern Illinois UP, 1996).

12. Charles Olson, *The Maximus Poems*, ed. George F. Butterick (Berkeley: U of California P, 1985) 5; hereafter cited parenthetically in text as MO.

13. Charles Olson, *Selected Writings*, ed. Robert Creeley (New York: New Directions, 1966) 92–93.

14. Olson, *Selected Writings* 113.

15. George F. Butterick, *A Guide to the Maximus Poems of Charles Olson* (Berkeley: U of California P, 1978).

16. Butterick, *A Guide to the Maximus Poems* 701–02.

17. Butterick, *A Guide to the Maximus Poems* xliv-lv.

18. Ekbert Faas, *Towards a New American Poetics: Essays and Interviews* (Santa Barbara: Black Sparrow, 1978) 57.

19. Ezra Pound, *Selected Letters 1907–1941*, ed. D. D. Paige (1950; New York: New Directions, 1971) 48; T. S. Eliot, *The Complete Poems and Plays, 1909–1950* (New York: Harcourt, Brace, 1971) 141.

20. William Blake, *The Complete Poetry and Prose*, ed. David B. Erdman (New York: Anchor, 1982) 18.

21. Clark, *Charles Olson* 125–26; Jarnot, *Robert Duncan* 108–09.

22. Ekbert Faas, *Young Robert Duncan: Portrait of the Poet as Homosexual in Society* (Santa Barbara: Black Sparrow, 1983).

23. Robert Duncan, *The Collected Early Poems and Plays*, ed. Peter Quartermain (Berkeley: U of California P, 2012) 12, 194; hereafter cited parenthetically in text as CEP.

24. Eliot, *Complete Poems* 48, 21–22.

25. Robert Duncan, *Letters: Poems 1953–1956*, ed. Robert J. Bertholf (Chicago: Flood Editions, 2003).

26. Robert Duncan, *The H. D. Book*, ed. Michael Boughn and Victor Coleman (Berkeley: U of California P, 2011).

27. Duncan, *The H. D. Book* 53.

28. Duncan, *The H. D. Book* 278.

29. Robert Duncan, *Selected Poems (Revised and Enlarged)*, ed. Robert J. Bertholf (New York: New Directions, 1997).

30. Robert Duncan, *The Collected Later Poems and Plays*, ed. Peter Quartermain (Berkeley: U of California P, 2013); hereafter cited parenthetically in text as CLP.

31. Faas, *Towards a New American Poetics* 56.

32. Robert Duncan, *Ground Work: Before the War* (New York: New Directions, 1984).

33. James Boswell, *Life of Johnson*, ed. R. W. Chapman (London: Oxford UP, 1953) 281.

34. Robert Creeley, *The Collected Poems of Robert Creeley, 1945–1975* (Berkeley: U of California P, 1982) and *The Collected Poems of Robert Creeley, 1975–2005* (Berkeley: U of California P, 2006); hereafter cited parenthetically in text as, respectively, CP1 and CP2.

35. Robert von Hallberg, *American Poetry and Culture, 1945–1980* (Cambridge, MA: Harvard UP, 1985) 13.

36. Robert Creeley, *Selected Poems, 1945–2005*, ed. Benjamin Friedlander (Berkeley: U of California P, 2008) 5.

Z-Sited Path

Late Zukofsky and His Tradition

Born in 1904, not half a decade into the new century, Louis Zukofsky was still reinventing himself at the beginning of the 1970s. He had kicked off his writing career in the 1920s with a savage and funny parody of Eliot's *Waste Land* ("Poem beginning 'The'") and with the opening movements of a *Cantos*-like long poem, *"A"*. In the first half of the 1930s, he had been the leader and primary theorist of the short-lived "Objectivist" movement, which in its few heady days of public prominence had counted among its members and fellow-travellers Williams Carlos Williams, Kenneth Rexroth, Carl Rakosi, Charles Reznikoff, and George Oppen. But the Objectivists had proved a mere blip on the radar screen of passing poetic trends, and for some thirty-odd years Zukofsky had worked on in the face of seemingly universal public indifference. He was sustained in part by his friendships and correspondences—with Williams, Basil Bunting, Lorine Niedecker—and in part by the sporadic interest of small presses and little magazines.[1]

By the 1970s, however, Zukofsky had begun to achieve somewhat broader public recognition. While James Laughlin still refused to print Zukofsky, Laughlin's New Directions Press revived interest in the Objectivists by publishing books by Oppen, Reznikoff, and Rakosi through the sixties. In 1968, the scholar L. S. Dembo consolidated the critical rediscovery of the Objectivist "movement" by inviting Zukofsky and the other three to the University of Wisconsin; the following year, he published his interviews with them in *Contemporary Literature* as "The 'Objectivist' Poet: Four Interviews." And Zukofsky's own work was becoming more widely available. *"A" 1–12*, a limited edition of which had been published in Kyoto by Cid Corman's Origin Press in 1959, was reprinted by Doubleday in its Paris Review Editions Series in 1966, and that publisher would publish *"A" 13–21* in 1969. W. W. Norton collected his shorter poems, hitherto available only in periodicals and small press editions, in the volumes *ALL: The Collected Shorter Poems 1923–1958* and *ALL: The Collected Shorter Poems 1956–1964*. In contrast to his earlier small press collections, these books were being reviewed in venues as prestigious as the *New York Times* and *The Nation*.

The Zukofsky of the 1970s, however, was a far different poet from the author of "'The'," the quasi-Imagistic short poems of the 1920s, and the early Poundian movements of *"A"*. "A"-21, for instance, written in 1967, was an impacted translation of Plautus's play *Rudens* ("The Rope"), in which Zukofsky compressed each Latin hexameter line into five words of English, striving at the same time to preserve something of the original sound. The result, while one could certainly imagine it on stage—the movement is, after all, dedicated to Zukofsky's friend, theater critic John Gassner, and to Zukofsky's elder brother Morris, who had taken the future poet to see Yiddish theater of the 1910s—is fast-moving, oblique, and oddly "hip": "My! while that sea operates / only tempest's in his nets. / Today's catch's cooked, slipped these / fingers, fluke vehement sea mar."[2] "A"-22 and -23, written between 1970 and 1974, compressed thousands of years of history—linguistic, literary, geological—into two thousand five-word lines of densely concatenated quotation, translation, and transliteration, and somehow at the same time managed to bring to remarkable closure the twenty-one formally various movements that had come before them. "A"-24 was the "L.Z. Masque," an arrangement for four voices and harpsichord of a plethora of Zukofsky texts; it was his wife Celia's present to him, and he appropriated it to end *"A"* on both a musical and familial note.

80 Flowers, in press when Zukofsky died in 1978, was a collection of eighty-one poems, each one eight lines long with, again, five words to the line, each (save the epigraph) named after a flower (or plant). As in "A"-22 and -23, syntax is radically open in these poems; in essence, they are deeply considered collages of quotation and translation, opening seemingly infinite regresses of suggestion and implication to the careful reader, while enforcing no single level of meaning. Late Zukofsky is continuous with early and mid-period Zukofsky in his concern with poetic form and with the musical value of verse, but Zukofsky's seventies-era poetics effect a quantum leap from his earlier work in syntactic openness, multiplicity of meaning, and sheer readerly difficulty. It is a poetry of deep, angular beauty, and of obdurate but tantalizing resistance. The last lines of "A"-23 are emblematic. The movement ends by naming both the four voices of the "L.Z. Masque" and by pointing out the "path" of a "z-sited"—a Zukofsky-sited?—tradition: "music, thought, drama, story, poem / parks' sunburst—animals, grace notes— / z-sited path are but us" (*"A"* 563).

The phrase "z-sited path" is a temptingly vague one to use in describing how younger poets have received Zukofsky's work. Influence studies, of course, are one of the hoariest of academic pursuits, and too many scholars have reduced Zukofsky to a case study of the influence of Ezra Pound, rather than paying attention to how radically Zukofsky's work differs from his friend's. Zukofsky himself, in a 1930 note on "Influence," argues intelligently enough that direct influence of the sort beloved by academics is really no more important than a writer's absorption of a tendency "in the air," or a writer's sense of kinship with another writer of a far different era—like, for instance, his own obsession with Shakespeare.[3] Zukofsky's own attitude toward poetic influence is a complex matter, to say the least, and his various statements work to undermine any clear-cut notion of how one poet's work makes a difference in the works of those who follow. To write about Zukofsky's "tradition," then, propels one into a minefield; one has a sense of flying in the face both of Zukofsky's own sense of poetic tradition, and of the actual, highly complex workings of literary history.

Zukofsky's own statements, and his increasing reclusiveness, did little to mitigate the impression that by the 1960s he was a "forgotten" poet. It is clear, however, that poets were reading Zukofsky in the years when his books could find no publishers. Robert Duncan, associated both with Charles Olson at Black Mountain College and Jack Spicer in San Francisco, had been reading Zukofsky since 1937, and by 1954 considered him among his "masters," though one of a foregoing generation. Through Duncan's and Edward Dahlberg's promptings, Robert Creeley would publish Zukofsky in 1955 in the *Black Mountain Review*, and would later visit the Zukofskys at their Brooklyn Heights home. For Creeley and others, Zukofsky represented an important living link with the modernism of Pound and Williams, a counter-establishment modernism that many of the poets of the "New American Poetry" saw as a crucial alternative to the academically sanctioned modernism of T. S. Eliot, W. H. Auden, and the New Critics. Throughout the late 1950s and the 1960s, then, a procession of poets committed to nonacademic verse would visit Zukofsky, among them Allen Ginsberg, Denise Levertov, Joel Oppenheimer, Jerome Rothenberg, and Paul Blackburn. Two of them, Robert Kelly and George Economou, would publish Zukofsky's *I's (pronounced* eyes*)* under the aegis of their Trobar Press in 1963. They found in Zukofsky far more than a relic of high modernism, but an active and exploratory sensibility that was still inventing, pushing beyond what Pound and Williams had done.

Some of the poets who read, corresponded, and spoke to Zukofsky would assimilate his work as a relatively minor influence, or would take it as an affirmation or explanation of poetics already substantially framed: Duncan, for instance, who was continually adding new ingredients to the multiply-"staind [coffee] / pot" of his own poetics,[4] and Allen Ginsberg, who had early in his writing career established an intense correspondence with Zukofsky's friend Williams. Other poets fell into more absolute, all-compassing relationships with Zukofsky's work. Perhaps the two most overtly "Zukofskyan" of such poets are Cid Corman and Frank Samperi. Corman had met Zukofsky in Florence in 1957. The editor of *Origin* (which published Zukofsky on a regular basis) and a close correspondent of Zukofsky for the last two decades of the latter's life, Corman over the course of some eighty-odd collections pursued a poetics of the formally compact. His (mostly) short-lined poems are deeply indebted to various Japanese and Chinese models, but his methods of deploying syntax and modulating line length owe more—at times, it seems everything—to Zukofsky. Frank Samperi, another writer associated with *Origin*, left as his major lifework the trilogy *The Prefiguration* (1971), *Quadrifarium* (1973), and *Lumen Gloriae* (1973), a sequence of eighteen shorter poems that strive to reinvent in American English the ecstatic-religious poem on a Dantescan scale.[5] In its word-count prosodies and visually based mysticism, the verse of Samperi's trilogy seems a continual allusion to Zukofsky. Samperi's work, however, whatever the interest of its dense scholastic philosophy and mystical vision, lacks the knotted and difficult lyricism that makes Zukofsky's work ultimately rewarding.

In contrast to those of his contemporaries who taught in poetry writing programs, Zukofsky's teaching position at the Polytechnic Institute of Brooklyn—an intensely pragmatic school, to say the least—was not conducive to the acquisition of poetic disciples. One of his students, however, Hugh Seidman, went on to appear in the Yale Younger Poets Series with *Collecting Evidence* (1970). In that volume, as well as in *Blood Lord* (1974) and *Throne/Falcon/Eye* (1982), Seidman shows himself deeply attentive to the sound values of Zukofsky's verse, marrying the sometimes harsh music and tentative syntax of mature Zukofsky to the surrealism of César Vallejo in poems that explore brutal and scarifying personal relationships with a frightening intensity.[6] In *Throne/Falcon/Eye*, perhaps his finest book, Seidman lays out a quintessentially urban—New York—vision, superimposing personal and social realities upon a framework of Greek and Egyptian mythology. Seidman's work has little in common with the various avant-gardes writing today: he has, most notably, no interest in purging the personal voice from his poetry. But the lessons he learned from Zukofsky—conciseness, music, and precise image—set his poetry apart from that of the workshop poets ubiquitous in the American academy.

Michael Heller, who also began as an engineering student, and who first encountered Zukofsky's work through Seidman's recommendation, is also a New York poet, but of a far less somber cast. Heller has written an important monograph on the five Objectivist poets (including Zukofsky's friend Lorine Niedecker), *Conviction's Net of Branches: Essays on the Objectivist Poets and Poetry*, and the texture and tone of his later work owe as much to Rakosi, Reznikoff, and Oppen as they do to Zukofsky.[7] Nonetheless, Heller's work is obsessed with questions of perception and epistemology—as evidenced in the title of his 1979 collection *Knowledge*—that have a definite family resemblance to those at the heart of Zukofsky's work and thought, and the fine precision of observation in his poetry is deeply akin to Zukofsky's.[8] Like Heller, Theodore Enslin is a poet who finds in George Oppen's work modes of thought and emotion more congenial than Zukofsky's rigors; nonetheless, Enslin's writing is fundamentally indebted to Zukofsky's musical sensibility. Enslin, who studied composition with Nadia Boulanger, spent much of his life in rural Maine, far from the urban and academic centers of American poetry. From the 1960s on, he published scores of volumes of poetry, many of them installments of such multivolume long poems as *Ranger* and *Forms*. Following the lead of Zukofsky's work, which often models its forms upon those of classical music, Enslin has systematically explored the ways in which one can write poetry that approaches the formal "condition of music." It is difficult to take in Enslin's whole achievement—his works run to many thousand pages—but his shorter lyrics often strike an extraordinarily Zukofskyan note:

The tide
        is dust
seeped in
        dry wells
are dark in
        deed.[9]

What most struck many of the younger poets reading Zukofsky in the last decades of his life—and what inevitably strikes readers encountering him now—is his sense of compressed form, of the overwhelmingly careful and intelligently weighed placements of his words within the lines of his poems, and the precise, almost fastidious, crafting of the movements from line to line, stanza to stanza. Often this craft is evident in short-lined poems; in his later works, it plays out in a word-count prosody, where each line has precisely two, or three, or five words, regardless of the number of syllables or stresses within those words. Traditional poetry in English is most often written in accentual-syllabic forms: in each line, a relatively fixed number of stresses occurs within a relatively fixed number of syllables—as in the classic iambic pentamenter line, which theoretically has five stresses placed at certain points within ten syllables. By making word-counts rather than syllable- or accent-counts the basis of his later prosody, Zukofsky radically redefines the balance between fixed order and individual variation that constitutes poetic form.

Zukofsky's sense of poetic form in general has had a profound impact on the work of Robert Creeley, the poet who was closest personally to Zukofsky for the last two decades of Zukofsky's life. Creeley's short-lined poems everywhere evidence the same precision of movement that Zukofsky's do, perhaps most clearly in the poems of *Pieces* (1969), a collection dedicated to Zukofsky: "Late, the words, late / the form of them, al- / / ready past what they were / fit for, one and two and three."[10] Creeley's impressive body of work stands as a thorough working-through of the implications of the Zukofskyan short lyric and lyric sequence. Robert Kelly, whose poetic corpus stretches (like Enslin's) over thousands and pages and encompasses numerous forms, would find the word-counted lines of Zukofsky's "A"-15 (1963) a vital model for his own volume *Axon Dendron Tree* (1967), which employs similar one- and two-word lines.[11] And Lyn Hejinian's *The Cell* (1992), a series of dated, densely philosophical journal poems, while not nearly as formally rigid as Zukofsky's late works, tends to gravitate toward a five-word line that bears a family resemblance to Zukofsky's.[12]

Among the most controversial of Zukofsky's mature poetic techniques was his method of phonetic translation, in which he sought to bring a foreign text into English first and foremost by reproducing its *sound*. Zukofsky's translations—or "transliterations"—represent an important innovation in poetics. While every formal decision a poet makes imposes a certain limitation upon the words of the poem, phonetic translation does so to an unprecedented degree: the *sound* of the foreign text, that is, becomes the more-or-less rigid template over which the poet must plot his language. As in so much of Zukofsky's work, which constantly deploys the rhetoric of aurality, of music in particular, his method of translation forces meaning—the traditional aim of the translator—into a position of belatedness. If the new text's "meaning" approximates that of the original, well and good, but more often the sounds of the foreign poem generate new and unsuspected significations in its English translation. Zukofsky's 1969 *Catullus* (in collaboration with his wife, Celia) is the most notable example of this process at work, but there are passages of such transliteration throughout the later movements of *"A"* and *80 Flowers*. Not many poets have taken up this gauntlet: Charles Bernstein has transliterated a poem of Dominique Fourcade's in *The Sophist* (1987), but the method is more expansively exemplified in David Melnick's *Men in Aida, Book One* (1983), a phonetic translation of the *Iliad* that gives Melnick ample space to pursue his own ludic directions—this *Iliad*, that is, seems to take place by turns on a Trojan plain, in a barroom, and in a San Francisco bathhouse.[13]

Bernstein and Melnick are both of course associated with the Language movement, a loosely organized coalition of east- and west-coast poets who came to maturity in the 1970s and public and academic prominence in the 1980s. Language poetry is an extraordinarily diverse phenomenon: it is easier and probably more accurate to describe it as a tendency within (and against) American literary institutions than to summarize any single set of poetic practices its adherents hold in common. I think it safe, however, to describe Language poetics as a generalized reaction to the speech-based poetics practiced (in far divergent forms) by both the workshop-trained poets of the academy and the mavericks of the "New American Poetry," as collected in Donald Allen's 1960 anthology of the same title. One of Language poetry's inaugural moments, for instance, is Robert Grenier's 1971 essay "On Speech," in which Grenier (himself a dedicated student of Zukofsky's work) proclaims, in no uncertain terms, "I HATE SPEECH."[14] For the Language poets, poetry finds its significance as both an exploratory mode of knowledge and a social critique in a renewed emphasis on the text *as* text, rather than as transcript of speaking or singing voice.

As so many revolutionary poetic movements have done, the Language poets (most of them products of the post–World War II baby boom) looked beyond their immediate predecessors for useful models of poetic technique, turning to an earlier generation of avant-garde writers that included Gertrude Stein and Louis Zukofsky. Ron Silliman, in the introduction to his influential anthology *In the American Tree*, cites Zukofsky and Stein as representatives of "a latent tradition of a poetics not centered on speech,"[15] and Charles Bernstein and Bruce Andrews' *The L=A=N=G=U=A=G=E Book*, an anthology of selections from their crucial 1970s journal *L=A=N=G=U=A=G=E*, includes numerous poets' responses to Stein and Zukofsky. While the Language poets' borrowings and adaptations of Zukofsky's techniques are as varied and idiosyncratic as their own poetics, Language poetry clearly represents the first generation of avant-garde American poets who have taken Zukofsky's work as a central inheritance of the modernist movement.

A few examples of Language poetry's debts to Zukofsky will have to suffice here. Bernstein, a poet who has experimented with a bewildering variety of forms, tones, and techniques in his work, is intimately familiar with Zukofsky's work, and often echoes him in his disjunctive syntax and almost reckless montage. Most interestingly, Bernstein seems to have internalized the *tone* of mid-period Zukofsky, a dry, wry, Jewish wit that veers from Catskillslevel humor to surprising pathos and profundity. Michael Palmer arranged for Zukofsky to read at Harvard University in 1963, an event commemorated in Zukofsky's poem "After Reading," and Palmer's own work is sprinkled with references to Zukofsky, perhaps most notably in the beautiful elegy "Notes for Echo Lake 3."[16] Palmer's early verse is clearly influenced by Zukofsky's sense of poetic form in its sharply chiseled, imagistic lines, heavily relying on the torque of enjambment; but his later work—both dreamlike and densely philosophical, rather like a marriage of Wittgenstein and surrealism—seemed profoundly imbued with the senses of space and time manifested in Zukofsky's later poetry.

On a more concrete level, one can note how the structure of Zukofsky's *"A"*—the only modernist poem of its magnitude actually *completed* during the lifetime of the Language poets—has influenced Ron Silliman's work. Silliman has noted with approval how Zukofsky, in the process of composing *"A"*, arrived at "a new conceptualization as to the function of part-to-whole relations in the formation of a longpoem [*sic*]."[17] Each movement of *"A"* "is a totalization, complete in itself, capable of entering into larger structures as an autonomous fact," according to Silliman, and Zukofsky's "recognition that the section of a large work must operate as a group, not as a series" is what enables him, in contrast to the authors of *The Cantos*, *Paterson*, and *The Maximus Poems*, to bring his long poem to completion. Just as Zukofsky decided early on that there would be twenty-four movements to *"A"*—no matter what material those movements would contain or what forms they would take—Silliman has organized his own (very) long poem, *The Alphabet*, around a similarly arbitrary (and similarly overdetermined) framework, that of the twenty-six letters of the alphabet. *"A"*, of course, is written in an astonishing variety of forms, from the paratactic free verse of its early movements, to the sonnets of "A"-7, the double canzone of "A"-9, the isolated *four words* of "A"-16, the recycled collage of "A"-17, and the word-counted lines of other later movements. The sections of Silliman's *Alphabet*, published in multiple, scattered venues and written—chronologically speaking—out of alphabetical order, manifest a similar formal and topical variety. *Paradise* (1985) is in what looks like prose, its levels of organization the single sentence and the paragraph, as Silliman theorizes in his essay "The New Sentence." *What* (1988) is a left-justified free verse internal monologue, reminiscent of parts of Zukofsky's "A"-13. *Hidden* (1992) is in two-line stanzas; *Xing* (1996) in three-line stanzas.[18] *The Alphabet* has all the makings of a major achievement in American poetry; at the very least, it is an unmatched record of the political, social, sensual, and informational *texture* of late-twentieth-century American life. Silliman, by clear-sightedly seizing upon and extending the implications of part-to-whole relationships within Zukofsky's *"A"*, has forged for his own poem a flexible and capacious formal armature within which he has explored a dazzling variety of experiences and issues.

Silliman (who has worked as an organizer for prisoners' and tenants' groups) has argued that poetic experimentation is best conducted within a closely knit movement of like-minded poets, a group in which, ideally, there can be mechanisms of "articulate self-discipline within the community."[19] He is inclined to scoff at the (admittedly tired) Romantic notion of the poet as individualistic outsider or solitary innovator. For Silliman, late Zukofsky's isolation is a consequence of the public and personal failure of the Objectivist movement, its failure to provide Zukofsky and his contemporaries a durable experimental community. What Zukofsky achieved was remarkable, and against tremendous odds: later poets pursuing individual extensions of Zukofsky's techniques without the support and constant critical exchange of a community such as the Bay Area Language poets—such poets, Silliman specifies, as Frank Samperi, John Taggart, and Ronald Johnson—run the risk of simply amplifying and repeating, sterilely, Zukofsky's innovations. One could argue on the contrary that individualistic—idiosyncratic, fundamentally personal—reconceptions of Zukofskyan poetics have led to some of the highest achievements of American poetry's latest fin-de-siècle: most notably in the cases precisely of Taggart and Johnson.

For his PhD at Syracuse University, John Taggart wrote the first dissertation extensively addressing Zukofsky's work, and in 1973 he devoted an issue of his periodical *MAPS* to commentary on Zukofsky's writings. Taggart's own poetry, more so than that of any of the poets in the Language movement (from which he has studiously distanced himself) is in large part a strikingly original development of elements explicit and implicit in Zukofsky's. His early work is very much in a chiseled, short-lined "objectivist" vein. Later, in the book-length poems *The Pyramid is a Pure Crystal* (1974) and *Dodeka* (1979), Taggart generates poems out of building blocks of strictly circumscribed verbal material, manipulating them through various "fugal" and canonic systems.[20] It is indeed a poetics of "process," but it results in strikingly lively and energetic poetry, and is a direct descendent of the poetry Zukofsky composed through such strict systems as the canzone of "A"-9 and the more recondite prosodies of later movements of *"A"*. In his more recent work, Taggart has meditated long and deeply on the implications of the connections, fundamental to Zukofsky, between poetry and music. But where Zukofsky looked to the fugal forms of Johann Sebastian Bach and other baroque composers for formal analogies in making his poems, Taggart has turned to the systems of repetition and variation in the compositions of contemporary "minimalist" composers—Steve Reich, Philip Glass, LaMonte Young—and in the playing of the great jazz instrumentalists—John Coltrane, Thelonious Monk, Eric Dolphy. By using such musics as a formal model, Taggart has created, in an ongoing series of volumes that includes *Peace on Earth* (1981), *Loop* (1991), *Standing Wave* (1993), and *Crosses* (2006), poems both short and long that manipulate verbal and cadential repetition in a subtle, shifting movement of great intellectual and emotional power: "Deepened by black red made deep by black / deepened and dark darker at the top / doorway without a door's always darker / deep red dark red always darker at the top."[21]

It is a poetry that demands reading aloud, but when the reader renders it the necessary patience and attention, it reveals moving aesthetic and spiritual depths. Taggart has gone on record rejecting much of Language poetics as a dehumanizing technologizing of poetry; his goal, repeated in work after work, is to construct a poetics that is capable of encompassing the spiritual aspect of human experience. Unlike Frank Samperi, however, who simply *asserts* the spiritual function of poetry, Taggart attempts actively to capture the experience of the numinous in his repetitive, hypnotic lines. While the "music" of his poetry has a far different sound from Zukofsky's, and is directed at a far different end, it nonetheless owes a profound debt to Zukofsky's conception of the interrelatedness of poetry and musical form.

Ronald Johnson died in March 1998, a little over a year after the long-awaited publication of his long poem *ARK* in its single-volume form. *ARK*, which was completed in late 1990, is an extraordinary achievement, a ninety-nine-section poem that evokes by turns Dante's *Commedia*, Merrill's *Changing Light at Sandover*, Johnson's immediate modernist forebears Pound, Williams, and Olson, and the gnarled later sections of *"A"*. In some sense, it is all a hymn to light, to the unbelievably complex and inexhaustible physical and chemical processes by which the energies of the stars are transmuted into the human eyes that behold them, the human language that praises them, and the human cultures that strive to emulate their beauty. It is as well a massive patchwork of found and invented bits of language, all woven together in a homegrown American aesthetic that Johnson compares to those of such visionary eccentrics as Simon Rodia (of the Watts Towers) or Harry Partch. And it is also a rewriting of *The Wizard of Oz*, beginning in Johnson's own childhood home, Kansas, and ending in the Oz of San Francisco—an Oz blighted, in the poem's later sections, by the shadow of the AIDS epidemic.

Johnson is quick to acknowledge, as he does in the afterword to *ARK*, that his chief poles of influence are Zukofsky and Olson: "the Minimalist and the Maximus."[22] But the compositional procedures, the collagistic aesthetic, and above all the musical *ear* of the poem—all these are Zukofsky's: in a passage elegizing Zukofsky himself, Johnson writes of a poetic "music"

in cherubim cliffed hayseed, rayed
clouds in plaster
forever
or near it
as consonance gets without
clef
(98)

Like Zukofsky, Johnson has freely borrowed, adapted, and above all *condensed* other texts for his poem: a section of BEAMS 21–23, the "Palms," consists of words abstracted from the Psalms, much as sections of "A"-14 and "A"-15 distill the words of *Paradise Lost* and Gibbon's *Decline and Fall.* As in *"A"*, the various sections of *ARK* have radically different forms, from prose paragraphs to actual musical notation to the center-justified unrhymed triplets of the poem's later sections. And, most strikingly, the *texture* of *ARK*—words and phrases set free from prescribed syntax, interacting one with another in multiple and shifting combinations, continually playing with and seriously weighing the implications of their own sounds—brings to mind that of Zukofsky's seventies-era poetry, verse in which the poet seems to be continually striving toward the upper reaches of his own integral: "upper limit music / lower limit speech." It seems to me that Johnson, of all the poets who have read and listened to Zukofsky's work, has come closest to capturing the intricate music of his elder.

Unlike Pound's *Cantos*, Silliman's *Alphabet*, or many of the movements of *"A"*, *ARK* is a long poem that emphatically resists Pound's definition of the epic as a "poem including history." In Johnson's own words, it is a "poem *without* history," a poem that, while including great masses of quotation and found materials, explicitly disclaims the utility of the source-hunting activities so beloved by Pound and Joyce scholars, and disclaims any immediate political, social, or didactic use-value.[23] The "histories" Zukofsky traces in "A"-22 and -23 are assemblages of words set free from originary names, dates, and social relations—"History's best emptied of names' / impertinence met on the ways" (*"A"* 511)—and Zukofsky would have us read the words of these movements, not referentially, as pointers to texts and ideas outside his poem, but as elements *within* the poem itself—"read, not into, it: / desire until all be bright" (*"A"* 528). Johnson's *ARK* presses this poetics to a further point: a long, obsessively formal, collagistic poem whose burden is neither personal, historical, nor didactic, but *aesthetic*. The essential tone of *ARK*, that is, despite its passages of self-doubt, of hushed awe, and of quiet mourning, is one of joyful play, of delight in the beauties of the sensible universe and of the language through which we apprehend and describe it. As much as the knotty, punning music of his lines, this rejoicing in cosmic order is Johnson's inheritance from Zukofsky. Johnson's is far from the only use to which contemporary writers have put the arsenal of techniques, forms, and intellectual stances Zukofsky has left them; but it is perhaps the most attractive.

Notes

1. For a detailed account of Zukofsky's career and writings, see Mark Scroggins, *The Poem of a Life: A Biography of Louis Zukofsky* (Emeryville, CA: Shoemaker & Hoard, 2007).

2. Louis Zukofsky, *"A"* (1978; New York: New Directions, 2011) 475. Hereafter cited parenthetically in the text.

3. Louis Zukofsky, *Prepositions+: The Collected Critical Essays* (Hanover, NH: Wesleyan UP, 2000) 135.

4. Robert Duncan, *The Collected Early Poems and Plays*, ed. Peter Quartermain (Berkeley: U of California P, 2012) 642.

5. Frank Samperi, *The Prefiguration* (New York: Grossman, 1971), *Quadrifarium* (New York: Grossman, 1973), and *Lumen Gloriae* (New York: Grossman, 1973).

6. Hugh Seidman, *Collecting Evidence* (New Haven: Yale UP, 1970), *Blood Lord* (New York: Doubleday, 1974), and *Throne/Falcon/Eye* (New York: Random House, 1982).

7. Michael Heller, *Conviction's Net of Branches: Essays on the Objectivist Poets and Poetry* (Carbondale: Southern Illinois UP, 1985).

8. Michael Heller, *Knowledge* (New York: Sun, 1979).

9. Theodore Enslin, *Carmina* (Dennis, MA: Salt-Works P, 1976) n. p.

10. Robert Creeley, *Pieces* (New York: Scribner's, 1969) 43.

11. Robert Kelly, *Axon Dendron Tree* (Annandale-on-Hudson, NY: Matter, 1967).

12. Lyn Hejinian, *The Cell* (Los Angeles: Sun & Moon, 1992).

13. Charles Bernstein, *The Sophist* (Los Angeles: Sun & Moon, 1987), David Melnick, *Men in Aida, Book One* (Berkeley, CA: Tuumba, 1983).

14. *In the American Tree: Language, Realism, Poetry*, ed. Ron Silliman (Orono, ME: National Poetry Foundation, 1986) 496.

15. Silliman, *In the American Tree* xvi-xvii; *The L=A=N=G=U=A=G=E Book*, ed. Charles Bernstein and Bruce Andrews (Carbondale: Southern Illinois UP, 1984).

16. Louis Zukofsky, *Anew: Complete Shorter Poetry* (New York: New Directions,

2011) 233; Michael Palmer, *The Lion Gate: Selected Poems 1972–1995* (New York: New Directions, 1998) 70–72.

17. Ron Silliman, *The New Sentence* (New York: Roof, 1987) 128.

18. All of these sections are collected in Ron Silliman, *The Alphabet* (Tuscaloosa: U of Alabama P, 2008).

19. Silliman, *In the American Tree* xix.

20. John Taggart, *The Pyramid Is a Pure Crystal* (New Rochelle, NY: Elizabeth P, 1974) and *Dodeka* (Milwaukee: Membrane P, 1979).

21. John Taggart, "The Game with Red," *Loop* (Los Angeles: Sun & Moon, 1991) 232. See also *Peace on Earth* (Berkeley: Turtle Island Foundation, 1981), *Standing Wave* (Providence, RI: Lost Roads, 1993), and *Crosses: Poems 1992–1998* (London: Stop P, 2006).

22. Ronald Johnson, *ARK* (1996; Chicago: Flood Editions, 2013) 311. Hereafter cited parenthetically in text.

23. Ronald Johnson, "Planting the Rod of Aaron," *Northern Lights: Studies in Creativity* 2 (1985–1986) 2.

The Palace of Wisdom and the Six-Minute Poem

Theodore Enslin

Two friends of mine were waiting at the maître d's desk in a posh New York restaurant, when one of them whispered urgently, "Look over at that table—there's Joyce Carol Oates! She's having dinner with a guy—and he's holding her hand. He must be telling her he loves her." "Naw," the other said, "he's just trying to keep her from writing during the meal."

"The road of excess," Blake proclaimed in one of his "Proverbs of Hell," "leads to the palace of Wisdom." A little further on, he was less metaphorical: "You never know what is enough until you know what is more than enough."[1] Both of these sentences ran through my mind as I looked back over Theodore Enslin's career in poetry—almost six decades of writing, over seventy books all told, among them more pages of long poems than Pound, Olson, and Merrill put together. It's hard to avoid the question: Has Enslin written too much? Has this gentle, retiring, bearded and ponytailed poet, jotting down poems in tiny notebooks as he walks his remote Maine farm, been riding a Harley-Davidson down the road of excess? And the palace of Wisdom—are we there yet?

Voluminous production has a long pedigree. The four hundred-odd plays we have by the Renaissance dramatist Lope de Vega are only a fraction of the 1,500 to 2,000 he is said to have written; it's no surprise that much of what survives holds (as Pound said) "merely antiquarian interest."[2] Writing for a hungry market seldom affords time for high art. After his financial smash-up of 1826, Sir Walter Scott spent the remaining six years of his life struggling to repair his fortunes, churning out a novel a year, in addition to a six-volume life of Napoleon, multivolume histories of Scotland and France, and heaven knows what else. He broke his health in the process, and the last few Waverley novels—the characters pasteboard cutouts, the plots incoherent and spotty—make dispiriting reading.

And then, for those who aren't so beset by deadlines, there's *revising* too much. I'm one of the sizeable minority who prefer the 1799 two-part version of Wordsworth's *Prelude*. Sure, there are remarkable moments in the 1805 thirteen-book version, but the emotional intensity and nervous movement of the shorter version have been sadly blunted. And *nobody* I know cares much for the final 1850 fourteen-book version, where the aged and respectable poet, wearing his laureate status like a dray horse his blinkers, muffles all the good bits in the wet blanket of pious hindsight.

Theodore Enslin has given the world a very large number of books, but I'm not sure you can accuse him of over-revising. Some of the later collections included in *Then, and Now* have composition dates appended to them, and some of those dates are enough to raise a reader's eyebrows. The two sequences that make up *Love and Science*, for instance, are dated "June 16—July 10, 1989" and "December 23, 1989—January 29, 1990." What, only eight weeks to write 78 short lyrics? Does Enslin ever sleep? His operating procedure, it would seem, is to write and publish continuously. One book is always pressing up against the next; there's always something in the pipeline. The notion of setting poems aside, revising them, or even discarding them, simply doesn't seem to have occurred to Enslin. "I wrote it in a space of about six minutes, and I know this exactly," he says of one piece, with a touch of adolescent glee.[3]

Enslin is one of a small group of poets (others include Cid Corman and Robert Kelly) whose writing has been deeply influenced by Williams and the Objectivists, and who have each published an enormous number of collections that have received only limited attention, either from the reading public or the critical community. (The verbosity and disregard, I would venture, are not unrelated.) All these poets came of age in the postwar years; Kelly, the youngest, was born in 1935. They all sought out, befriended, and learned from Louis Zukofsky, and they have all found publishers willing to print book after book of their poetry. Kelly has had over twenty of his sixty-odd books published by John Martin of Black Sparrow Press. Corman, tucked away in far Kyoto, has been less lucky in finding sponsors: some twenty-seven of his over ninety(!) books bear the imprint of his own Origin Press. And while it's hard to name a little press that hasn't at some point done a Theodore Enslin book, his most longstanding support has come from Jim Weil of the Elizabeth Press (twelve volumes) and Tom Bridwell of the Salt-Works Press (nine volumes).

The very fact of Enslin's unstoppable productivity—almost a book and a half per year—makes assessing his work, or even pinpointing what's best, a chancy thing. I buy an Enslin book when I see one; I must have a score or so on my shelves, some of which contain poems I like very much indeed, others of which fail to move me. But I've always been reluctant to pronounce on the man's work as a whole: How do I know that there isn't some volume out there I've never seen, a collection that will entirely alter my view of the poet?

The publication in 1999 of two volumes of selected Enslin—*Then, and Now: Selected Poems 1943–1993* and *Re-Sounding: Selected Later Poems*—seems finally to hold out some promise of a vantage point.

Then, and Now is a selection of Enslin's shorter poems spanning fifty years and twenty-three books (thirteen of them in their entirety), edited by Mark Nowak, a poet and editor of the journal *Xcp: Cross Cultural Poetics*. I approach selected editions put together by someone other than the poet with the same trepidation that I do a "best of" package assembled by a singer's record label—is this really going to be the best stuff, or some bean-counter's idea of the "greatest hits"? In the case of a poet as prolific as Enslin, the question is whether the editor's opted to present us with a selection of the most vital Enslin, or simply a representative cross-section. Jackson Mac Low's *Representative Works: 1938–1985*, for instance, gives a fair picture of Mac Low's aleatory poetics, but I doubt the collection would be any less—or more—interesting if one swapped its contents for any other 300 pages of his work.[4] It really does make a difference in Enslin's case, however, for this is a poet who—to put it bluntly—isn't always "on." Nowak, to his credit, has chosen discerningly. Of course he has his own preferences. Nowak is keenest on the poetry written to musical models (more on this later), so such collections—*Carmina* (1976) and *Music for Several Occasions* (1985), for instance—get heavy rotation. And Nowak's selection, almost two-thirds of which dates from the eighties and nineties, gives the impression—appropriately, I think—that Enslin is a poet who's improved with age.

There's no introduction to *Then, and Now*; instead Nowak glances back over Enslin's career by means of a lengthy interview, in which the editor tells the poet which of his poems are going into the big book, and the poet, scratching his head—seemingly the only extraneous noise that isn't picked up by Nowak's tape recorder and dutifully transcribed—tries to remember when he wrote that one. Setting aside any irritation one feels at Nowak's ethnographical enthusiasms, all those "yeahs" and "(laughs)" and clocks chiming, the interview is actually a rather refreshing change from the standard "editor's introduction." We are spared the usual huzzahs and accolades, as well as the editor's (often misplaced) assertions about which poems are the best. Instead, we get a leisurely, sometimes rambly walk-through of Enslin's career, attaching names and places to poems that might otherwise seem as though they floated in a void.

* * *

Very near the beginning of *Then, and Now* stands "Witch Hazel," a poem that wants to serve as an *ars poetica*. Enslin, in "straight-flying fury," is tired of the oneiric haze of Romanticism, the fuzz of abstraction. He will have none of

The dead bone of poetics buried
under sacramental clouds
of sleep or of wine, or too much
awareness of the things that are not there:
Ghosts.

The solution? A Frost-like return to nature. The poet will cut himself a branch of witch hazel, both an astringent switch to "whip old ghosts / through sunsets to the morning," and a dowsing rod that will lead him to water, "An old cellar hole / dropping away to the infinite side of the hill and the sunset" (TN 18–19).

"Witch Hazel" is a homely but likable poem, energetic in its syntax and plain in its vocabulary. And it's a polemic, rare enough for Enslin, who tends toward observation and rumination. There's a sly jab against Eliot's poetics of cultural mosaic, fragments shored against ruins—"straight-flying / is my time of day, and no ruins / but for rocks to build"—and a reverent nod to Whitman: "Nostalgia is along the way / and very well, but no stopover" (TN 19). Of course, in terms of mystery and intensity, "Witch Hazel" is nowhere near the poem its mid-section evokes, Frost's "Directive," where the "belilaced cellar hole" of the abandoned homestead glowers near "A brook that was the water of the house," and the narrator offers the reader "A broken drinking goblet like the Grail":

(I stole the goblet from the children's playhouse.)
Here are your waters and your watering place.
Drink and be whole again beyond confusion.[5]

"Directive" is a scary, deep poem about the return to origins (and, for my money, Frost's best); "Witch Hazel," for all its energy, is hunting far smaller game: "The dead bone of poetics."

Once you're a few score more pages into *Then, and Now*, you start wondering how much of this *ars poetica* has really stuck. The thrust of "Witch Hazel" isn't all that different from what Pound and Williams had called for decades earlier. "Don't use such an expression as 'dim lands *of peace*'. It dulls the image. It mixes an abstraction with the concrete," wrote Pound way back in 1913, "Go in fear of abstractions."[6] "I am not in search," says Williams in *Spring and All*, "of 'the beautiful illusion.'"[7] What Pound and Williams were up against was a poetry that lost itself in ideas and abstractions, "Dim lands of peace," blurry evocations of Keats's "faery lands forlorn." The early Enslin seems little tempted by such vapors. But there are other sorts of abstractions to go in fear of than just the Romantic variety, and while the concrete image may be something to strive for, the directness of a poet's observations doesn't guarantee the success of his poem.

Most of the first third of *Then, and Now* consists of poems chiseled out of moments of everyday experience, set down in standard-issue post-Williams free verse. A man tinkers with his custom car in "Hot Rod":

> Among the tall yellow flowers
> (ten petalled helianthus)
> he works over the rusted body,
> greased rods of a cut down truck—
> something he made for himself.

Walking away, this shade-tree mechanic steps "back through the flowers / without noticing / them" (TN 46). (The poet, of course, both precise and sensitive, has been able to name and describe the blossoms—a gesture wholly in keeping with the disdain for industrial society that runs through Enslin's work.) Enslin observes, records, and implies a conclusion, having something to do with the natural and the man-made—the worker, absorbed in steel, but blind to the beauties of the flowers. Not a subtle point, to be sure, but it's a modest poem.

The 1962 sequence *New Sharon's Prospect* (included in its entirety in *Then, and Now*) reads like an Imagist boiling-down of James Agee's *Let Us Now Praise Famous Men*. It consists of a number of interspersed poems and dated journal entries recounting Enslin's sojourn among the Tibbettses, a back-country family that earns its precarious living cutting firewood (the men) and making Christmas wreathes (the women). The prose sections give us the family in all its appalling fecundity, its subsistence-level scraping-by, and its rather creepy mixture of penny wisdom and imaginative poverty. The poems are freeze-frames of particular moments, reminiscent of Jonathan Williams at his most serious or Wendell Berry at his most offhand:

> baldwin's mill
>
> was burned last summer.
> The roof had bowed:
> slight curve, but unsafe.
> Looking at the charred trees there
> and the cracked chimney
> smothered in snow,
> I asked him about it:

"Baldwin came from New Hampshire.
Sawed hard wood there
until it warn't no use." (TN 29)

There is a certain modest pleasure to spare poems like this, but one can only work the resonances of short lines and plain speech so far before getting into the realm of what my erstwhile creative writing professor Wyatt Prunty once called "emaciated poetry."[8] In "Baldwin's Mill" Enslin foregoes two-thirds of the resources of his form: the Wile E. Coyote drop-offs of unexpected line breaks, the surprises of slightly off-kilter syntax. We're left with the bare statement, which is just barely enough.

New Sharon's Prospect is by far the most unified run of poems from the earlier work here, and makes the most satisfying use of its perceptions. Enslin is able to elicit both sympathy for the lives of these New England Snopeses and amusement at their expense. More often, Enslin's brief verses clamp down so heavily upon a moment as to squash it underneath:

Not that it is
                    more than
the tree flowering
                            next to it,
not that its branches,
                broken in winter,
compose well.
                    I doubt
if it bears fruit;
                        but the recognition
of it,
        on another errand,
makes a part
                    of the day.
("View of a Flowering Plum," TN 117)

Depending on your point of view, this poem is either an anorexic version of "I Wandered Lonely as a Cloud" or a Dom DeLuise version of "The Red Wheelbarrow." There are lots of such moments in *Then, and Now* and *Re-Sounding*. They read like journal jottings, the poet's wrestling of daily experience into significance through tricks of lineation. After going through a few dozen such pieces, one's patience begins to flag. "In a Station of the Metro" is a dandy poem, but Pound only wrote it *once*.

When Enslin has no immediate experience at hand, however, he tends to turn his portentous beam upon the processes of his own thought. The result is too often a tortuous and terribly serious mulling over of abstract issues, as in the fourth section of "The Poem of No Shadow":

> I began—
> but I found there
> no beginning,
>   nor as an end
> a period—
>   finality
> was no part of it.
> The human condition formed
> in clusters—
>   grew upon the vine
> as grapes,
> and at any point
>   picked up
> it involved the rest of it—
> totality
>   which was more
> and less than
>   total. (TN 80–81)

As an exercise in post-Olsonian lineation and dry, post-Zukofskyan sound manipulation, this poem isn't bad—if it doesn't taste great, it's at least drinkable. As *logopoeia*, the "dance of the intellect among words," however, it's definitely less filling. The vine-like tangles of the "human condition" is a pretty good image (though one winces at that last phrase), but the conclusion—"totality / which was more / and less than / total"—is not so much truly paradoxical as *easy*, a grammatical sleight-of-hand.

Too often Enslin's thoughts coil themselves into miniature Celtic knots and then, like a temporary tattoo in the shower, wash off the page before your eyes. By the time one reaches the halfway point of *Then, and Now*, and the poems seem to toggle almost mechanically between these two modes—irritatingly fastidious observation and abstract statements dressed up as revelation—one begins to sigh at the great vistas of pages yet to read.

* * *

And then things change. Enslin's poetry starts becoming something else altogether, something far more moving. The idea of music has taken hold of the poet, pushing him in new formal directions. While he may use it only intermittently, Enslin has always been a poet with quite a good ear. Listen to "Road or River" (1943), the first poem of *Then, and Now*, which ends with three sonically ravishing lines: "The night, for river or for road, / will move its silence, and a few / night singers: Crickets, and the wind in wheat" (TN 17). (I hear Keats's "To Autumn" there—"hedge-crickets sing.") But it's only in his later work that Enslin begins thinking of the poem as a music-like composition, and begins to subordinate his small-scale structures of looking and thinking to more ambitious, musically derived principles of order.

The jacket copy of *Re-Sounding: Selected Later Poems* is anxious to key us in to Enslin's musical connections: "Theodore Enslin's poetry, writer Herschel Silverman has said, 'is actually musical composition.' A student under Nadia Boulanger, Enslin also attended the New England Conservatory of Music."[9] I don't care for that "actually," and I don't think Enslin would quite endorse the statement, but the overall import is clear. As Enslin puts it to Nowak, "I've often said that I like to be considered as a composer who happens to use words instead of notes. That's all. That is, if you want to flatter me, say that. Don't call me a poet. Don't call me a writer. Don't call me . . . anything. Composer" (TN 418).

When we harp on the conjunction of poetry and music, we're on a marshy and treacherous ground beloved of the modernists. Was it Pater who started it all, with his claim that "All art constantly aspires to the condition of music"? At any rate, Pound picked up that ball and ran with it. "Poetry is a composition of words set to music," he wrote in 1918 (picking up also on a suggestion of Dante), "poetry withers and 'dries out' when it leaves music, or at least an imagined music, too far behind it."[10] Despite his tendentious tone, Pound has some pretty solid historical backing here. Scholars will tell us that what such archaic Greek poets as Sappho made—*mousike*, or *melos*—was not lyric poetry as we know it, but an art form in which the words were inseparable from the tune to which they were sung. The great Tudor lyricists—Campion, Wyatt—wrote to a composer's tune. But for the most part, the equation of lyric poetry and music is a rhetorical one, an analogy, and has been such at least since the time of Longinus's *On the Sublime*. Catullus may have called his poems *carmina*, "songs," but he knew that they were being read, not sung.

The real shift comes when poets begin to think of the relationship between music and poetry, not in the familiar terms of harmonious words, lyrical "music" (Pound's *melopoeia*), but in terms of *structure*. In the nineteenth century, this relationship was only dimly perceived, out-dazzled by Wagner's *Gesamtkunstwerk*, the ultimate art form that would incorporate all of the lesser forms—music, poetry, drama, and so forth. In 1895 Mallarmé told a Cambridge audience that "our present task . . . is to find a way of transposing the symphony to the Book: in short, to regain our rightful due."[11] Twenty years before, that other Wagnerian Sidney Lanier (himself a professional musician of great gifts), had written "The Symphony," a rather dreadful poem that attempted not merely to describe the thematic and harmonic development of a Romantic symphony, but also to use that development as the model for its own argument.

The modernists certainly weren't anywhere near Lanier in their understanding of the technicalities of music, but they were far readier to strip the old accentual-syllabic machine down and rebuild it on new principles. In 1927, groping for analogies to describe the form of *The Cantos* in a letter to his father, Pound hit upon the fugue: "Rather like, or unlike subject and response and counter subject in fugue."[12] Fugal form is a tough fit for poetry—the fugue depends upon the simultaneous sounding of different but complementary musical themes, while a poem has to be read one line, one string of sound, at a time. That didn't stop Pound's brightest protégé Louis Zukofsky from experimenting with "fugal form" throughout the first half of his long poem "*A*", and Zukofsky's friend Basil Bunting would describe his own long poems as "sonatas."

So Enslin is working within a well-established modernist tradition, albeit one based on a problematic analogy. The value of a poetic method, however, doesn't lie in its accuracy or plausibility. The test is simple: does it produce interesting poems?

More often than not, Enslin's overtly "musical" poems offer pleasures far more compelling than his earlier work. His "Slow Theme with Nine Variations" begins by stating its "theme," a precisely phrased stanza of only somewhat discernable import:

> Cut it down
> to the stem,
> or let it dwindle
> to the pinch
> that holds its waist.
> Hourglass with trace
> of sand along its measure,
> in the just proportion
> as it moves away—.

Deflects the cut.
Restores—it deepens
sound or color   deepens
as it moves
between and deepens. (TN 226)

The cadences here are tentative, circling around a series of phrases—"Cut it down," "to the stem," "to the pinch"; the timbre is crisp, not at all mellifluous. Where Milton's music was a many-stopped organ, Enslin's is Webern's piano.

"Slow Theme with Nine Variations" shows Enslin moving beyond his earlier work. Instead of simply exfoliating from a given group of lines and images, he's held himself to the classic "theme and variations" form, a clearly stated opening passage followed by a finite set of variations of more or less the same duration as the theme from which they depart. The first variation, for instance, has indeed "cut down" its theme, but evokes new, related images—the pinched waist of a hussar, or a wasp.

Pinch
        hold in
waist
        hussar
and wasp
to breathe
is to
      instill
as steel
          to stellar
stelae
        sand
that deepens. (TN 226–27)

The long **e** of "between" and "deepens" has become a key sound in the variation—"breathe," "steel"—the repeated action of "breathing" picking up the time-keeping sense of the theme's "Hourglass." Breathing "instills" oxygen in the blood, and sets off a string of **st** sounds—"instill / as steel / stellar / stelae," so that the pinch-waisted hourglass of the theme has become, in the variation, a tall, narrow stele—a formal pun which should be taken, as well, in its botanical sense. It's hard to say precisely what's being *meant* here, what the poem's talking about, though I suspect Enslin has taken the pruning of shrubbery as his occasion. Subject-matter becomes secondary to the poem's play of words.

Later variations introduce new material still. The fourth, which begins "This thinking's labyrinth, / fly-blown and with vinegar, / this passage where the thread is lost" (TN 226), ropes in the Classical (the labyrinth of Daedalus), the vernacular ("You catch more flies with honey than with vinegar," as my mom used to say), and the philosophical: the hourglass is now the fly-bottle of Wittgenstein's *Philosophical Investigations.* (§309: "What is your aim in philosophy?—To shew the fly the way out of the fly-bottle."[13]) "Variation Seven," in parallel columns, associates the dwindling of the Hourglass's sand with a range of Ovidian shape-shifters—Daphne, Echo, Narcissus:

Diminished	pinch
dwindling	waist
a young girl	in a forest
clothed	in leaves
Ah! Daphne	echoes
holds	to purpose
still	pool
narrows	deep (TN 229)

(The pool, Narcissus's looking-glass, has been foreshadowed in the fifth variation—"glass to see by" [TN 228].) Once you get past the fact that these columns can be read either vertically (one at a time) or horizontally (line by line), a neat but rather flimsy trick, you see how the variation both picks up clusters of words from previous sections and forms itself around particular rhythmical units. "Dwindling" and "pinch" appeared in the "Theme"; "waist" in the first variation, "narrows" in the fifth, and "Diminished" in the sixth. Like the "Theme," "Variation Seven" plays with a series of triplets: "Diminished," "a young girl," "Ah! Daphne," and "to purpose."

Music for Several Occasions, the collection that includes "Slow Theme with Nine Variations," also contains "A Chromatic Fantasy," "Passacaglia," "Rondo," "Chaconne," and "Concerto for Solo Voice and Chorus" (with a clutch of poems designated "songs," to boot). I'm not qualified to say how accurately Enslin has imitated these forms in each poem, but these poems strike one with a shapeliness previously lacking. Once in a while, of course, this poetry of repetition and variation gets mechanical. "Motet," for instance, shuffles and recombines the phrases "burnished arrows," "morning light," a "bending bow," and "glowing air" over a full four pages, until one wants to scream "Shoot the bloody thing already!" More often, however, Enslin's variations are subtle, surprising, and aurally satisfying.

In more recent poems, I sense a development parallel to that of Enslin's friend John Taggart. Taggart spent much of the seventies and early eighties developing a poetry heavily influenced by jazz and American "minimalist" classical music, a poetry in which lines and groups of lines are repeated with minor but constantly accreting changes. Works like Taggart's *Peace on Earth* (1981) are perhaps the verbal equivalent of, for instance, Steve Reich's fifty-six-minute *Music for 18 Musicians*. To the right listener, in the right mood, hearing music gradually shift and change is an almost orgasmic experience; to everyone else, it's like watching paint dry. Similarly, you can't silently read through *Peace on Earth* for more than fifteen pages without your eyes beginning to glaze over; read aloud, however, the poem becomes a hypnotic, moving experience. Taggart's more recent poems make use of repetition in a far more understated, supple manner, and his way of deploying repeating and slightly varied phrases from line to line, and within the line, is very similar to what Enslin achieves in many of the later poems of *Then, and Now*.

"Sonata for a Sextet," for instance, begins with a description—or more accurately, an imitation—of the six instrumental voices "leading" one another, then merging into a general tone:

> Just as the voices
>   lead one to another
> just in parts
>   six lead
>   open to one
> another one just voice
>   leading
> down the ice
>   to fire rise
> in moves of one to another
> rising   just part
>   six strands
> the talking various
>   multiplied
> in layers just as parts
> to another no longer
>   parted
>   toned (TN 290–91)

Note how the verbal echoes mime the echoing lines of the instruments, while never falling into exact repetition: "*Just* as the voices . . . *just* in *parts* . . . *just* voice . . . *just part* . . . *just* as *parts* . . . no longer *parted*" (to follow only one "line" of several). The "meaning," of course, is quite unparaphrasable, and Enslin's telling Nowak that the piece is based on the Opus 18 of Brahms doesn't really pin it down any better (TN 407). (That's the B-Flat Major Sextet of 1859–1860, by the way, though Enslin doesn't tell us so.) One can only read the words aloud, slowly, and marvel at the shifting, interlocking patterns—which is what, after all, Pater meant by the "condition of music": a purely formal art, patterns without content.

It's a bravura performance, this "Sonata for a Sextet," a sophisticated updating of Lanier's "The Symphony" sustained over four movements and nine printed pages. Along with "Abendmusik," "La Foglia," and a number of other poems that don't have explicit musical tags in their titles—"Aberrant Rock," "Small Pastoral Displaced," and others—it bears comparison with Zukofsky's "A"-13, a five-section imitation of Bach's Violin Sonata in D Minor. However, Enslin eschews Zukofsky's range of cultural reference, the magpie sensibility that makes room in "A"-13 for Hermes Trismegistus, Nikita Krushchev, William and Henry James, Montaigne, the anonymous gentleman reading the paper on the Brooklyn Heights Promenade, and (probably) the kitchen sink. Enslin is content to work harder a more limited palette of images or references. In "Small Pastoral Displaced," that palette contains the key term "gold," the secondary terms "elixir," "sulfur," "iris," a set of solar observations, and a number of allusions to alchemy. The poem resolves on a quiet acknowledgement of the sun's continual "gilding" of the day—"a day / another / as another day" (TN 354)—but the shuffling and variation that lead up to this redeem the ending from commonplace.

There are, I hasten to add, more pleasures to be had from *Then, and Now* than simply watching Enslin unfold his meta-musical elaborations. The long, lovely sequence *The Weather Within* is also a sort of theme with variations, but in these poems Enslin is responding to poems, lines, and ideas he's found in George Oppen's work. Oppen deals with weighty issues—the nature of community, the possibility of communication through poetry, the meaning (one can't avoid the cliché) of life. Enslin's plainspoken, brief responses have about them the same tentativeness of Oppen's longer, more scattered poems, yet achieve a lucidity that often eludes Oppen.

"Her Signature Herself," the first of the paired sequences *Love and Science*, is a series of unabashed love songs. The first, "Love Song in Silver," is worth quoting in full, both for its cheeky forwardness, its Steinian singsong, and the delicacy with which Enslin manipulates its surprisingly regular meter:

My love's a cleft
cleft peach her lips
her sex a cleft
off center cleft

that I may enter her
or so I think to take
ripe fruit so cleft
yet as she is not owned
herself the cleft
a cleft her own
not mine unless she wills it so (TN 299)

("Horny" is not an adjective one immediately applies to Enslin, but someone has "cleft" on his mind in this poem.) The entire sequence is a warm, compelling, adult, and unromanticized set of poems on conventional Romantic themes. It's as if Enslin, out on recess from watching nature à la Williams or Basho, or wrestling with the infinite à la Oppen or Bronk, has found new energy in climbing the jungle gym of good old Eros.

* * *

Enslin at his best is often a *quiet* poet, and the poems of *Re-Sounding: Selected Later Poems* are quiet indeed. ("Selected," by the way, seems a bit of a misnomer—most of the material is previously unpublished, and the book as a whole feels like two or three of Enslin's shorter books bunged together.) There are more evanescent haiku-like things here—"Sickle cut of ice / the darker waters / of the pond reflecting / nothing" (RS 103)—some lovely moments of seeing, like "Honey in the Snow"—

Not to look too closely
but is there anything
quite like a woman's blonde hair
freshly braided flecked
with tiny snowflakes
as she stands talking
to a friend and the snow
passes over both of them? (RS 56)

—and even flashes of welcome, if unsubtle, humor. (It wouldn't be fair to call Enslin a *dour* poet, but let's say that the earnest element far outweighs the playful in his poetry.) The great majority of the poems in *Re-Sounding* are less than a page long; Enslin is content to walk Pegasus around the pony-riding ring rather than letting him rip on the five-mile course. The poems here have all the shortcomings and strengths of the rest of Enslin's work. They can be portentous, mawkish, and almost absurd in their quest for the profound behind the inconsequential. But they benefit from Enslin's delicate ear and meticulous sense of lineation, and display the tentative stance of a wide-eyed observer, continually prepared to be surprised by what comes next. The best poems dwell on leave-taking, loss, and ageing. This is something of a shame, for *Then, and Now* leaves me with the vivid impression of a poet not just ageless, but actively *young*. (The "Her Signature Herself" poems, written when Enslin was in his mid-sixties, make the poems of Robert Creeley's *For Love* seem like a codger's reminiscences.) No longer. Now a bare tree, which would once have sparked the poet to a meditation on the branches' framing of the sky, produces an evocation of melancholy leaf-drift: "Overnight the litter below / of leaves grown suddenly ancient" (RS 96). Enslin's work has acquired a new pathos without sacrificing the old delicacy:

> Of age which gnarls and hardens   rock and bone
> left bleaching to the open sea
> its storms bring in the news   and in detritus
> what has fallen aimless   aimed in currents
> caught in tides   comes in ashore
> to founder there until a blaze removes it
> bare once more   a fire in its drifted wood
> sings age to age   a gentle ash
> to cover what's to come
> and what's to come to age again
> the gnarl of aging and a promised wind.
>   ("Fait Accompli," RS 68)

For the first-time or time-strapped reader, *Then, and Now* is a fine distillation of the Enslin *oeuvre. Re-Sounding* feels like a coda to that collection, but I wouldn't bet on its being anywhere near Enslin's last (lo and behold!, a quick Amazon.com search shows that two new Enslin titles have just become available). And I wouldn't discourage anyone—another editor, or just an interested reader—from wading out into the trackless pastures of Enslin's planting. There's lots of grain to be found in those overgrown fields.

Notes

1. William Blake, *The Marriage of Heaven and Hell*, ed. Sir Geoffrey Keynes (Oxford: Oxford UP, 1975) plates 7 and 9.
2. Ezra Pound, *The Spirit of Romance* (New York: New Directions, 1968) 182.

3. Theodore Enslin, *Then, and Now: Selected Poems 1943–1993*, ed. Mark Nowak (Orono, ME: National Poetry Foundation, 1999) 390; hereafter cited parenthetically in text as TN.

4. Jackson Mac Low, *Representative Works: 1938–1985* (New York: Roof Books, 1986).

5. Robert Frost, *Collected Poems, Prose, and Plays*, ed. Richard Poirier and Mark Richardson (New York: Library of America, 1995) 342.

6. Ezra Pound, *Literary Essays*, ed. T. S. Eliot (1935; New York: New Directions, 1968) 5.

7. William Carlos Williams, *Imaginations*, ed. Webster Schott (New York: New Directions, 1970) 89.

8. Wyatt Prunty, "Emaciated Poetry," *Sewanee Review* 93.1 (Winter 1985): 78–94.

9. Theodore Enslin, *Re-Sounding: Selected Later Poems* (Jersey City, NJ: Talisman House, 1999); hereafter cited parenthetically in text as RS.

10. Pound, *Literary Essays* 437.

11. Stéphane Mallarmé, *Selected Prose Poems, Essays, and Letters*, trans. Bradford Cook (Baltimore: Johns Hopkins UP, 1956) 42.

12. Ezra Pound, *Selected Letters, 1907–1941*, ed. D. D. Paige (1950; New York: New Directions, 1971) 210.

13. Ludwig Wittgenstein, *Philosophical Investigations*, 3rd ed., trans. G. E. M. Anscombe (1953: New York: Macmillan, 1968) 103e.

Truth, Beauty, and the Remote Control

Anne Carson

Never short of cheek, Ezra Pound printed the following three lines, ellipses and all, as a complete poem in his 1916 collection *Lustra*:

> Spring . . .
> too long . . .
> Gongula . . . [1]

"Papyrus" is of course a (barely) plausible translation of what remains of three lines from one of Sappho's poems, preserved on a scrap of parchment (not papyrus) first transcribed and published in 1902. ("Gongula," who also appears in Fragment 211, is Sappho's heart-throb of the moment.) There's an idealism involved in speaking of Sappho's "poems," because none of them, save for a single twenty-eight line lyric, now exists complete. Clumps of words, groups of lines, and lone letters—quoted by classical grammarians and critics, or made out by turn-of-the-century German scholars peering themselves blind—are all we have of the seventh century BCE.

And yet, as Guy Davenport writes, these "mere words and phrases . . . were once a poem, and, like broken statuary, are strangely articulate in their ruin."[2] Certainly many twentieth-century poets have found them so. Where the Romantics had embraced Winckelmann's notion of Periclean culture as the apex of beauty and grace, the modernists made space at the table for Sappho's fragments, stripped of the padding and conjectural reconstructions within which Victorian translators had swaddled them. There was a new respect for the fragment, a fascination we can see not only in "Papyrus" but also in, for instance, Rilke's "Archaic Torso of Apollo" and the "fragments" Eliot shores against his ruin at the close of *The Waste Land*. The classical fragment, dating from "the springtime of the world," comes into its own in the modernist period, and it's no surprise that so many of the modern poets—Pound, Cummings, H. D., Zukofsky—were Classicists of an unorthodox stripe, revolting against philology, the deadening Germanic discipline in which Pound had been trained at Penn. These were *poems*, after all. If some silly University of Chicago Classicist couldn't recognize *Homage to Sextus Propertius* as an adaptation rather than a translation, how could he see the poetic energy that radiated from three words of a Sappho fragment?

Following squarely in this tradition, Anne Carson launched her meteoric career—she has won a basketful of prizes, sold quite a few books, been profiled in *The New York Times Magazine,* and is writing her way through a multivolume contract with Knopf—with a meditation (mostly) on Sappho called *Eros the Bittersweet: An Essay* (1986). Suddenly, out of the drab woods of Classical scholarship—those stolid Clarendon editions of Greek medical texts, those sociological examinations of burial practices—sprang this glittering nymph of a little book, thirty-six brief chapters dwelling on, caressing, unraveling erotic desire as Sappho and her contemporaries conveyed it. In limpid, pointed prose, *Eros the Bittersweet* shows the power of desire to unseat reason, to loosen limbs, to destroy cities. By the time I've gotten to the last page, where Carson rests her case—"It is a high-risk proposition, as Sokrates saw quite clearly, to reach for the difference between the known and the unknown. He thought the risk worthwhile, because he was in love with wooing itself. And who is not?"[3]—I'm willing to forgive the inflated rhetorical question and count myself in.

Part of the appeal of *Eros the Bittersweet* is that while it treats of fragments and may seem, on the surface, to be (in the manner of Pound's choppy *Guide to Kulchur*) rather fragmentary itself, in fact there's a logical order behind the dips, swoops, and veers of these aphoristic mini-essays. The book began as a doctoral dissertation—Carson being, as everyone knows, a Classics professor by trade—and the traditional argumentative structure of the academic paper still lurks behind its modular form. Each two- to nine-page chapter builds upon the ones before it, and Carson sets observations, speculations, and interpretations upon each other in a balanced and seemingly inescapable progression.

Yet can the same be generally said, *mutatis mutandis,* of her poetry? For here too Carson is irresistibly drawn to fragments, even if she refuses to acknowledge it. (In a hilarious *Iowa Review* interview with John D'Agata—who, armed with all the slings and arrows of an MFA vocabulary, seems as frustrated as his subject—Carson, when asked about "fragmented narratives," impatiently responds, "What do you mean by a 'fragment'?" She'd rather speak of "Painting with thoughts and facts.") At the same time, she would have her poems manifest a quality known to the Greeks as *charis,* which she defines for D'Agata as follows: "The Greeks used the word for the grace of a poem, the charm that makes it a poem and makes you want to remember it. So for them to make a poem is to make something that will be so charming that it will be a gift that the world wants to receive and also give back precisely because it's so good."[4] But how does a poem achieve this grace, this memorability, when the poet is so attracted to the fragmentary, the broken, the enigmatic bit? What sorts of "charm"—if any—is Carson able to conjure out of her shards of language and emotion?

* * *

Carson's favorite trick over the years has been to juxtapose or overlay elements, usually taken from sources that are widely disparate, either culturally or temporally, or both. Sometimes such juxtaposition seems to serve a didactic purpose; more often, it just elicits a pleasant shock of the strange (a shock which often doesn't survive multiple readings). "The Glass Essay," the longest poem of Carson's second collection *Glass, Irony and God* (1995), manages to give us at once a seemingly autobiographical narrative and a meditation on the works and lives of the Brontë sisters.[5] For *Autobiography of Red* (1998), her "novel in verse," Carson went back to the fragments of the seventh-century BCE poet Stesichoros and refashioned his narrative of the monster Geryon so that Geryon becomes pretty much your average backpack-carrying, artistically inclined, self-consciously gay teenager—burdened, incidentally, by being winged, bright red, and in love with a Don Juan named Herakles.[6]

All this, needless to say, is very modernist indeed, not very different from what Joyce did when he plopped Odysseus down in 1904 Dublin in the person of a petit-bourgeois Jewish ad canvasser, or what Eliot did when he had Tiresias play peeping Tom to the amours of a bored typist and a repulsive office clerk. But the strategy has served Carson well enough, and she continues to experiment with it in her 2000 collection *Men in the Off Hours.* In the twinned poems "Hokusai" and "Audubon," she contrasts the two painters, one Japanese, the other American. (Our approval is meant to go to Hokusai, because he doesn't have to kill and wire up his tigers to paint them, as Audubon his birds.) In "Lazarus (1st draft)," the resurrected brother of Mary and Martha quotes *War and Peace.* In "Hopper: *Confessions,*" short poems responding to Edward Hopper paintings are counterpointed with passages from St. Augustine's *Confessions.*

But such overlaid perspectives are freshest in Carson's "TV Men," parts of which first appeared in *Glass, Irony and God.* The sequence has been expanded and made more complex in *Men in the Off Hours*, and now it even has a pseudo-epigraph: "TV makes things disappear. Oddly the word comes from Latin *videre* 'to see.' (Longinus, *de Sublimitate*, 5.3)."[7] (That, I take it, is a joke, though a rather labored one: Part Five of *On the Sublime* has only one section.)

While at least some of these poems were inspired by Carson's experience working with Boston public television on a series about Nobel Prize winners, she admits not owning a set and seems to sport the standard intellectual disdain for the medium: it boils complex issues down to sound bites; it promotes flashy images over intelligent discourse; it turns our youth into couch-bound lotus-eaters, and so forth. But Carson's approach has less to do with TV as experienced by a regular viewer than with her own take on how it produces its shiny, ephemeral illusions. "TV Men: Hektor" (*Glass, Irony and God*) lays down portentous one-liners ("TV is ugly, like the future," "TV is inherently cynical. It speaks to the eye, but the mind has no eye," "TV is loud, yet we do not awake") as it transports the Trojan hero to Death Valley, where he is being filmed in his own death scene:

> He had constructed throughout Troy a system of gutters,
> which ran along both sides of every street,
> squared with stone
>
> in alternating blocks of polished and unpolished agate.
> Waters ran quietly out of Troy.
> Now Hektor worries
>
> that stains on the back of his clothing will be visible
> from the helicopter as he turns
> to run.[8]

W. H. Auden might have chuckled; in his 1969 poem "Moon Landing," he noted that "Hector / was excused the insult of having / his valor covered by television."[9]

In the later, more fully realized poems of the sequence, Carson takes the odd distancings and awkward dissonances inherent to her conception of television and uses them as jumping-off points. In some poems, she explores the juxtapositions that occur between image and voice-over in documentaries. "TV Men: Tolstoy" crosscuts a narrative of moments in the novelist's life (often interior) with the visuals (often not "visual" at all) over which that narrative might be spoken:

A curiously tender man and yet
even after their marriage he
called his desire to kiss her
"the appearance of Satan."

Her in right profile against the light, all the music in the room streams toward the blue frosty window. (MO 75)

In other poems, she worries the relationship between life and script, the accidental or nefarious telescoping involved in cramming experience and thought into a twenty-inch screen and a thirty-minute time slot. Antigone, walking behind her father, the blind Oedipus, pauses to deliver a forty-two second speech into the microphone. "For sound-bite purposes," the director notes, "we had to cut Antigone's script from 42 seconds to 7 . . ." The resulting six lines, cobbled together out of the original fourteen, are indeed more sound-bite-worthy:

Other things I like: a lot of money!
The way we live, light and shadow are ironic.
Projects? yes: physics. Anarchy. My father.
Here, twist a bit off.
Freedom is next. (MO 101)

There's one of Carson's judgments on television: from Sophokles to Jerry Springer.

The most striking of these video odes is "TV Men: Lazarus," which spreads itself over three sections. The first is a "voiceover" from the Director of Photography, who is both a technician and something of a theorist; he knows what TV is all about, "how the pull is irresistible. The pull to handle horrors / and to have a theory of them" (MO 87). He is about to film Christ's raising of Lazarus from the dead, and while not entirely sure of the theological implications of that resurrection ("if / God's gift is simply random, well / for one thing / it makes a / more interesting TV show"), he knows the Platonic implications of his own medium: "Lazarus is an imitation of Christ,"

As TV is an imitation of
Lazarus. As you and I are an imitation of

TV. Already you notice that
although I am merely
a director of photography,

I have grasped certain fundamental notions first advanced by Plato,
e.g. that our reality is just a TV set

inside a TV set inside a TV set, with nobody watching
but Sokrates,
who changed
the channel in 399 B.C. (MO 88–89)

But the director is not interested in repetition, how Christ's resurrection will replay that of Lazarus, nor in the "Before and after"—there won't be any "home videos of Lazarus / in short pants," or "footage of Mary and Martha side by side on the sofa / discussing how they manage / at home / with a dead one sitting down to dinner" (MO 90). Instead, his documentary will focus "entirely on this moment, the flip-over moment" of resurrection:

I put tiny microphones all over the ground
to pick up
the magic
of the vermin in his ten fingers and I stand back to wait
for the miracle. (MO 91)

That final detail—"the vermin in his ten fingers"—succeeds, to some degree, in making the entire monologue come alive, redeeming it from the director's irredeemable vulgarity (not to mention the flat, prosaic lines in which he speaks).

Would that Carson could sustain the balance of "Director of Photography: Voiceover" in the middle section of the poem. "Lazarus Standup" attempts to narrate the experience of being raised from the dead, a tall order that Carson isn't quite up to. She falls into overheated metaphor, a hyperbolic miming of the "blooming, buzzing confusion" of sensation that leads up to an embarrassing climax, deflated not nearly enough by the director's voice: "We know the difference now / (life or death) / For an instant it parts our hearts. / *Someone take the linen napkin off his face,* / says the director quietly" (MO 95). The final, ekphrastic section, "Giotto Shot List," consists of four looks at Giotto's Lazarus fresco in the Scrovegni chapel. "Giotto," Carson writes, addressing Lazarus, "slips / you / sideways into time." Lazarus's eyes "have the power of the other world. Barely open, / narrow shock slits / whose gaze is directed—simply, nowhere" (MO 97, 99). The painting is described lovingly, even painfully, and with an intensity Carson denies the video medium.

It's hard not to read a moral here, and a rather obvious one at that: TV may capture the moment as it happens, and it may be where the money gets made, but when it comes to real miracles, give me that old-time religion of Renaissance frescoes. One can't help feeling that Carson is looking at television from only one end of the tube. In her fascination with the fractious goings-on that take place behind the camera and in the script doctor's office, she overlooks the oddly seamless reality that the medium presents to viewers on their couches. She's less the restaurant critic assessing the andouille than the health inspector wrinkling her nose at what goes into the casings. (Inevitably, in some future installment of "TV Men," Carson will latch onto the remote control, the magic wand that zaps us through thirty worlds a minute, and I'm not sure whether to look forward to that moment with pleasure or trepidation.)

As mixed as the results may be, one has to admire Carson's originality and audacity in taking television production as a formal model. In fact, this is just one example of her refusal to be bound by generic conventions. She seems determined to make every form she touches new, to twist it out of the expected. One hesitates to call Carson a formalist—there's not a sonnet to be found in her books, nor a ghost of meter (though one turns up a very occasional rhyme)—but her work shows a continual fascination with casting ideas into different forms.

The seven little "Epitaphs" sprinkled through *Men in the Off Hours,* for example, have the brevity, shapeliness, and conceptual snap that we associate with the genre, yet they entirely resist the specificity, the human connection it demands. "Epitaph: Zion" paints in shades of Celan—

> Murderous little world once our objects had gazes. Our lives
>   Were fragile, the wind
> Could dash them away. here lies the refugee breather
>   Who drank a bowl of elsewhere. (MO 9)

—while "Epitaph: Thaw" flirts with early Auden at his most Edward Learish, in the process pointing up Carson's fondness for the awkward and the faux-naïf:

> Little clicks all night in the back lane there blackness
>   Goes leaking out the key.
> "It twindles," said Father to April on her
>   Anvil of deep decree. (MO 127)

Another form that Carson extensively tinkers with—or perhaps eviscerates—in *Men in the Off Hours* is the essay poem. (Like *Glass, Irony and God,* the book includes a traditional essay, "Dirt and Desire: Essay on the Phenomenology of Female Pollution in Antiquity," reprinted from a scholarly venue and trailing a cloud of footnotes. So far as I'm concerned, Carson should keep such work out of her poetry books.) "Essay on What I Think About Most" is pretty much what its title claims: a little essay on "Error / and its emotions," beginning with Aristotle's claim that metaphor "causes the mind to experience itself / / in the act of making a mistakes" (MO 30) and then musing over a computational error in an Alkman poem. The fact that it's broken into verse lines doesn't make it any less an essay, a brief bit of expository writing. Its follow-up poem, however, "Essay on Error (2nd Draft)" is something else altogether, a brief, enigmatic monologue by an unnamed poet:

> It is also true I dream about soiled suede gloves.
> And have done so
> since the day I read
> in the third published volume of Freud's letters
> (this was years after I stopped seeing him)
> a sentence which I shall quote in full.
> Letter to Ferenczi 7.5.1909:
> "He doesn't look a bit like a poet except for the lashes."
> Freud hesitates to name me
> but
> let me tell you
> that was no
> pollen stain.
> Here
> I could paraphrase Descartes
> *The hand that busy instrument*
> or just let it go.
> After all
> what are you and I compared to him?
> Smell of burnt pastilles.
> I still remember the phrase every time I pass that spot. (MO 37)

Who speaks here? What was that yellow stain on those suede gloves? Above all, who has made the "error"? I don't have a problem with the poem's esoteric references, but I'm not running to the library to check out Freud's letters or thumbing through my Descartes, either; the poem's learning seems no more than a nimbus of teasing mystery. Carson might call this an "essay" all she wants, but it has nothing to do with anything Cicero or Plutarch pioneered. (As she tells D'Agata, her idea of the essay is on the Ciceronian model, "to have something to say and to do so"; she has no time either for Montaigne's self-revelation or his recursive ramblings.[10]) "Essay on Error (2nd Draft)" is a fragment of speech, half of a long-distance telephone conversation. It belongs on the same shelf as Pound's "Papyrus" or Eliot's "Prufrock." One reason Carson's poem isn't in the same league as Eliot's, however, is her mostly inert, unmusical lines. She has no gift for rhythm, and her unsubtle line breaks—"but / let me tell you" or "Here / I could paraphrase Descartes"—read like an undergraduate's touching attempts to jazz up a piece of prose.

Finally, *Men in the Off Hours* also includes several translations, if one can call them that. When Carson translates Sappho or Archilochos in *Eros the Bittersweet,* she seems more interested in getting across Greek word order than in recreating poems; her versions of Sappho aren't a patch on Davenport's or Mary Barnard's. In *Men in the Off Hours*, however, she joins the ranks of iconoclastic modernist translators. Pound covered his tail by calling his Propertius an "Homage." Zukofsky was less shy—the zany, slangy, phonetic transliterations he (in collaboration with his wife Celia) did of Catullus were meant "to breathe the 'literal' meaning" of the *Carmina.*[11] Carson ups the ante in "Catullus: *Carmina*," where she adapts fifteen of Catullus's lyrics in a manner that would give my high school Latin teacher conniption fits. "Passer Deliciae Meae Puellae," where the poet moans about the attention his beloved is giving her sparrow (rather than him), becomes a grim, slightly perverse contemporary snapshot:

On her lap one of the matted terriers.
She was combing around its genitals.
It grinned I grinned back.
It's the one she calls *Little Bottle* after Deng Xiaoping. (MO 38)

The old chestnut "Odi et Amo" ("I hate and love. Why I do so, perhaps you ask. I know not, but I feel it, and I am in torment," in F. W. Cornish's stolid paraphrase[12]) becomes a Dick Higgins-like Fluxus piece:

Hate hate hate hate hate hate hate hate hate.
Hate hate hate hate hate hate hate love hate.
Love love love love love love love love love love.
Love hate love love love love love love love love.
Why why why why why why why why why why.
Why why why why why I why why why why why.
I I I I I I I I I I I I I I I I I I I I I I I I I I I I I I I I I I I.
I I I I I I I I I I I I I I I I why I I I I I I I I I I I I I I I I I I.
(MO 42)

That, I fear, wears less well on each rereading. Far more compelling is Carson's reduction of "Si Quisquam Mutis Gratum Acciptumve Sepuleris"—a lovely poem in which Catullus comforts his friend Calvus on the death of his wife—down to a *Cathay*-like flutter of words:

As tree shapes from mist
Her young death
Loose
In you. (MO 43)

* * *

Carson's determination to explode and splice forms is even more pronounced in her most recent book, *The Beauty of the Husband,* which is provocatively subtitled *A Fictional Essay in 29 Tangos.* Not surprisingly, the book isn't really an essay at all, but rather a narrative poem in twenty-nine sections, or "tangos." "The word 'tango,'" María Susana Azzi gushes in the liner notes to yet another Astor Piazzola recording, "conjures up images of Buenos Aires, of a dimly lit dance floor, the smoke of a cigarette curling up into the air, a beautiful woman in the arms of a man, surrendering to a rhythm that is at once love and dream, pain and reality."[13] Carson is briefer: "A tango (like a marriage) is something you have to dance to the end."[14] The poet may be less prone to imaginative flights than Azzi (and most everybody else who's written on the dance), but Azzi's images fit *The Beauty of the Husband* pretty well: While it may not feature romance or trance, there's love, pain, and a woman's "surrender" to a rhythm—a rhythm of desire, which in the poem is inextricable from the rhythm of marriage.

The rest of the book's dust-jacket copy (aside from the definition of "tango") reads as follows: "*The Beauty of the Husband* is an essay on Keats's idea that beauty is truth, and is also the story of a marriage." The relationship of Keats to *The Beauty of the Husband* is worth pondering, though I doubt I've worked it out. The tangos are introduced with little quotations from Keats, some of them from the odes but most from the dreary piece-work tragedy *Otho the Great* and the ham-fisted, unfinished satire *The Jealousies: A Faery Tale, by Lucy Vaughan Lloyd of China Walk, Lambeth* (better known as "The Cap and Bells"). Many of those quotations are, in the best Susan Howe style, deleted lines and questionable readings, and frankly, only God and Carson know their relationship to the tangos they introduce. And, of course, to speak of "Keats's idea that beauty is truth" is to open a whole other can of worms. Strictly speaking, Keats didn't say that—the Grecian urn did. What Keats himself said, in his

22 November 1817 letter to Benjamin Bailey, was, "I am certain of nothing but of the holiness of the Heart's affections and the truth of Imagination—What the imagination seizes as Beauty must be truth—whether it existed before or not—for I have the same Idea of all our Passions as of Love they are all in their sublime, creative of essential Beauty."[15] One could read through a whole shelf of critical studies arguing out the implications of this statement, along with a few other passages in which Keats addresses the truth/beauty business, but Carson is interested in a far more concrete sense of beauty. As the long-suffering Wife of her poem says:

> . . . why did I love him from early girlhood to late middle age
> and the divorce decree came in the mail?
> Beauty. No great secret. Not ashamed to say I loved him for his beauty.
> As I would again
> if he came near. Beauty convinces. You know beauty makes sex
> possible.
> Beauty makes sex sex. (BH 9)

To summarize in the quickest and nastiest fashion, *The Beauty of the Husband* tells the story, largely from the point of view of the Wife, of a marriage in which the Husband is the sort of serial adulterer whose dalliances derive their savor from being committed in spite of the enamored and madly patient spouse to whom he always eventually returns. His attraction lies neither in his brains nor in his character, but in his "beauty"—this is all we know, and all we need to know.

The poem's narrative (the Wife, by the way, eventually shakes off this inexplicably attractive schmuck, if not his memory) is matter for a Jeanette Winterson novel, or a *New Yorker* short story. It is sturdily told, and at times reaches rather frightening emotional pitches. One scene unfolds in a hotel room in Athens, where the Husband has taken the Wife "after three years of separation . . . for adoration, for peace," but still must "telephone New York every night from the bar / and speak to a woman / who thought he was over on 4th Street / working late" (BH 99). There is a confrontation, an argument, and then, just as the two have reached an impasse (the Wife's mind running over Parmenides), "His nose begins to bleed."

> Then blood runs down over his upper lip, lower lip, chin.
> To his throat.
> Appears on the whiteness of his shirt.
> Dyes a mother-of-pearl button for good,

Blacker than a mulberry.
Don't think his heart had burst. He was no Tristan
(though he would love to point out that in the common version
Tristan is not false, it is the sail that kills)
yet neither of them had a handkerchief
and that is how she ends up staining her robe with his blood,
his head in her lap and his virtue coursing through her

as if they were one flesh.
Husband and wife may erase a boundary.
Creating a white page.

But now the blood seems to be the only thing in the room.

If only one's whole life could consist in certain moments.
There is no possibility of coming back from such a moment
to simple hatred,
black ink.

If a husband throws the dice of his beauty one last time, who is to
blame? (BH 100–01)

As a narrative climax, and as the crossing-point of a number of interlinked images and motifs—the nosebleed, the sail from *Tristan and Isolde,* the white page and black ink—this is a gripping passage. But, as with far too much of Carson's work, it leaves much to be desired as poetry. For one thing, I'm not fond of Carson's propensity for emphasizing her line breaks with syntactically uncalled-for full stops ("Creating a white page."). It calls attention to the generally loose lineation of the verse, which might well be chopped-up prose. In her interview with D'Agata, Carson speaks of "a novel I've written that was all prose at first and very thick. Then I thought, 'What if I break these lines up a bit? Maybe they'll move along more smartly.' So now the novel's in verse."[16] Breaking up one's prose is an efficient way of producing poems, I suppose, but the finished product often leaves something to be desired. (Read a few pages of late MacDiarmid, for instance.) I'm an anti-Laodicean here: if you choose to write in lines, you ought to make damn sure those lines are doing every bit of work for you they can.

And then there's the matter of melopœia, the music of the language. Carson's lines have a ruthless clarity, a simplicity that is sometimes graceful Shaker and sometimes just plain rude Puritan. The best Guy Davenport can say for Carson's poetic language, in his introduction to *Glass, Irony and God,* is that "truth and observation are more important than lyric effect or coloring. If a good line happens, it happens."[17] In *The Beauty of the Husband,* the sans-serif type seems almost to emphasize the resolute prosiness of the phrasing:

> They are both serious.
> Their seriousness wracks her.
> People who can be serious together, it goes deep.
> They have a bottle of mineral water on the table between them
> and two glasses.

Many of the "tangos" trudge forward in this clipped voice, reserving their moment of lyricism for a final sucker punch:

> A cold ship
>
> moves out of harbor somewhere way inside the wife
> and slides off toward the flat gray horizon,
>
> not a bird not a breath in sight. (BH 111)

There is a moment of magic here—a very brief one—but too often we're left scanning the flat gray horizon of the language for some glimpse of bright plumage that never shows up.

Despite its generally undistinguished language, *The Beauty of the Husband* offers a number of pleasurable moments, some quite modernist and others more traditional. There are the eight quirky elegiacs quoted by the Wife in Tango XXVI (out of her manuscript, she explains, of 5,820!):

> This Wind at Night carrying it all over the Sky like Quartets
> Or Dido surviving between Lightning Sets
>
> Against this Wall, the way Brothers tear at
> one another's Heads with their Love, it fought (BH 124)

There are subtly repeated leitmotifs: Kutuzov and Napoleon at the Battle of Borodino, Keats's scratching a bit of misspelled graffiti on a window and prefiguring his own name "writ in water." There is the sheer pleasure of learning things, or having known things repeated in a new, seductive manner: the varieties of European and American grapes in Tango VI, the rape of Persephone in Tango IX, the minutiae of Nahum Tate's revision of *King Lear* in Tango XXI, the appalling details of the Battle of Epipolai (413 BC) in Tango XXV. And throughout the poem, as through much of *Men in the Off Hours*, there is a compressed emotional intensity that seems able to find its outlet only in intellectual statement.

The story doesn't so much end as peter out. The Wife, older and wiser, returns to the Keats saw: "To say Beauty is Truth and stop, / Rather than to eat it. / Rather than to want to eat it. This was my pure early thought" (BH 139). Like Persephone or Eve, however, she has been unable to resist the object of desire. A painter named Ray, who works in a diner, eats mashed potatoes for breakfast, enjoys speaking in rhyme, and has been both her confidant and the Husband's, has the penultimate word, and a banal one it is:

> Well life has some risks. Love is one. Terrible risks.
> Ray would have said
> Fate's my bait and bait's my fate.
> *On a June evening.*
> Here's my advice,
> hold.
>
> Hold beauty. (BH 141)

But that's not all. A final, unnumbered tango gives us the voice of the Husband:

> Some tangos pretend to be about women but look at this.
> Who is it you see
> reflected small
> in each of her tears.
>
> Watch me fold the page now so you think it is you. (BH 145)

This final turn, where the villain steps forward and announces that he's been the central character all along, is too clever by half. We've already been shown the Husband's monstrous self-centeredness in a dozen ways—why this last twist of the knife? And that metafictional gambit—Dear Reader, look into your own heart and find yourself in this story—simply doesn't ring true.

Perhaps my specific dissatisfaction with *The Beauty of the Husband*—apart, that is, from my general disquiet with the texture of Carson's verse—rests ultimately with that blunt, totalizing "beauty." *Eros the Bittersweet*, when it addressed the complex, social, and often baffling experience of desire, did so in a nuanced and painstaking manner; it took very few conceptual shortcuts. *The Beauty of the Husband* explains all of its anguishes through the simple ideogram of "beauty," and in the end "beauty" can't stand up as an explanation of the erotic complications Carson's poem dramatizes. *Eros the Bittersweet* analyzed—painstakingly, painfully—Sappho's triangulated desire (the lover, the beloved, and the other); here, it's become a bad old-fashioned love triangle

Carson has been schooled by the earliest—and still the keenest—dissectors of the heart in the Western tradition, whose pain, lust, and clarity are still sometimes aglow in her lines; we hear those antique frustrations echoing, even through the static and montage of our own era. As Carson's televised Sappho laments, worried that the changing foliage of the Place de la Concorde will cause continuity problems in the video play in which she's acting,

> You cannot erase.
> Is this a law?
>
> No, a talent. To step obliquely
> where stones are sharp.
> Vice is also sharp.
>
> There are laws against vice.
> But the shock stays with you. (MO 62)

"You cannot erase." You may smash them into fragments to be reassembled into an Absolut vodka ad, or you may clip and telescope them into a Ken Burns documentary, but the maxims, epitaphs, and cries of baffled desire of Carson's archaic precursors will not be erased. Her own poems are mosaics of such desire, scrambled by the video snow of arbitrary juxtaposition and muffled by the bluntness of her language. If she can imbue her verse with some of the grace and music of her ancestors, then perhaps her poems as well can be acts of *charis,* "the charm that makes it a poem and makes you want to remember it."

Notes

1. Ezra Pound, *Poems and Translations,* ed. Richard Sieburth (New York: Library of America, 2003) 289.

2. *Archilochus, Sappho, Alkman: Three Lyric Poets of the Seventh Century B.C.* (Berkeley: U of California P, 1980) 14.

3. Anne Carson, *Eros the Bittersweet: An Essay* (Princeton: Princeton UP, 1986) 173.

4. John D'Agata, "A __________ With Anne Carson," *Iowa Review* 27.2 (1997): 17.

5. Anne Carson, *Glass, Irony and God* (New York: New Directions, 1995).

6. Anne Carson, *Autobiography of Red: A Novel in Verse* (New York: Knopf, 1998).

7. Anne Carson, *Men in the Off Hours* (New York: Knopf, 2000) 61. Hereafter cited in text as MO.

8. Carson, *Glass, Irony and God* 59.

9. W. H. Auden, *Selected Poems*, New Edition, ed. Edward Mendelson (New York: Vintage, 1979) 294.

10. D'Agata, "A _________ With Anne Carson," 16–17.

11. Louis Zukofsky, *Prepositions+: The Collected Critical Essays* (Hanover, NH: Wesleyan UP, 2000) 224.

12. *Catullus, Tibullus, Pervigilium Veneris* (Loeb Classical Library), trans. F. W. Cornish, J. P. Postgate, and J. W. Mackail (Cambridge: Harvard UP, 1962) 163.

13. Trans. Richard Haney-Jardine, from Yo-Yo Ma, *Soul of the Tango: The Music of Astor Piazolla*, Sony SK 63122, 1997.

14. Anne Carson, *The Beauty of the Husband: a fictional essay in 29 tangos* (New York: Knopf, 2001) dust jacket. Hereafter cited in text as BH.

15. *The Selected Letters of John Keats*, ed. Lionel Trilling (Garden City, NY: Doubleday, 1956) 99.

16. D'Agata, "A _________ With Anne Carson," 20.

17. Carson, *Glass, Irony and God*, viii.

Still Diving the Mauberley Trench

John Matthias

It's a rule—not as immutable as the Second Law of Thermodynamics, but at least as unavoidable as the unwritten prohibition on smoking in church—or perhaps a karmic principle: every successful revolution becomes at best another style, at worst an orthodoxy. The trim young militant at the barricades ages into the thick-jowelled commissar dispensing favors from behind a desk. The ripped shirts of London punks circa 1977 show up as part of somebody's 1982 ready-to-wear collection. Even modernism, that series of cultural upheavals so violent it seemed to some observers that the world as they (and Queen Victoria) had known it was coming to an end, has been comfortably processed by our civilization's cast-iron digestive tract. I remember vividly from my own undergraduate days a rumpled and mustachioed music appreciation lecturer gleefully recounting the semilegendary 1913 premiere of *The Rite of Spring*. "It was practically a riot! The audience was booing so loudly the dancers couldn't hear the orchestra," he said, before settling the needle onto a record so that we could experience some of this incendiary music. A football player sitting next to me—who probably hadn't even seen *Fantasia*—was unimpressed. "Sounds like a movie soundtrack to me," he muttered.

The American composer George Antheil (1900–1959), self-dubbed "bad boy of music," himself embodied that transition of revolution into style. Antheil had begun his career at the center of 1920s modernism, living upstairs from Sylvia Beach's Shakespeare and Company in Paris (he would swing up to his window by the shop sign when he'd forgotten his latchkey), hanging out with Hemingway, Cocteau, and Stravinsky, and serving as Ezra Pound's poster boy for what was new and exciting in music. But by the 1940s, Antheil was living in Hollywood, writing slushy neo-Romantic symphonies and churning out B-movie soundtracks by the cartload (*Tokyo Joe*, *Serpent of the Nile*, *Panther Girl of the Kongo*).[1] Antheil's music, early and late, hasn't aged well, and that includes the work for which he is best remembered: the "Ballet mécanique," a thunderous romp for sixteen synchronized player pianos, a raft of percussion instruments, and divers noisemakers (sirens, electric bells, an airplane propeller).

Antheil's Paris was a city of roiling artistic experimentation where Pound, Joyce, Picabia, Léger, and others were assiduously renovating their respective arts and testing the possibilities of such new forms as the cinema. "Automystifstical Plaice," the first of the two long poems that make up John Matthias's 2002 volume *Working Progress, Working Title*, aims to remind us of precisely how exciting that modernist moment was.[2] One of the poem's central reference points is Antheil's 1923 performance at the Théâtre des Champs-Élysées, where the pianist's violently rhythmic music (the climactic piece was entitled "Mechanisms") seems to have prompted any number of fistfights and upended seats. Unbeknownst to its participants, that riot was being filmed, and the footage would be incorporated into Marcel L'Herbier's silent movie *L'Inhumaine*. Here's Matthias's account:

> A camera's panning the audience, picks out the famous:
> Picasso and Joyce, Duchamp, Milhaud and Satie.
> We see them there with Leblanc as Lescot in the film
> but we don't hear a sound Mr. Pound leaping
> right out of his seat and shaking a fist as people begin
> to walk out on Antheil himself . . .[3]

Movies and music bounce off one another as Matthias's poem unfolds: the outrage provoked by Antheil's "Mechanisms" becomes part of a film; "Mechanisms" itself inspires another film, Fernand Léger's *Ballet mécanique*, for which Antheil in turn composes his own "Ballet mécanique."

L'Inhumaine starred Georgette LeBlanc in the role (in Antheil's words) of "an 'inhuman' opera songstress" named Claire Lescot. Lescot, a robot-woman like the siren of Fritz Lang's *Metropolis*, speaks much of "Automystifstical Plaice," casting a cold base-two eye from her current digs "at MIT in some robotics lab" over the frenetic techno-fascination of 1920s Paris (CLP 267). They were before their time, those machine-struck moderns:

> No one could actually *play* that piano roll A wrote into the score,
> the digitals moving at speeds and at intervals
> nobody's ten carboniferous digits could match. (CLP 248)

And there was no way Antheil could realize his initial conception of "Ballet mécanique" on sixteen pianolas: the instruments—enormously complex music-boxes, really—simply couldn't be synchronized closely enough. Not, that is, until the era of computer-driven, Midi-linked digital pianos: "He hadn't met the Midi, technical cousin of Claire, his digital and instrumental interface," notes Matthias (CLP 252). Schirmer music publishers can now rent you a full set of Midi software instructions for performing Antheil's work, and Matthias "quotes" some of their online schemata in "Automystifstical Plaice."

The poem takes us in thirty tightly woven pages through twenty years' worth of modernist-related arcana: Antheil's progress both as avant-gardist and Hollywood hack; the writings of his bulldog Pound; Léger's machine aesthetic; the experimental silent film scene; and the career of the Hollywood diva Hedy Lamarr (born Hedwig Kiesler), from her nude debut in the German film *Ecstasy* to her friendship with Antheil in the 1940s, when the two designed, of all things, a radio-controlled torpedo: "Find me George Antheil. / We're going to sink the Herzenbergers / and the Krupps with my torpedo," Matthias imagines her saying (CLP 263). (Lamarr's first marriage was to a German armaments manufacturer, we are told, and she did a good deal of listening in when designs for new weapons were being discussed around the house.) The torpedo was patented but never built; some of the basic principles of its design, however, would eventually prove crucial to the invention of cellular telephone networks. The roots of things are cunningly and surprisingly intertwined: "What lengths what loops," as Matthias puts it in another poem.[4]

"Automystifstical Plaice" is an assured yet zany poem, deriving much of its verbal energy from Mother Goose–like internal rhymes and an Oulipo-like reliance on the dictionary to suggest the next word ("the mogul / and the moilers make a single molecule for a moment / as modalities come into play" [CLP 358]). It's suffused with nostalgia for that first moment of "heroic" modernism, when it seemed to a certain group of artists—Antheil, Léger, Wyndham Lewis, the Futurists—that the new technologies of electricity and internal combustion would become the basis of a new, dynamic aesthetic whose madonna was Picabia's mechanical "fille née sans mère."[5] Matthias both pays homage to the machine aesthetic of early modernism and makes a stab at a digital aesthetic for the twenty-first century. His poem, stocked with factoids garnered from the Internet, punctuated by the static and dropped-out words of a cellphone conversation, is partly given over to the dream that all human culture is somehow available, in a vast surrealist *musée imaginaire*, to whomever can plug the right set of search terms into Google.

At the same time, "Automystifstical Plaice" is a very old-fashioned modernist poem. While it may be telling us to plug into the World Wide Web, vast stretches of its material can be "sourced" in a printed document, Antheil's autobiography *Bad Boy of Music*, just as one sources Pound's "China" *Cantos* in J. A. M. de Mailla's *Histoire générale de la Chine*. But where Pound hunts for "luminous details"—a single line in a Canto can be meant as shorthand for an entire significant passage or event in Mailla—Matthias looks for fruitful suggestions: Antheil's brief account of screening *Un chien andalou* for Cecil B. DeMille (he "was a pale green when the lights went up. He got up and left without a word"[6]) prompts a darting collage in which Dalí and Buñuel's surrealism comes smack up against the demands of early-forties Hollywood:

> so we play this little coup de vache
> on every scatalogue and watch the ants emerge
> from his stigmata, no? the way he's roped
> to this machinery he drags, pianos stuffed with putrefying
> donkey and dos padres, si? the priests tied up and
> on their backs in bondage of some kind as part of this
> contrivance & DeMille out of his seat by now
> and saying brother rat [?] or bugger that [? the file at
> this point labeled diction inconsistent] so
> we'll give them Custer Lincoln Hickok Cody Hopalong
> and Jesus Christ at Rancho Grande, George
> but what the hell is this? (CLP 258)

And what the hell is *this*?, the reader of "Automystifical Plaise" might ask. Well, it's a backward glance at modernism, from a confirmed if somewhat belated practitioner.

* * *

That football player in my music appreciation class was right: Stravinsky *does* sound like movie music—but only because movie music for the last forty years has sounded like Stravinsky. The shocking creative idioms the modernists pioneered have become the environment of our turn of the century, from the cinematic montage of pop music videos to the Bauhaus lines of Ikea furniture to the slushy faux-Cubism paintings you can buy at the discount furniture store. One *verbal* idiom that never quite caught on, however, was that of the mature Pound, a cross-cutting of lush lyricism and esoteric literary-historical references. At its best, this kind of poem is a shimmering intersection of immediate experience and all the bright bits of history in the poet's mind; at its worst, it is grumpily didactic, rapping our knuckles for not knowing the details of Justinian's law code or the Albigensian Crusade.

Louis Zukofsky pursued that idiom for maybe the first half of his long poem *"A"*, before that work shifted into a series of dazzling formal experiments and a mode of even more radial collage. Charles Olson and Robert Duncan took Pound's "ideogrammic method"—a poetic principle only slightly more clearly defined than Williams's notorious "variable foot"—and ran with it in far more open-ended, associative directions. Matthias, who has read and learned from both Olson and Duncan, is, like them, a poet very much in the Pound tradition. But unlike those Black Mountaineers, he has cannily shied away from opening his poems out to whatever infinity the poet's imagination might strain toward. There's much to admire in such open-ended sequences as Olson's *Maximus Poems* and Duncan's "Passages," but I'm not sure the world needs more complex, esoterically learned, and painfully incomplete poetic torsos. Instead, Matthias has given us a series of highly finished medium-length efforts: one *Briggflatts* after another, rather than a single "poem of a life."

Matthias first collected his longer poems in the 1995 volume *Beltane at Aphelion*, which presented eight twenty- to forty-page poems written between 1965 and 1990.[7] Once Matthias has gotten some youthful kinks out of his system—there's way too much alchemy in "Poem in Three Parts," and "Bucyrus," a prose poem marrying Gertrude Stein, L. Ron Hubbard, and Bright's *Anglo-Saxon Reader*, is simply weird (and not in a good sense)—this *Mauberley*-length form proves a remarkably flexible canvas. One model at which Matthias's long poems seem to nod is Pound's early "Near Perigord," an agreeable tramp through the countryside of the Troubadours.[8] Like "Near Perigord," Matthias's are often *topographical* poems, works that focus upon a single place or cluster of places. "Northern Summer" is a Scottish poem; "Facts from an Apocryphal Midwest" cruises the riverways around Lake Superior in the company of La Salle and the French explorers, the ancient copper-mining "mound people," and Francis Parkman; "An East Anglian Diptych" traces the ley lines and rivers of Cambridgeshire, Suffolk, and Norfolk; and "A Compostela Diptych" travels the French and Provençal pilgrimage routes to Santiago de Compostela, the old stomping grounds of Roland, El Cid, and Pound's troubadours.

Matthias has been at it a long time, this late harvest of the fields of high modernism. One can't imagine that he got much encouragement from the crusty Yvor Winters, his teacher at Stanford, who by the 1960s had become the intransigent advocate of traditional form. But of that mid-sixties crop of Winters's students, two of whom (Robert Pinsky and Robert Hass) would go on to become poets laureate, another two, John Matthias and John Peck, would fashion themselves into the most accomplished neo-modernist poets of their generation.[9] Matthias has published over a dozen books of poetry since 1970 and is probably slightly better known than the astonishingly gifted and remarkably difficult Peck. Both men's work has suffered the misfortune of falling between stools: readers and reviewers have never been able to shuffle it into the ready-made categories that so often spare one the difficulty of actually *reading*. For one thing, Matthias's work really isn't at all *post*modern, at least in the most widespread sense of that squishy term. In the last four decades or so, more and more poets have taken up a stance toward language in which the human subject itself is seen as little more than the spot where a variety of linguistic and social codes converge. A rather busy stop on the Paris Métro: call it Station Barthes, Station Foucault, Station Derrida. Matthias isn't having any of that: as far-ranging as his poems might be, as zany as their unexpected juxtapositions might strike us, he's still comfortable with an old-fashioned unified subject behind it all. He may, as in some of the more word-salady moments of "Automystifstical Plaise" and "Pages," be willing to "cede the initiative to words" (Mallarmé's phrase[10]) *a bit*, but there's always a nodding and winking Wizard of Oz pulling the levers behind the curtain.

On the other hand, while Matthias has written often and affectingly of himself, his family, and his experiences (usually in his short poems), he has rarely gone in for either the well-turned personal epiphanies that characterized so much American magazine verse of the 1970s and 1980s or the stream of consciousness, notebook jottings of the post-Williams poets crowding the small-press fringes. Instead, he's pursued a post-Poundian aesthetics of *inventio*—not so much "invention" as "finding."

On a local level, Matthias's longer poems are often bound together by the repetition of themes and phrases. "Northern Summer," for instance, begins with a handful of lines from the Swedish poet Göran Sonnevi, which Matthias will put through various paces for the rest of the poem:

> *The flight of sentimentality through empty space.*
> *Through its heraldic hole*
> *an heraldic blackbird's*
> *black wings, yellow beak, round eyes, with the yellow*
> *ring, which defines its inner empty*
> *space* (CLP 33)

Matthias finds himself spending the summer in a folly—an architectural one, mind you—between a coal mine and a castle overlooking the Firth of Forth. As he trawls through local history, muses on the almost-abandoned technology of Victorian coal-mining, replays in his mind's eye the high scenes of Scottish history (John Knox badmouthing Mary Queen of Scots, Bonnie Prince Charlie inspecting Holyrood Castle at the height of his brief bid to regain Britain for the Stewarts), and relives his mother's reading him Stevenson's

Kidnapped, that "heraldic blackbird" continually pokes its yellow beak into the pages, surveys the poet's "flight of sentimentality" with quizzical round eyes.

This isn't Wallace Stevens's blackbird, which appears in a baker's dozen of different syntactic and imaginative guises. Instead, Matthias's blackbird darts into and out of the poem as a complex emblem of the poet's mind brooding upon his present surroundings and the history that lies behind them, arranging those materials into a poem:

> Language
> moving upon consequence
> Consequence
> upon a language: Flight
> of an heraldic bird
> through space that is inhabited. (CLP 34)

These lines refer to King Edward's order that Sir Michael Wemyss be considered a traitor and stripped of his lands—language of "consequence," indeed. Other language, like the voices hailing Bonnie Prince Charlie's return to Holyrood, move "upon inconsequence / and consequence / at once" (CLP 40); they are both empty and meaningful. The tension between the languages of consequence and inconsequence runs through "Northern Summer," parallel to the tension between the high "sentiment" of Scottish patriotism and the debased "sentimentality" of Macpherson's fake Ossian or the tourist-directed Scottish "heritage industry": "Sentiment's transfigured into history, / and history to sentiment" (CLP 42).

At times the poet cannot help fearing that his own shifting attention amounts merely to a "Flight of sentimentality through empty space." But Matthias thinks not; rather, his musings on place and the past have opened the poem into a space in which the voices of the past can themselves speak unexpectedly and sometimes eloquently:

> I stare quizzically at what I've written here,
> at language that has used me one more time
> for consequential or inconsequential ends that
> are not mine. (CLP 47)

* * *

The long poems in *Beltane at Aphelion* range from prentice work to masterful; I would especially single out "A Compostella Diptych," in which Matthias pursues his unfinished pilgrimage before a backdrop of both his own illness and his daughter's (told of in the shorter poem "Dedication to a Cycle of Poems on the Pilgrim Routes to Santiago de Compostella" [CSP2 53–4]). But those long poems are much of a piece: dense, sometimes bookish evocations of the historical resonances that echo in particular locations. Matthias doesn't expect us to take his research on trust—at the end of the book he provides exhaustive lists of his sources (over two pages for "A Compostella Diptych" alone). It's a gesture of acknowledgement for debts incurred, but less ponderous or frivolous than, say, Eliot's notes for *The Waste Land*, that "remarkable display of bogus scholarship" that kept professors busy for so many years.[11]

Another poet with a penchant for annotations was the Anglo-Welsh modernist David Jones, who is perhaps the most important of Matthias's acknowledged masters. In his preface to *The Anathemata*, his lambent and widely woven exploration of the "matter of Britain," Jones describes his own method by quoting the Latin historian Nennius: "I have made a heap of all that I could find."[12] The poem may be "a series of fragments, fragmented bits, chance scraps really, of records of things," but they are "Pieces of stuff that happen to mean something to me and which I see as making a kind of coat of many colours, such as belonged to 'that dreamer' in the Hebrew myth."[13] Poetry, for Jones, "is a kind of *anamnesis* of, i. e. is an effective recalling of, something loved."[14]

An effective recalling of something loved: that's a fair description of the working method of Matthias's long poems. What in the hands of a less involved, less *loving* poet might seem a tourist's scrapbook of diverting facts and anecdotes from regions visited, is transfigured into something rather more compelling: one is always aware of the consciousness perceiving, selecting, and arranging his materials. Matthias is treading a fine line, though: a poetry of place that relies so heavily on the testimony of documents constantly runs the risk of becoming a versified travelogue.

We see this perhaps most poignantly in "Northern Summer." Near the beginning there's a fruitily lyrical description of the poet's environs—"Large, magnificent, commodious / with rock nearby and wood and water to afford / the eye a picture of a rare / and charming beauty"—a description immediately deflated: "the sight of which / could not but amply compensate et / cetera / the language of a tour book / threading aimlessly / through sentimental empty space" (CLP 33). This is a moment, I'm inclined to think, of self-revelation. The poet has lost his summer home in Suffolk ("the place where I had done most of my writing for fifteen years or more," he tells us in the afterword to *Beltane*[15]), and is desperately seeking to regain some grounding, some connection to place—a difficult matter when one is summering in an unfamiliar

Scotland. We can almost feel Matthias straining throughout the poem ("Only Connect!" booms E. M. Forster subsonically), and the closest thing to a real connection he can think of—his mother's reading him *Kidnapped* at "eight or nine"(CLP 41)—proves in the end all too tenuous:

> There is a space
> I have not learned to fill
> somewhere between printed marks and sounds
> and I am lost in some way too
> among the heather, frightened of the distances
> when all I want to do is drift on lang
> uage into dream. . . . (CLP 41)

The long poems of *Beltane at Aphelion* read more smoothly when we sense the affection and enthusiasm Matthias feels for his location—his at-homeness. When his connection to the place is more tenuous, as in "Northern Summer" and "A Compostella Diptych," the poem becomes (among much else) the record of the poet's longing for such connection, such grounding. While the "settled" poems are perhaps more finished and masterful, the "unsettled" poems, with their grand and sad old themes of exile, hejira, and homeless wandering, pack more emotional punch.

* * *

Matthias collected his long and short poems in the two volumes of *Beltane at Aphelion* and *Swimming at Midnight*[16] in 1995, but in the two decades since, he has shown neither a waning of his powers nor a desire to rest on past achievements. In a turn-of-the-millennium trio of long poems—"Pages: *From a Book of Years*," "Cuttings," and "Automystifstical Plaice"—Matthias seems to have shifted from a concern with *place* to a concern with *time*. (Not an uncommon shift, one might add, for a writer heading into his sixties.) Time has always been of the essence in Matthias's work, but while "Northern Summer," "A Compostella Diptych," or "Facts from an Apocryphal Midwest" build palimpsests of temporally receding texts upon particular locations, like the layers of various "Troys" Heinrich Schliemann excavated beneath the single mound of Hissarlik, "Pages" especially is less concerned with place—Matthias's boyhood Ohio, a college trip to Turkey, graduate school at Palo Alto—than with the passage of time itself.

There's something ostensibly haphazard about "Pages: *From a Book of Years*."[17] The poem is divided into five sections, each of them focusing upon a particular year: 1959, 1941, 1953, 1961, and 1966. Each section is, in turn, composed of five numbered parts, largely prose interspersed with lineated passages. (These subsections' equivalent lengths is due to another incursion of technology into Matthias's bag of tricks: "Pages" is the first poem he composed directly on the word processor—"I wrote until I hit the bottom of the computer screen, and then began another part," he explains in an interview.[18]) Each section concatenates the happenings of its respective year, from world-historical events, the deaths of celebrities, the entry of new words into the dictionary, to Matthias's own emotional and erotic life. Section II of 1959, fairly representative, begins:

> Disasters 1959: Rio de Janeiro plane crash
> Guadalajara bus and train Formosa
>
> earthquake Istanbul a fire Western
> Pakistan a flood & in the Persian Gulf typhoons
>
> a caved-in mine in Merlebach and just
> northeast of Newfoundland a sunken ship,
>
> *Blue Wave*
> I put my hand directly up her skirt and she did not say no don't do it
> didn't say a thing and so I kept it there a moment just above the knee
> and then began advancing slowly with my finger tips in little steps
>
> *blue wave, blue wave*
>
> And out there somewhere Viscount Charles John Lyttelton Cobham.
>
> This year Raymond Chandler died and so did Abbott's friend Costello. It's hard to think of Abbott all alone his eyes upon Costello's derby hanging on the hatrack in the hall. For days you keened in grief for Errol Flynn your only child's Robin. General Marshall, Admiral William Halsey also on the list. And Ike in tears. Who'd say weep my love for
>
> John Foster Dulles (CLP 204–05)

Where in his earlier long poems Matthias had seemed something of a "library cormorant" (in Coleridge's phrase), in "Pages" his sources are more humble: the collection of yearbooks—encyclopedia yearbooks, fashion yearbooks, chess yearbooks, horse racing yearbooks—that his father had accumulated in a closet of his Columbus home. Matthias finds himself shuffling through these yearbooks alone in the house, having returned to Ohio on one of the most heartrending errands of middle age: to move his mother, suffering from Alzheimer's, into a nursing facility and to clean out the home of his childhood before putting it up for sale. His mother's voice enters the poem time and again, always repeating the same mantra: "Take me home she said don't sell the house I can't remember quite which one you are you know I don't really live here I'm only visiting."[19] In the face of such erosion of memory, "Pages" is a frantic attempt to remember, to shore up fragments against the ruin of inexorable age. It is *anamnesis* at the edge of oblivion.

In the *Phaedrus* Plato warned that the written word would be the death of human memory ("Why should I memorize something I can look up in a book?" Einstein said when asked his phone number), and *ars memoriae* has been cultivated since Classical times, with Renaissance figures such as the Jesuit Matteo Ricci bringing it to elaborate perfection.[20] The yearbooks Matthias ransacks are the tabulated and bound tombs of such organic memory arcades, marking the demise of the memory arts. Where the humanists had proposed memory systems organized by multibranched logic, relating the data memorized to the intellectual structure of the human world, the yearbooks rely on the contingencies of the alphabet, on the one-damn-thing-after-another logic of the calendar. (Since the fading of his youthful commitment to Marxism—a strong element only in his early work—Matthias's poetry has shown no tendency to seek a progressive logic, Hegelian or otherwise, in the history of which he writes.) Like some local historian, the poet of "Pages" is attempting to reconstruct his own past on the basis of some thousands of pages of random data, and on the basis of his own vivid—but, he fears, faltering—memory.

* * *

In 2004, Matthias gathered his work once again in the hefty *New Selected Poems*. In the afterword to this almost four-hundred-page volume, Matthias reflects on his experience as a poet of both long and short forms, like Auden and Rexroth before him. *Swimming at Midnight*, which collected his short poems, was well received and reprinted in paperback; *Beltane at Aphelion*, the book of long poems, "sold very few copies indeed."[21] A pity, because however keenly observed Matthias's short poems might be, the longer poem is really his métier. *New Selected Poems* presents a comprehensive collection of both Matthias's long and short writings, in hopes "that a reader of short poems will also become a reader of longer ones." The most ephemeral of the early long works—"Bucyrus," "The Stefan Batory Poems," and "The Mihail Lermontov Poems"—have been omitted (to the good), and some of the other long poems have been abridged. The volume proceeds roughly chronologically, and makes clear that Matthias has devoted himself as often to the single-page *New Yorker*–sized lyric as to the more expansive and complex—more modernist—long poem.

Leafing through *New Selected Poems*, one is constantly reminded of sides of Matthias that one perhaps overlooked. There are numerous shorter poems that are handshakes to various writers and artists—Verlaine, Mandelstam, Augustus John, the Henry Miller-Lawrence Durrell-Anaïs Nin trio; there is a wonderful run of poems addressing various composers—Percy Grainger, Stravinsky, Janácek, Messiaen, Samuel Barber, Schoenberg; there are poems that return to Matthias's Ohio roots, his forebears and relatives; and there is a handful of plainspoken poems addressing Matthias's wife, his daughters, and his unborn grandson. I'm frankly not as fond of Matthias's shorter works as I am of his longer poems. It's a bit like when the star pitcher puts on his batting helmet and steps up to the plate; you're not at all surprised if he gets a single or double, but you know that he's doing something other than what he does best. Pound was wont to cram as much music as possible into his shortest lyrical utterances, and David Jones's rare short poems have an incantatory lyricism that's very enchanting indeed. Matthias's work, by contrast, tends to have a flat, Midwestern, speech-like quality that works well in long poems, where he builds up the incremental structures, but that can seem simply prosy in short ones.

But a clipped, prosaic language serves Matthias well in "Swell," the sweetly melancholic final piece of *New Selected Poems*. The poem both sums up Matthias's life and career and hearkens back to yet another modernist forebear: Ernest Hemingway, whose spare prose is the model for his own flat and precise lines. Matthias and his wife are on Michigan's Walloon Lake, looking back fifty years to when he was photographed there with "my one fish, a bass," and beyond that to 1920, when Hemingway summered on the same lake. While the bulk of Matthias's previous poetry has wandered across Britain and Europe, this interlude on Walloon Lake suggests that he's finally coming to terms with America:

> The rich are different from the rest of us, said Scott.
> They have bigger boats. Ours is maybe fifteen feet, plus outboard.
> In a larger craft than this, I did in fact reach Paris.
> Reached Pamplona, too. It's taken a lifetime to prefer it here. (CLP2 104)

The poet, now in his sixtieth year, has settled down. Once upon a time, it was all about sex; no longer. One of the meanings of "swell" upon which the poem plays is that of tumescence: "E. P.: who said to Lowell that he'd started with a swollen head / to end with swollen feet. Hem, who measured Scott's / small cock and told him, Look: it only counts engorged with blood" (CSP2

105). ("The rich are different from us, said Scott. / They have bigger boats.") Hemingway, early and late, was much obsessed with sex and tumescence, and Matthias has been a Hemingway reader for almost fifty years. Hemingway was Matthias's initiation into the world of books. The two men's shared time on Walloon Lake, mediated as it is by the kitsch of the Hemingway Industry—the proprietor of the Red Fox Inn has given Matthias "gummed labels saying / *Purchased from the heir of Volie Fox, fishing guru who taught / Hemingway his tricks*" (CSP2 106)—is yet another of the "overlays" of history that have so fascinated Matthias.

In contrast to the political, cultural, and literary histories that have occupied his other poems, the history of "Swell" is a largely personal history, a story of one man's reading. The poem ends anticipating a scene of reading like that at the end of the posthumously published Nick Adams fragment "The Last Good Country":

> Left unfinished, Nick's last story stops at *Sure* when Littless
> asks *And will you read it? Or is it too old to read out loud?*
> Too old to read out loud? She's brought along *Wuthering Heights.*
> Or did she mean Am *I* too old to ask you for this gift?
> He'll read it to her. It's swell, and so is she. She cuts her hair
> like Catherine on the Cote d'Azur, calls herself a boy.
> She says that they'll have children, swings her child's legs
> astraddle on his hips. Sure, he says, I'll read. (CSP2 105)

Reading in some sense has been Matthias's life, and now, in the boat at dusk, he looks forward to his wife's bedtime reading to him, to hold his melancholia at bay:

> This started out to be a poem about a bass I caught when
> I was ten. And never once again.
> You'll read to me tonight, I know. Whether Proust or
> Mother Goose, it does its work. It's no big show
> at the Chautauqua with a smell of gaslight, but it's exactly swell
> enough, no more. It's great. In my life it's starting to get late.
> We haven't yet found Windemere
> And now the sun has set entirely on the lake. (CSP2 109)

I shouldn't take that note of leave-taking finality too seriously: in the decade since "Swell" Matthias has published two more mid-length poems ("Laundry Lists and Manifestoes" and "Kedging"), the book-length poem *Trigons*, and some 150 pages of short poems.[22] But closing *New Selected Poems* with "Swell" seems absolutely right ("Just fine," as a Hemingway character might say). By so doing, Matthias has placed his own career in the frame of one of the oldest human stories, and one beloved of the modernists: he is Odysseus, returned to his Ithaca of the Midwest after decades of spiritual and poetic wandering.

Matthias's poetry rarely rises to lyrical heights, and only rarely makes the outrageous gestures that sometimes still astonish us in the old modernists: the "Cress" letters in Williams's *Paterson*, the lyrical bursts in the *Pisan Cantos*, Mina Loy's extraterrestrial metaphors, Gertrude Stein's sublime flouting both of the canons of sense and the limits of any sane reader's patience. Instead, Matthias's work moves at a level of constant and thoughtful intelligence: his is a sensibility enchanted with the verbal survivals of the past, the shiny pageant of history, geography, and culture. It is a very good thing to have this body of work available, both as an *anamnesis* of these things that Matthias has known and loved, and as a reminder that a valid mode of art—while there are always those anxious to move beyond it—is never dead so long as there are those willing to master its disciplines. The modernists, by making poems out of "heaps of all that they could find," risked making those poems museums of history. But modernist poetics, Matthias's work argues, are by no means ready for the museum.

Notes

1. For a lively account of Antheil's career, see his autobiography, *Bad Boy of Music* (1945; Hollywood: Samuel French, 1990).

2. John Matthias, *Working Progress, Working Title* (Cambridge, Eng.: Salt, 2002).

3. John Matthias, *Collected Longer Poems* (Bristol, Eng.: Shearsman, 2012) 247; hereafter cited parenthetically in text as CLP.

4. John Matthias, "Easter 1912 and Christmas 1929: Blaise Cendrars and Garcia Lorca in New York (a second take)," *Collected Shorter Poems, Volume 2: 1995–2011* (Bristol, Eng.: Shearsman, 2011) 34; hereafter cited parenthetically in text as CSP2.

5. Picabia's 1916–1917 watercolor is reproduced in CLP 245.

6. Antheil, *Bad Boy of Music* 301.

7. John Matthias, *Beltane at Aphelion: Longer Poems* (Athens: Sparrow P/Ohio UP, 1995).

8. Ezra Pound, *Poems and Translations*, ed. Richard Sieburth (New York: Library of America, 2003) 302–08.

9. Robert Archambeau, *Laureates and Heretics: Six Careers in American Poetry* (Notre Dame, IN: U of Notre Dame P, 2010) is a fascinating study of Winters and five of his students: Matthias, Pinsky, Hass, Peck, and James McMichael.

10. "L'œuvre pure implique la disparition élocutoire du poëte, qui cède l'initiative aux mots"; Stéphane Mallarmé, "Crise de vers," *Œuvres complètes II*, ed. Bertrand Marchal (Paris: Pléiade, 2003) 211.

11. T. S. Eliot, *On Poetry and Poets* (1957; New York: Noonday P, 1961) 121.

12. David Jones, *Epoch and Artist: Selected Writings*, ed. Harmon Grisewood (New York: Chilmark P, 1955) 107.

13. Jones, *Epoch and Artist* 129–30.

14. Jones, *Epoch and Artist* 118.

15. Matthias, *Beltane at Aphelion* 195.

16. John Matthias, *Swimming at Midnight: Selected Shorter Poems* (Athens: Swallow P/Ohio UP, 1995).

17. First published in *Pages: New Poems and Cuttings* (Athens: Swallow P/Ohio UP, 2000), and as the second half of *Working Progress, Working Title*.

18. Joe Francis Doerr, "Interview with John Matthias," in *The Salt Companion to John Matthias*, ed. Joe Francis Doerr (Cromer, Eng.: Salt, 2011) 211.

19. First at CLP 208, then 218, 224, 232, 240.

20. See Frances A. Yates, *The Art of Memory* (Chicago: U of Chicago P, 1966).

21. John Matthias, *New Selected Poems* (Cambridge, Eng.: Salt, 2004) 377.

22. "Laundry Lists and Manifestoes" and "Kedging" are included in CLP; the new short poems make up the bulk of CSP2; *Trigons* (Bristol, Eng.: Shearsman, 2010) as yet stands alone.

Dark Matters

Peter Gizzi and Rae Armantrout

On the back cover of his 2003 collection *Some Values of Landscape and Weather*, we're told that Peter Gizzi is "on the quixotic mission of recovering the lyric."[1] While I had no idea we'd lost it, I suppose the blurbist has a point. Gizzi, who during the late 1980s and early 1990s co-edited the excellent and eclectic journal *O-blēk*, writes within an avant-garde tradition that sometimes views melopœia with suspicion, or else discounts it entirely. What place song in the ranks of savage, analytic parataxis? I'm happy to report that whether the lyric actually needed "recovering," *Some Values* presents a range of wonderfully musical moments, as in the title poem to the book's "History of Lyric" section, a Pre-Raphaelite idyll in a world of electronic static:

I lost you to the inky noise
just offscreen that calls us

and partly we got stuck there
waving, walking into the Percy grass.

A sinking pictorial velvet spray
imagining vermilion dusk.

You lost me to your petticoat
shimmering armor

saying it is better here
on my own amazon.

Why can't we or is it
won't you leave your solo ingle

beside the page. Did we never
consider life lyric interruption

to the idyll, laboring to rescue
real time, lost in affection. (SV 11)

Here the old lyric voices strive to break out of a Creeleyesque jaggedness ("Why can't we or is it"), and even a comforting line of iambic tetrameter ("imagining vermilion dusk") makes an embattled appearance.

One gets the feeling that Gizzi, if he had his druthers, might be a thirteenth-century Occitan troubadour, or an Andalusian singer of the *cante jondo* (his sequence "Masters of the Cante Jondo" is a wonderful attempt at re-imaging that particular tradition), or even a Delta blues musician. "Plain Song" strings together comfortable clichés and almost-clichés into an engaging lyric. It begins:

> Some say a baby cries for the life to come
> some say leaves are green 'cause it looks good against the
> blue
> some say the grasses blow because it is earth's instrument
> some say we were born to cry (SV 89)

Two pages later, the poem winds up with a bit of Steinian riffing and some "you say 'to-may-toe,' I say 'to-mah-toe'" back-and-forthing that leaves us, like Dante, in "heaven":

> Some say "the good way," some "stuff"
> some say yes we need a form
> some say form is a simple thing some say yes the sky is a
> form of what is simple
>
> *
>
> Some say molecular some open others porous some blue
> some say love some light some say the dark some heaven (SV 91)

The "love" slipped into that last line is key: while Gizzi doesn't allow his romantic side as much space as a sentimental reader like myself would like, he's a delicate love poet. "To his wife far off in a time of war" is a beautiful reworking of the "distanced lovers" trope, while "Add This to the House" finely situates spousal affection in the furnishings, fittings, and routines among which it dwells:

> Not a still life into which artifice may enter
> but a labor to describe the valves

and cordage that entwine this room;
the voltage is enough to kill.
Who in morning dish-gray light
can fathom the witless parable of waking,
the bed, the cask, the zoned spaces
we pass through. It would be lovely
to say floorboards pose in firelight,
coals are banking down, the room
comes up by degrees. Instead, the day
has begun, shadows dispelled by the clock,
by the promise of work, Clorox,
the phone. I can see you by that metaphor,
the house, the door, the car heading out
to meet the sun, then again hours
later returning, your back to it. (SV 17)

Gizzi is acutely aware of his own nostalgia for a premodern setting, for "firelight," "coals" and morning illuminating the room "by degrees," but instead must settle for a room "entwined" in potentially deadly "valves / and cordage," a day whose harbingers are the paraphernalia of contemporary bourgeois life: "the clock, / . . . the promise of work, Clorox, / the phone"—another cluster of "objects" closer than the mirror-watcher might realize, or might like.

In "Objects in mirror are closer than they appear," Gizzi lists a number of eighteenth-century artifacts, reminders of a time when Americans were as yet "England's, still colonials" (as Frost put it in "The Gift Outright"[2]): "a dirty blotter / its crusty bottle, a plume," "a treatise on rotating spheres," "a few doubloons, powder horn / musket bag and tricorne hat" (SV 4). But the immediate objects through which Gizzi moves in *Some Values* are mostly *American*, and the new poetic values he seeks to establish are values within an American context. (The short poems "Hawthorne" and "Edgar Poe" nod toward the "American Renaissance," that first major blossoming of a homegrown culture.) "To Be Written in No Other Country" voices a kind of cultural despair. "It is a sorry day for the pollster and body electorate / for the mildewed pages of a wound dresser," Gizzi writes in the face (one assumes) of a mishandled election, an event that would bring sorrow to Whitman (the "wound dresser," of course). "As a youth did Grant wonder / that he would become both a drunk / and president and die like Melville, forgotten, / buried under ambition and guilt?" Contemporary Americans can only look back in regret at the nation's cultural icons, "lost as we are in the kiddy section of Wal-Mart" (SV 46).

Perhaps the most "American" of the poems in *Some Values of Landscape and Weather* is "Revival," a tremendous elegy to the beat poet Gregory Corso, a first-generation American whose name might be bigger in Italy these days than in the land of his birth. "It's good to be dead in America," the poem begins, and Gizzi rambles on through a genial accounting of the clutter of European culture with which one doesn't have to deal:

> To be dead in America at the movies
> distracted by preview music in the dimming lights.
> I never once thought of Alfred Deller
> or Kathleen Ferrier singing Kindertotenlieder.
> It's good to be lost among pillars of grass.
> I never once thought of My Last Duchess
> or the Pines of Rome . . . .
> It's good to share molecular chasm with a friend.
> I never once reached for Heisenberg
> or The Fall of the Roman Empire. (SV 47–48)

But as strenuously as Whitman, and after him William Carlos Williams, sought to forge an American culture free of old-world influences, for the European-American poet the "mind of Europe" (Eliot's phrase) is continually shaping one's experience of the immediate present:

> I was talking about rending, reading, rewriting
> what is seen. Put the book down and look into the day.
> I want an art that can say how I am feeling
> if I am feeling blue sky unrolling a coronation rug
> unto the bare toe of a peasant girl
> with vague memories of Jeanne d'Arc,
> or that transformation in Cinderella. (SV 49)

While the European past continually shadows the poet who attempts to capture daily reality, he is just as hampered by the utilitarian materialism of American society (a materialism, mind you, about which writers have been complaining for a century and a half): "This pageant demands too much, / that we work and not break, that we love / and not lie, and not complain. / It's good not to break in America" (SV 49–50). Gizzi concludes, saluting the dead Corso, that there is no single "American life," only the disparate lives of Americans brought together in a single multivoiced song that once promised salvation:

These parts wobble, stitching frames
to improvise a document:
all this American life. Strike that.
All our life, all our American lives gathered
into an anthem we thought to rescue us,
over and out. On your way, dust. (SV 52)

A grim, unhopeful ending to a lively, polychrome elegy: over and out, indeed.

* * *

All sorts of red flags (in more senses than one) go up at the title of Gizzi's more recent collection, *The Outernationale*.[3] Eugène Edine Pottier wrote "L'Internationale" in 1871 in the immediate aftermath of the Paris Commune. He meant it to be sung to that weathered French revolutionary tune "La Marsellaise," but it's most familiar in an 1888 setting by Pierre De Geyter. The song, appealing to the downtrodden of all nations, is certainly stirring—"Debout, les damnés de la terre, / Debout, les forçats de la faim," it begins ("Arise, wretched of the earth, Arise, convicts of hunger"). Its title designates a proletarian movement that transcends borders. But what is one to make of Gizzi's title, an apparently nonsensical nonce word that pulses with implications: what exists outside the nation-state? Can one be simultaneously a citizen and not a citizen? What, a hundred and thirty years on, has become of the utopian hopes of the Paris Commune, the Bolshevik Revolution, the American Wobblies?

While Gizzi's earlier work tended toward a spare, notational obliquity or echoed the "Martian" broadcasts of Jack Spicer (whose lectures and poetry Gizzi has edited[4]), his more recent, lusher poetry has a habit of falling into the accents of Walt Whitman. Indeed, much of *The Outernationale* reads like a series of riffs on *Leaves of Grass*. "A child I became a question / sitting on the grass" (O 13), runs the opening of "Stung," and here Gizzi seems to have reshuffled the sixth section of "Song of Myself," which includes lines such as "A child said *What is the grass?* fetching it to me with full hands." To Whitman, grass in part represented "the flag of my disposition, out of hopeful green stuff woven."[5] To Gizzi, the color green has less positive connotations. In "Aubade and Beyond," the "signal green" of spring is obscured, nearly overwhelmed in descending "sheets":

Everything seems to be falling in sheets today.
Sheets of glare and sheets of wind, paper

sheets and more, more sun, glint
near the monument. Such sheets in stone. (O 26)

"Nocturne," a poem of Edward Hopperish edges and garish, urban lights, presents a series of color slides in which the natural and the man-made collide: "bright-bright Gatorade green / green dusky as gray forest-shade green" (O 43). "Human Memory Is Organic" seeks to unwind the tangled relationship of physics, time, and consciousness, and finds all of them coming together in a "green" that concludes in "tears" (perhaps *lacrimae rerum*?):

Let us examine green. Let us go together

to see it all unstable and becoming
violent and testing gravity

so natural in its hunger.

The organic existence of gravity.
The organic nature of history.

The natural history of tears. (O 28)

Once you start looking for Whitman in *The Outernationale*, he turns up everywhere. I find it difficult not to think of the poet of *Drum-Taps* and the Civil War passages of *Specimen Days* when I read "On What Became of Mathew Brady's Battle Photographs." Brady was, of course, Whitman's photographic counterpart, documenting the war's devastation in over 10,000 plates (most of them made by his corps of photographers). "After the war," Gizzi tells us in a note, "Brady's glass negatives were sold wholesale to farmers to build greenhouses" (O 118), and the visual record of the Republic's agony was bleached to invisibility in the sun:

Sunlight and plant light
glass and stain
the campaign the conflict
the dead frozen in air
the sun and the sweat
the swell of fetid flesh
the tears the ache
the heat of loss
the nerves burn
and the shock

of never returning burns
in the belly
and the brain alike
these images lifting off
into air, dissolving
into heat and light
defy gravity
lifting off
they are going now
Mother, they are gone (O 86–87)

As have many other poets in recent years, Gizzi has felt compelled to respond to the Iraq War. "Protest Song" is in the tradition of neither Eugène Pottier nor Peter Seeger nor even Bob Dylan, but offers itself as a bitter commentary on Auden's "Poetry makes nothing happen":

This is not a declaration of love or song of war
not a tractate, autonym, or apologia

This won't help when the children are dying
no answer on the way to dust

Neither anthem to rally nor flag flutter
will bring back the dead, their ashes flying

This is not a bandage or hospital tent
not relief or the rest after

Not a wreath, lilac, or laurel sprig
not a garden of earthly delights (O 88)

"This won't help when the children are dying" is terrifically bathetic, as is "Neither anthem to rally nor flag flutter / will bring back the dead," but I suspect it is an intentional bathos, leading up to the more delicate modulations of "not a bandage or hospital tent / not relief or the rest after." The poem protests not so much against the devastations of war as against the uses to which poetry has been put, the "Martian generalities" purveyed by the "Out-weariers of Apollo" (as Pound's Sextus Propertius puts it[6]) or the tender-hearted laments that serve mostly to salve the consciences of powerless poets. This song is not a "wreath" for the tomb of some Unknown Soldier, nor a laurel sprig to decorate some hero, nor a bit of lilac, that most Whitmanian flower of mourning. Nor is it, in the tradition of Hieronymus Bosch, a "garden of earthly delights," an allegory of sin, fallenness, and corporeal nature. It is an exercise in painful and necessary self-limitation, an acknowledgement of sublunary ills and the inability of the poet's art to mend them.

Whitman, encompassing multitudes, made his poems more than just a paean to democracy: they became a teeming microcosm of the American body politic, all of whose inequalities and contradictions were to be transcended in the gradual upward spiral of democracy. (In his later years, Whitman became not a "right" Hegelian or a "left" Hegelian, but a just plain *vulgar* Hegelian.) *The Outernationale*, while presenting a vivid array of particulars that at times rivals Whitman's, can't muster anything like his optimism. The first of the collection's two poems entitled "The Outernationale" begins with another nod to the good grey bard—"Leaves arch over everything / they are so democratic / to us our viewer in a world of secrets"—but then settles into a kind of grim musing: "Something is something / when the administration of money flows backward" (O 20–21). Even the freshness of seasonal change is somehow darkened by a life in which the most prominent light is the "little sheen of products / in rows behind glass":

In summer we open and opening
we wander and
before we were happy
we were unhappy.
Such is the dialectical
awakening everyone
is hankering to embrace. (O 21)

Watching sports on TV, "We find purpose / in the game and together," Gizzi admits (echoing Williams's "The Ball Game" [*Spring and All*]); but in the end, dusk leaves him in a dreary, questioning mood, unsure of the state of the body politic:

When the pistons call,
when I was a wedge of sun
over steel mills,
when I asked what happened
I meant what happened to us? (O 22)

Gizzi's second take on "The Outernationale" is a long, bravura performance cast in the first person plural, a meditation on where "we" stand in the natural world and where we're headed. "Start from nothing," he admonishes a listener with "the book in your hand," "and let the sound reach you" (O 93). The sound is of course the sound of words, which in this poem are apt to break into shards of suffixes: "I was raised into / out of the incubator / -obic, -etic, istic / the stain of the world got on me" (O 94). Something like original sin has broken our language, our society:

> If we could only open
> our hardware
> to rewrite the software
> down deep, the body
> coming to, inside
> this wooden structure
> -archy, -ology, -ocracy. (O 95)

Gizzi is disgusted by the canards of the media and the stench of the city—"The box is spitting electro- / magnetic lies into the room / again," "a boulevard / rich with dog shit and perfume / carbon monoxide and subway grates"—and history seems, when it is not forgotten, to come down to a "bad history" (O 96, 99). (It's probably no coincidence that Gizzi here echoes the title of Barrett Watten's "counter-epic" of the First Gulf War, *Bad History*.[7])

To "rewrite" our own "software" is a draftily utopian goal, but perhaps no more deluded than Pottier's call for the "wretched of the earth" to arise and gird themselves for the "final struggle," or Whitman's faith in the "Endless unfolding of words of ages!" "The Outernationale" winds down not with a burst of cheerleading, but a solemn call to consider the heavenly host:

> Throw back your head
> to the milky tears.
> All types and shapes
> of silent light.
> Here the crab, the bear,
> the dipper, the wheel
> and the little tightnesses
> that keep us wanting.
> The wanting that keeps us
> looking hard into the dark.
> The dark we hope to unpack
> and move into
> that one day
> we might find ourselves lit up. (O 102)

The progression from constellations to "tightnesses," from "wanting" to "dark," and from there—surprisingly—to a new illumination, is like an unexpected burst of fireworks, a hope that lights up all the darknesses of the poem, and of *The Outernationale* as a whole.

* * *

If Gizzi in recent years has come to resemble a reticent, dubious Whitman—golly, not much Whitman left in that description—a superficial comparison might be drawn between Rae Armantrout and Emily Dickinson. Armantrout has none of Dickinson's reclusiveness, and very little of her antinomianism, but she resembles Dickinson in the brevity of her poems, her fond familiarity with the Bible and with fairy tales, and the way the cosmic or noumenal irrupts into her poetry by way of an unpacked metaphor or an unexpected turn of phrase. Dickinson's bird, for instance, in "A Bird, came down the Walk –," is a closely observed slice of otherness, even as the poet strives to assimilate it to the human world, remarking its courtesy to the passing beetle, offering it a crumb. It's only when the bird takes flight that the poem spreads its wings into a brightly plumaged metaphorical fugue:

he unrolled his feathers
And rowed him softer Home—

Than Oars divide the Ocean,
Too silver for a seam,
Or Butterflies, off Banks of Noon
Leap, plashless as they swim.[8]

Rather than leaping into metaphor like this, Armantrout prefers a more calculated approach, often arranging her poems into dovetailed and counterpointed sections in which a given motif flickers between concreteness and metaphor. Note how the color yellow (or "golden") moves through "Away," from the witch's house of *Hansel and Gretel*, to the yellow eyes of a crocodile in a children's book (I suspect this one is Roy Gerrard's *Croco'nile* of 1994), to the bits of color the poet observes in the sidewalk:

The boy and girl leave
the tired woman behind
gladly.

They are off
to find their real mother,

she of the golden
edible house, the
cunning hunger.
*
From your snort of recognition
I can tell

that you are the baby
crocodile,

adrift
on a floating mat
of papyrus.

In your yellow, crescent eye
an insouciant attention.
*
Yellow flecks
of glitter
in the cement—
clusters?—

each a faraway
answer

to an ill-posed problem.[9]

We travel from the human (the children) to the animal (the croc) to the inanimate (the cement) in these three vignettes, and the yellow upon which the poem hinges grows larger and larger in its implications, until the "flecks of glitter" have become a kind of metaphysical stardust.

Like Dickinson, Armantrout is a poet of the quotidian. "My poems," she writes, "respond to everyday life by using happenstance; whatever happens by within a certain time frame can enter them. So they are penetrable, interrupted and yet, I hope, they hang together somehow (sometimes)."[10] In the hands of a poet less deft and quirky than Armantrout, such a poetics of the everyday—what Guy Davenport once called the poetics of the "shirt-cuff note"—would result in acres of trivia. But Armantrout's intelligence is continually probing beneath the surface of what she observes, drawing offbeat conclusions from ordinary data:

The very old man shuffles very slowly
not between

the white lines of a crosswalk
but down one of them.

Like a figure in a dream,
his relation to meaning
is ominous. (NL 26)

I'm not nuts about that "Like a figure in a dream," which seems all too easy a simile, but I find the vague, "ominous" manner in which he becomes a figure for the radically inexplicable rather compelling. Or consider the way a restaurant's décor leads Armantrout to a keen observation about our relation to the past: "General Foods ads from the '50s line a restaurant's walls. / It's not nostalgic; nostalgia requires a place / to which we might want to go back."

It's our felt distance
from the supposed past
as collectible,

our credulities and
incredulities
as collectibles. (NL 63)

While Armantrout's poems have a range of registers, those she most often explores are the flat but suggestive ones of mass media. "Headline Song" (*Next Life*) is simply a string of headlines: "Bush vows victory / over terror. // For the orphans, / nightmare lasts," etc. (NL 31). In "The Subject," the always-unpredictable World Wide Web casts the web-surfing poet from the world of Hans Christian Andersen into the realm of clock-watching citizenship:

I was just going to click
on "Phoebe is changed
into a mermaid
tomorrow!" when suddenly
it all changed
into the image
of a Citizen watch. (NL 18)

The poem is all about change, from the reverse Kafkaesque metamorphosis of its first section ("we've just been turned human / in order to learn / that the beetle we've caught / and are now devouring / is our elder brother") to the "restless" stutter of attention in the final section: "'What is a surface?' / we ask, // trying to change the subject." The subject that gets changed, after all, is not merely the topic of conversation, but the speaking subject herself: subjectivity shifts in tandem with whatever enters the field of attention.

"We can't change the country," Stephen Dedalus grouses to Bloom in the "Eumaeus" episode of *Ulysses*, "Let us change the subject."[11] Changing the subject (in all senses), or at least radically dislocating the language, has been one of the signature moves of the Language poets, most of whom would like nothing better than to change the current order of things. Armantrout has been bunged in with the Language cohort for some two or three decades now. "I do feel that I share some elements of a poetics with them," she once told an interviewer. "It's more than our use of parataxis, ellipsis or polyvocality (or whatever we're calling it now)"—the gentle put-down is classic Armantrout —"I think it comes down to a sense that critical intelligence and pleasure or, better yet, critical intelligence and play are not enemies. They can unite in poetry."[12]

It's the notion of "play" that hooks me on Armantrout's work. Humor pervades her work, as if the poet were wryly winking at us as she holds up her bits of overheard language and everyday observation. For instance, in "Thing," a bit of Christopher Smart pastiche turns into a smarty-pants jab at the right-wing bias of Fox News:

> We love our cat
> for her self
> regard is assiduous
> and bland,
>
> for she sits in the small
> patch of sun on our rug
> and licks her claws
> from all angles
>
> and it is far
> superior
> to "balanced reporting"
>
> though, of course,
> it is also
> the very same thing. (NL 15)

That's none too subtle, and I must confess finding that "of course" a trifle smarmy, essential though it may be to the culminatory rhythm of the last lines.

More characteristic is the first little section of "Promise": "Canary yellow of the school bus; / school bus yellow of the SUV" (NL 45). Here Armantrout remarks the odd slippage of our ordinary epithets, how the school bus's yellow gets described in naturalistic terms, while the SUV (massive, ungainly, the epitome of wasteful consumerism and American self-assertion) gets taken down a notch by being compared to a big box used for carrying kids around. A monster approaches a girl's bed in "A Distance," while the "girl's doll" watches "With contempt." "But whose contempt is it?," asks Armantrout (NL 20–21).

Armantrout is always tinkering with language, wondering what works and what doesn't, and why. "Try this," she writes in "Reversible": "Shadows of leaves / between shadows of venetian blinds // bounce // like holes // across the scroll of a / player-piano." A serviceable enough simile, perhaps a minor detail in someone else's poem. "But are similes reversible?," she asks:

> Try this.
>
> Trunk of a palm tree
> as the leg
>
> of a one-legged
> ballerina. (NL 29)

This simile, at least, just plain can't be reversed (try it); a one-legged ballerina is after all a preposterous notion, and comparing her leg to the trunk of a palm tree isn't going to make her existence any more possible.

The second section of "Reversible" begins with another bit of ordinary metaphor-making ("That's a bad / Sean Connery, but / a good Prince"—I assume Armantrout means The Artist Formerly—and yet again—Known as Prince), and then strikes out into weirder territory:

> We wake up to an empty room
> addressing itself in scare quotes.
>
> "Happen" and "now"
> have been smuggled out,
>
> to arrive safely in the past tense.
>
> We come home to a cat
> made entirely of fish. (NL 29–30)

There's a wonderful interplay here of old-fashioned surrealism (the room's interior colloquy, the piscine cat—I suppose if you feed your cat nothing but sardines she's in some sense made of fish) and purely linguistic speculation, with immediate events—"'Happen' and 'now'"—tucked into an irretrievable past. But the "safety" of the past tense, in which things don't happen "now" because they've already happened, is undercut by the slightly unsettling resonances of "empty room" and "scare quotes."

One might be tempted to call Armantrout a kind of laureate of the everyday, if that title weren't being vied for by so many poets. I'm tempted instead to think of her as the laureate of the *uncanny*, the *Unheimliche*, that which is familiar and unsettling at the same time. To read the world as Armantrout does, constantly tinkering with and unpacking its signs, is to render familiar, even shopworn surfaces new and vivid. Viktor Shklovsky called this *ostranenie*, or "defamiliarization." It's one of Dickinson's stocks in trade. When she observes how the bird on her walk "bit an Angleworm in halves / And ate the fellow, raw," there's a sudden shock of defamiliarization in that "raw": while we wouldn't expect a bird to eat his worms otherwise, the rawness of the meal suddenly underlines the alienness of the bird world.

For Armantrout, sad to say, the world has recently turned more alien in a threateningly intimate way. In June 2006 she underwent surgery for adrenocortical carcinoma, a rare and aggressive cancer that is difficult to treat. Her work since then has been written in the shadow of the disease; as she puts it in *The Grand Piano*, the Bay Area Language poets' ongoing "collective autobiography," "My recent cancer diagnosis is, of course, the ultimate unexpected input. It's as if some god said, 'Let's see you work around this.'"[13]

The metaphor Armantrout has seized on for her cancer is "dark matter." Physics knows dark matter as a kind of paradox, matter that cannot be detected but only inferred through its gravitational effect on visible matter. Like the "undiscovered tumor" that "squats on [the] kidney" of a woman whose photo is on the mantelpiece in "Apartment," dark matter is a silent, invisible, but looming presence.[14] Physicists now estimate that up to 95% of the universe's gravitating matter is dark matter.

The second section of *Versed*, Armantrout's 2009 collection, is titled "Dark Matter," and the poems are shot through with a melancholy and foreboding that, while by no means absent in her earlier work, had been offset by jauntiness. She has often transcribed her dreams in her poetry, but they rarely cut as close to the bone as in the middle section of "Around":

Chuck and I are pleased
to have found a spot
where my ashes can be scattered.
It looks like a construction site

now
but it's adjacent
to a breathtaking, rocky coast.
Chuck sees places
where he might snorkel.
We're being shown through
by a sort of realtor.
We're interested but can't get her
to fix the price.

"The future is all around us," the poem concludes: "It's a place, // any place / where we don't exist" (V 67–68).

It's sobering to realize that one ironclad definition of the future is *a time when we shall be dead.* Intimations of mortality have a way of waking one up to the limits of one's powers and ambitions. ("Depend upon it, Sir, when a man knows he is to be hanged in a fortnight," said Samuel Johnson, "it concentrates his mind wonderfully."[15]) Musing on the "dark matter" invading her body, Armantrout can ask brightly, "Who am I / to experience a burst of star formation?" But such playful Whitmanism, in the face of grave illness, is apt to dwindle: "after the first rush / of enthusiasm // any idea / recedes and dims" (V 69).

Armantrout has opted to face her illness with neither histrionics nor large gestures, but with the same curious equanimity she has brought to bear on the other "inputs" of her daily life. The final poems in *Versed* include a number that gesture toward the grand summing-up ("Passage" begins, "I held the framework / of my life in mind / with some precision" [V 119]), but time and again they veer from big statements to something smaller, quirkier, and more intimately compelling. The first section of "Hoop" starts at the very beginning, the pre-creation scene of Genesis 1:

God twirled
across the face of
what cannot be named
since it was not moving.

God was momentum then,
that impatience
with interruption,

stamping time's blanks
with its own image

The poem then moves on to Armantrout's own situation:

> Now her theme will be
> that she has escaped
> certain destruction,
>
> that she is
> impossibly lucky.
>
> This theme should be jaunty
> but slightly discordant,
>
> coming in, as it does,
> so late.

Armantrout's survival is not merely a late-arriving, almost incongruously bouncy theme in the midst of a somber symphony, but a fact that marks her out from the crowd:

> The character
> associated with this theme
> should be dressed
> in markedly old-fashioned clothing—
>
> a hoop skirt perhaps—
> while everyone else
> is in cut-offs,
>
> ready for the barbeque. (V 110–11)

No backward-looking pillar of salt, Armantrout has donned, along with a hoop skirt, a Dickinsonian seriousness that sets her apart from her casual peers, awaiting life's next event like a cookout.

"Fact," the last poem in *Versed*, turns a characteristically raised eyebrow toward whatever the day has to offer. Its first two sections juxtapose the Iraq War with the tedium of a hospital visit:

> Operation Phantom Fury.
>
> *
>
> The full force
> of the will to live
> is fixed
> on the next occasion:

someone
coming with a tray,

someone
calling a number.

"Operation Phantom Fury" was the code name for the Second Battle of Fallujah; here the phrase also signals, of course, the battle within Armantrout's own body. What delight, then, when in the final section of "Fact" she turns her attention, all her characteristic curiosity and questioning intact, to the enigmas the world continues to pose her:

Each material
fact
is a pose,

an answer
waiting to be chosen.

"Just so," it says.

"Ask again!" (V 121)

"I know I am solid and sound," Whitman booms in "Song of Myself," "To me the converging objects of the universe perpetually flow, / All are written to me, and I must get what the writing means."[16] Armantrout echoes him, albeit in a subtler, more subdued key. "Dark matter" is, after all, another "material fact" to be assessed, a "converging object of the universe," "an answer / waiting to be chosen." And with what gusto she echoes that "Ask again!"

Notes

1. Andrew McCord, back-cover copy to Peter Gizzi, *Some Values of Landscape and Weather* (Middletown, CT: Wesleyan UP, 2003); hereafter cited parenthetically in text as SV.

2. Robert Frost, *Collected Poems, Prose, and Plays*, ed. Richard Poirier and Mark Richardson (New York: Library of America, 1995) 316.

3. Peter Gizzi, *The Outernationale* (Middletown, CT: Wesleyan UP, 2008); hereafter cited parenthetically in text as O.

4. *The House That Jack Built: The Collected Lectures of Jack Spicer*, ed. Peter Gizzi (Hanover, NH: Wesleyan UP, 1998) and *My Vocabulary Did This to Me: The Collected Poetry of Jack Spicer*, ed. Peter Gizzi and Kevin Killian (Middletown, CT: Wesleyan UP, 2008).

5. Walt Whitman, *Complete Poetry and Collected Prose*, ed. Justin Kaplan (New York: Library of America, 1982) 192, 193.

6. Ezra Pound, "Homage to Sextus Propertius," *Poems and Translations*, ed. Richard Sieburth (New York: Library of America, 2003) 537.

7. Barrett Watten, *Bad History* (Berkeley: Atelos, 1998).

8. *The Poems of Emily Dickinson: Reading Edition*, ed. R. W. Franklin (Cambridge, MA: Belknap P of Harvard UP, 1999) 163.

9. Rae Armantrout, *Next Life* (Middletown, CT: Wesleyan UP, 2007) 27–28; hereafter cited parenthetically in text as NL.

10. Rae Armantrout (with Carla Harryman, Kit Robinson, Tom Mandel, Barrett Watten, Ted Pearson, Lyn Hejinian, Bob Perelman, Ron Silliman, and Steve Benson), *The Grand Piano: An Experiment in Collective Autobiography, San Francisco 1975–1980, Part 4* (Detroit: Mode A, 2007) 86.

11. James Joyce, *Ulysses (The Corrected Text)*, ed. Hans Walter Gabler et al. (New York: Random House, 1986) 527.

12. Rae Armantrout, "'Poetry Isn't Built on Hope': An Interview with Tom Beckett," *Collected Prose* (San Diego: Singing Horse P, 2007) 131.

13. *The Grand Piano, Part 4* 87.

14. Rae Armantrout, *Versed* (Middletown, CT: Wesleyan UP, 2009) 107; hereafter cited parenthetically in text as V.

15. James Boswell, *Life of Johnson*, ed. R. W. Chapman (London: Oxford UP, 1953) 849.

16. Whitman, *Collected Poetry* 206.

Ronald Johnson

Four Essays

1. Marrow-Bones and Turkish Delight

While my own native greens-and-ham-hock Southern cuisine is a hard sell to my friends with more refined palates, my mother's pecan pie recipe has always been well received. A simple concoction: in a single bottom piecrust (homemade or store-bought) you set out a layer of halved pecans, then pour over them an inch or so of beaten eggs and heavy corn syrup. In the oven, the pecans rise to the top to be crisped in the heat, while the syrup-egg mixture congeals into a hard gel. Crunchy pecans, flaky crust, and a center of unadulterated, primordial sugar: what's not to love (if you aren't diabetic, that is)?

The poet Ronald Johnson (1935–1998), who worked as a chef and caterer and who made most of what little money writing brought him from his excellent cookbooks, offers a variation of the traditional southern pecan pie in *The American Table* (1984). (My own copy has reached the stage of broken-spined, gravy-spattered dilapidation that marks a personal classic in the genre.) Instead of "the usual bottled dark 'Karo,'" Johnson's pie is based on a syrup made of sugar, orange juice, and the thinly sliced peels of two oranges.[1] It's still a pecan pie, the nemesis of dieters everywhere, but a pecan pie with a sophisticated twist, the orange peel adding a sour, slightly bitter zest like the tang of remorse.

It's hard not to be aware of Johnson's culinary vocation as one reads his poetry. An epicure's palate is evident in some of his early lines, as in "Quivera":

> On that soil, later to be stripped
> for prairie sod-houses,
>
> wild turkeys
> flocked among the persimmons

their flesh succulent from golden sand-plums,
bitter

with china-berries.[2]

Johnson chews and savors words with a gourmet's passionate discernment, as well. Watch the play of long "e"s, short "i"s, "r"s, and "t"s in these stanzas from *ARK* 61, *Fireworks II*—

gear aerie
the real article
heaven fled to ledge

limbed unsealed from limb
for wings'
alert machinery

& wield a torch
as sphere
held arch of time[3]

—coming to an emphatic close on the long "i" of "time."

The oral pleasures of speaking poetry are surely akin to those of eating. Once, when we were chatting on the phone about how much of the attraction of Louis Zukofsky's late verse lies in sheer *sound*, I asked Johnson if the same were not equally true of Swinburne. Yes, he replied, "but Swinburne's like eating Turkish delight. Now Zukofsky, that's gnawing a *marrow-bone*." Much as he would have us take him for a master chef of marrow-bones, all too often Johnson serves up a Swinburnean confection studded with alliteration and jingling rhymes, as in the final stanza of *ARK* 61:

rhyme twine
mirror rim mirror
to remind mired any moral
stiles arrayed,
choir
prise air
(A 190)

For some four decades, Johnson explored a variety of poetic modes stemming from the most radical experiments of the "high" modernists. He aimed to fuse the scattered and juxtapositional forms of Pound, Olson, and Zukofsky with the visionary poetics of Blake, Milton, and Dante, to tell the "tale of the tribe" as one episode in the evolution of a self-conscious, unbelievably complex but ultimately harmonious cosmos, and to mirror the harmony of that cosmos in the music of his lines. His is, in the end, a poetry of wonder, a happy poetry. (The text to which his text is commentary might be Herakles's climactic exclamation in Pound's version of *Women of Trachis*: "come at it that way, my boy, what / SPLENDOUR, / IT ALL COHERES."[4]) My mother's pecan pie is perhaps the basest of desserts, heavy candy served with a fork on a china plate; Johnson's is candy for grown-ups. Much the same can be said of his poetry, an endlessly literate, proliferatingly complex art with, at the end, a gooey sweet center.

* * *

Johnson spent his childhood in prairie Kansas, playing in the lumberyard his father owned, reading L. Frank Baum, and dreaming of escaping to Oz. His escape came in the form of a relationship with the poet and publisher Jonathan Williams, who introduced Johnson to contemporary poetry and to contemporary poets—William Carlos Williams, Louis Zukofsky, Charles Olson—and whose Jargon Society published his first book, *A Line of Poetry, a Row of Trees*, in 1964.[5] Those early poems, which can be sampled in *To Do As Adam Did*, Peter O'Leary's selection of works from the whole range of Johnson's career, are wholly credible exercises in an Olsonian late-modernist idiom. Quoting extensively from various source texts, they linger over the details of history, as in "Quivera," which follows Coronado's search for El Dorado; they hunt out the mythical resonances of the natural commonplace ("Sunflowers," "Indian Corn"); and, as Olson's *Maximus Poems* did with his own beloved Gloucester, they dig deep into specific places, in particular Johnson's native Kansas: "Canceas, Cansez, Kansies, Konza: the Indian word / meaning smoky"; or, more simply, "Kansas, of / sand plums & muddy rivers / from where I come" (TD 23, 25).

Johnson, however, is no Olson. His enthusiasm for the big man's collage poetics stops short of the headlong, "projectivist" untidiness of Olson's verse and thought, a rapacious bookishness that issued forth in lectures, essays, and poems that are models of incompletion, mazes of blind alleys and suggestions for further reading. Almost as counterweight to his own mentor Olson, Jonathan Williams had introduced Johnson to the spare, ascetic verse of Louis Zukofsky, then nearing the final stretches of his long poem, *"A"*. While Olson was cramming his multifarious reading into the shaggy, exfoliating lines of *The Maximus Poems*, Zukofsky was perfecting a poetics of concision, shaving his quotations down to single phrases and syllables to fit into the angular music of his word-count lines. The traces of Zukofsky's obsession with finish, with precision and closure, are everywhere evident in Johnson's early work, from his careful, almost overdetermined line-breaks to his subtle (and not-so-subtle) sound repetitions. For Johnson, Zukofsky and Olson are "The Minimalist and The Maximus—such opposing poles of influences: parities" (A 311).

Neither Zukofsky nor Olson, however, would have much truck with the two obsessions Johnson first cultivates in *A Line of Poetry, a Row of Trees*, and which he would pursue for the rest of his career: the magical, "Orphic" role of the poet himself; and the amazing architectures and symmetries of the nature which it is his task to celebrate. "Shake, Quoth the Dove House," which opens *To Do As Adam Did*, lays out the poet's calling as that of a gardener, shaping the nature around him:

> This is the Garden, where all is a poet's
> topiary. Where even the trees
> shall have tongues, green aviaries,
> to rustle at his will.
> . . . .
>   Here–
> both lines of poetry, rows
> of trees,
> shall spring all
>
> seasons
> out 'of the lust of
>
> the earth,
> without
> a formal seed.' (TD 3–4)

As O'Leary points out in the introduction to *To Do As Adam Did*, the prelapsarian Adam had but two tasks: to name the animals, and to cultivate the Garden of Eden. In Johnson's poetics, these charges are fused, and the very act of naming nature becomes that of conjuring it into garden-like form.

In his "mower" poems, Andrew Marvell regretted the opposition between fructive natural formlessness and the densely espaliered, pruned, and parterred spaces of typical seventeenth-century gardens:

Luxurious man, to bring his vice in use,
 Did after him the world reduce,
And from the fields the flowers and plants allure,
 Where nature was most plain and pure.
He first enclosed within the gardens square
 A dead and standing pool of air . . .
'Tis all enforced, the fountain and the grot,
 While the sweet fields do lie forgot:
Where willing nature does to all dispense
 A wild and fragrant innocence:
And fauns and fairies do the meadows till,
 More by their presence than their skill.[6]

In Johnson's horticultural poetics, however, there is no opposition between the formalized constructions of the garden and the seemingly shapeless growth of uncultivated nature. On the contrary: nature itself, as he sings it in "Four Orphic Poems," is itself the most wondrously regular of forms:

There is an exquisite movement, like it were chaos,

but of a sweet proportion
& order:
the atoms, cells & parsley-ferns

of the universe.
. . . .
Nebula, whirlpool, mist & cloud; knotted, asymmetrical
branchings

formed like a labyrinth

— are form, even as a sphere, crystal
& flower.

'Patterns

are temporary boundaries', the moving countries

where nothing
is seen in isolation. (TD 9, 13)

These will be the obsessions of Johnson's writing life. On the one hand, a celebration of the many-layered complexities and symmetries of natural process, a celebration in which the findings of the scientific method will time and again prove grist for the aesthetic mill, raw material for the Wonder Factory. (An early example: "Newton / —it is said—did not show the cause of an apple falling, / only the similitude between the apple / & the stars" [TD 14].) And on the other, a celebration of the poet's ability—figured as often as not in terms of the mythological singer Orpheus, whose music "made the trees bend and the animals one" (A 313)—to unfold and celebrate those complexities and symmetries.

Of the handful of books that determined the direction of Johnson's writing life, second only in importance to *The Wizard of Oz* was Elizabeth Sewell's *The Orphic Voice: Poetry and Natural History* (1960), which Johnson seems to have picked up in the early sixties and rarely laid down thereafter. He used the book as a mine of source material, repeatedly plundering its illustrative quotations and epigraphs for lines to incorporate into his own poetry, but he also attended to Sewell's arguments, and took them to heart. *The Orphic Voice* is a survey of the Orpheus figure in poetry from Shakespeare through Rilke; more crucially, it is a manifesto on behalf of "post-logical" thinking, exemplified for Sewell in the myth of Orpheus and the various "Orphic" poets she treats. Such postlogical thinking represents the convergence of *Naturphilosophie* and poetry as two closely related—perhaps, ultimately, identical—means of grasping the processes and structures of the world. "Poetry," Sewell writes, "is the most inclusive form of thought we have yet devised, a conscious call upon those resources of myth which underly all language and all thinking . . . Poetry, metaphor, mythology are highly realistic and down to earth. It is logic and mathematics which are the imaginative and fantastical exercises."[7] "In the Orpheus story, myth is looking at itself. This is the reflection of myth in its own mirror. It promises to give Orpheus a special significance: for myth as living thought and the very type of thought is an action, and for all those other reflexive or self-reflective forms; for the human organism as an indivisible whole trying to understand itself and its universe; for language and poetry reflecting back to the organism its own countenance and activity; for biology reflecting on the whole span of life in which thinking man appears as the last enigmatic development."[8] Heady stuff, indeed, and highly combustible fuel for the imagination of a young man who had spent his childhood in Ashland, Kansas, wondering what imaginative alchemy might change his surroundings to a polychrome Oz.

From early on, Johnson sets himself up not merely as an Orphic poet of Sewell's illustrious band, but as a *visionary* poet, a member of that ecstatic company that includes Thomas Traherne, William Blake, and the prophet Ezekiel. The visionary element is strong in Johnson's "breakthrough" volume,

The Book of the Green Man (1967), a long poem stemming from Johnson and Jonathan Williams's 1962–1963 walking tour of England and Wales. *Green Man* is a justly celebrated series of meditations on both the naturalists' and the visionaries' Britain, a land in which the "green man" of the title, an ancient nature avatar bearded with foliage, can be found on ordinary village pub signs or among the carved ornaments of piously serene country churches. In the green man, Johnson has tapped into a potent perennial symbol, from *Sir Gawain and the Green Knight* through Robin Hood, the Jolly Green Giant, and even the cinematic Shrek. (I'm surprised that a recent burst of green-man-interest among the New Age types hasn't brought Johnson's volume back into print.)

The first of *The Book of the Green Man*'s four sections, "Winter," begins with the poet in Grasmere Churchyard, listening to nighttime birdsong and the sound of the River Rothay, contemplating how he might forge his English experience into "something circular / seasonal . . . some // flowing thing in its / cycle—an image of our footsteps // planted in homage // over each ridge // & valley."[9] The Wordsworths—Dorothy and William, by whose grave he mediates seem as it were two halves of a single, ideal poet. William, with his peerless visions of the vast forces of nature, his "inner country / of deep, clear Lakes," "could not see daffodils" (never mind Wordsworth's reputation as the preeminent daffodil-poet in the tradition) "only / 'huge forms', *Presences* & earth 'working / like a sea'" (GM 15–16). It was Dorothy

who brought home

lichens & cushions of
moss,
 who saw

these Lakes
in all their weathers –

'dim mirrors',
'bright slate',

—the sheens like herrings
& spear-shaped
streaks

of polished steel (GM 16)

—who actually observed the nature about her, and fixed it in vivid and memorable language in her journals. *The Book of the Green Man* oscillates between lively, precise natural description (and here Johnson often relies on such classic naturalists as Gilbert White and Francis Kilvert) and ecstatic visionary experience. In its most successful moments, it manages to do both at once, to fix concrete experience and to translate it into striking visionary metaphor, as in "Upon First Opening a Cuckoo":

> I saw the sweet-briar & bon-fire & strawberry wire now
> relaxed into intricate thicket.
> It was as if seen in strong sunlight, flat
>
> & tapestried, all edge & definition. Here, an airy bone shaped
> like a plowshare, there, vibratory membranes within a space
>
> from which the song must come: a syrinx (hollow
> pipes of reeds) now silent
>
> in return to the 'Salliter' of earth.
>
> *Little more than*
> *a drift of air, brought*
>
> *into form by plumes.*
>
> Mulch to stone.
> Yeast of the clouds. (TD 37)

For the most part, Johnson's visionary effusions in *The Book of the Green Man* remain firmly anchored in observed natural reality. It's an unusual sort of visionary rapture, but one wholly in keeping with Sewell's description of the Orphic poet, able to imaginatively capture the processes that make up the natural world and that escape conventional logic. "There are connections in these," Johnson writes in "The Oak of the Maze,"

> – between an earth, sentient with moles,
> & the owl's
> radiant eyes –
>
> fine as a web drawn
> by spiders,
>
> close as the grain of oak . . .
>
> from earth, to mistletoe, ivy & lichen, to owl's-
> wing, to thunder, to lightning, to earth—& back.

There are many ways

to look at an oak, & one, with its
own eyes:

the blunt, burning push
of acorns

in an earth full

of movements, slight rustlings, as a passage of night-birds (TD 32)

I can't help hearing in these lines—and even more strongly in other passages of *Green Man*—an echo of the 1814 preface to Wordsworth's *The Excursion*:

> How exquisitely the individual Mind
> (And the progressive powers perhaps no less
> Of the whole species) to the external World
> Is fitted:—and how exquisitely, too—
> Theme this but little heard of among men—
> The external World is fitted to the Mind;[10]

And I can't help but recall what Blake scribbled next to this passage in his own copy of Wordsworth: "You shall not bring me down to believe such fitting & fitted I know better & Please your Lordship."[11] Blake, famously, had no patience with the visible, "corporeal" world, which he saw as the corpse of fallen reason, obscuring the bright visions available to the unfallen imagination: "He who does not imagine in stronger and better lineaments, and in stronger and better light than his perishing mortal eye can see does not imagine at all."[12]

For Blake, true imagination saw Ezekiel's wheels within wheels, Jacob's ladder to heaven, Isaiah's vision of the Lord on a throne "high and lifted up," the panorama of destruction and exultation that makes up the book of Revelation. He would have little patience with the rapture of botanical and cosmological process that Johnson pursues in *Green Man* and its sequel, *Valley of the Many-Colored Grasses* (1969).[13] On the other hand, Blake's lovely imagined dialogue from "A Vision of the Last Judgment"—"When the Sun rises do you not see a round Disk of fire somewhat like a Guinea 0 no no I see an innumerable company of the Heavenly host crying Holy Holy Holy is the Lord God Almighty"[14]—seems to me *echt* Johnson.

* * *

At the beginning of the 1970s, Johnson, long parted from Jonathan Williams and settled in San Francisco ("Everybody wanted to get to Oz and San Francisco is," he told one interviewer[15]), got himself caught in what I've come to regard as the flypaper of twentieth-century American poets: an epic-length poem. Its working title was the rather hokey *Wor(l)ds*, but Johnson rethought that when Guy Davenport counseled him that one shouldn't title anything with a word readers couldn't pronounce. *ARK* was the name he settled on, a polysemic syllable if ever there was: Noah's ark, which bore all animal life safe over the flood; the Ark of the covenant, containing the tablets of the deity's agreement with humanity; *arc-en-ciel*, the rainbow, the aerial prism that splits sunlight into a visible spectrum.

Radi os, the "revision by excision" of the first four books of *Paradise Lost,* which Johnson undertook in the mid-seventies, was for some time intended to serve as a sort of tailpiece to *ARK*, a dome of stars over the architecture of the whole. As Davenport notes in his afterword to *Radi os*, the Romantics were obsessed with Milton—Blake "rewrote" *Paradise Lost* at least twice, in *Milton* and *The Four Zoas*, and Wordsworth's *Prelude* begins with clear allusions to Milton—but by the twentieth century, far fewer poets were finding immediate inspiration in the Puritan polemicist. The high modernists looked to Homer and Dante instead; and by the 1970s, I would hazard, a large proportion of the late- and postmodernist poets following them, perhaps influenced by Pound and Eliot's notorious dismissals, had barely read Milton, much less acknowledged him as a master.

Significantly, it is under the aegis of the Romantic visionary Blake that Johnson makes his own approach to the seventeenth-century epic poet. *Radi os* is, Johnson explains, "the book Blake gave me (as Milton entered Blake's left foot—the first foot, that is, to exit Eden), his eyes wide open through my hand. *To etch* is 'to cut away,' and each page, as in Blake's concept of a book, is a single picture."[16] Blake's own method of producing his illuminated books is known as "relief etching": he would draw the designs and words (backward, of course) on a copper plate in a mixture of candle-grease and salad oil, then cover the plate with an acid bath that ate away the surrounding areas, leaving him a raised surface with which to print in various colors.[17] The method itself was as slow and painstaking as can be imagined—but then, Blake was trained as an engraver, the slowest and most painstaking of artistic trades—and it came to carry a powerful ideological charge for him, as he explains in *The Marriage of Heaven and Hell*: "But first the notion that man has a body distinct from his soul, is to be expunged; this I shall do, by printing in the infernal method, by corrosives, which in Hell are salutary and medicinal, melting apparent surfaces away, and displaying the infinite which was hid."[18] In *Radi os* Johnson has applied infernal corrosives to the first four books of *Paradise Lost*, burning all of Milton that stands in the way of his own vision of truth: burning away the narrative and the characters, from the defiant and paradoxically heroic Satan and the company of fallen angels, to the sententiously self-righteous Lord and his eager-to-please Son.

What's left is clearly a Ronald Johnson poem, though one whose vocabulary has been supplied by John Milton. (This very fact makes the poem more Johnsonian, given the degree to which all of his work is woven of quotation.) It begins:

O   tree
                                    into the World,
                                                                        Man

                                                                the chosen

Rose out of Chaos

                                                                        song (R 3)

—in place of Milton's magnificent opening invocation, "Of Mans First Disobedience, and the Fruit / Of that Forbidden Tree, whose mortal tast / Brought Death into the World, and all our woe, / With loss of *Eden*" and so forth, down to "I thence / Invoke thy aid to my advent'rous song"(1.1–13).[19]

Much of *Radi os* (and of the in-progress *ARK*) is encapsulated in this first picture-page: the "tree," a complex instrument for transmuting the sun's energy and the nutrients of the soil in which it is rooted into a complex, ramifying structure that reaches toward the sun (perhaps represented by the large "0"); the complex interrelationships of plant life ("tree") and humanity ("Man"), the only terrestrial inhabitant capable of consciously recognizing its place in this complex ecosystem ("the chosen"), within "the World"; the "Rose" (which as so many words in *Radi os* can be taken as both noun and verb), a perennial symbol of beauty and order, evoking both the Rose of the Blessed at the climax of the *Paradiso* and Pound's "rose in the steel dust"; and how all of this rose—and continues to rise—"out of Chaos," this will be the burden of Johnson's "song."

Radi os is a long poem that a longtime reader of Milton is apt to find endlessly frustrating or endlessly delightful (or both). A comic book adaptation of *Paradise Lost*, or the movie version I keep hearing is in production, will perforce give one a simplified Milton, but at least a Milton that retains some of the comfortable "story" elements of the poem as one knows it. But Johnson's composition by corrosives has so thoroughly evacuated *Paradise Lost* of character, setting, event, and argument that what is left is as it were a series of gestures toward divine, ecstatic utterance—but none of the majestic architecture of thought and image Milton erects.

Radi os contains an ongoing series of local modifications and reversals of Milton that at times one can't help but find amusing, as when Johnson takes Satan's bitter reflections on Adam and Eve's married felicity—"Sight hateful, sight tormenting! thus these two / Imparadised in one another's arms / The happier *Eden*, shall enjoy thir fill / Of bliss on bliss, while I to Hell am thrust" (4.505–08)—and replaces them with a flash of sly homoeroticism: "Imparadised in one another's / thrust" (R 80).

More telling, however, is Johnson's adaptation of a passage at the beginning of Book Three of *Paradise Lost*, where God watches Satan's progress toward Earth, predicts to his Son that Man will succumb to the tempter's stratagems, and justifies (rather smarmily, to my ears) the punishment that must be meted out: "So will fall / Hee and his faithless progency: whose fault? / Whose but his own? ingrate, he had of mee / All he could have; I made him just and right, / Sufficient to have stood, though free to fall" (3.95–99). After all, what pleasure could God take in receiving obedience from creatures who could not choose otherwise: "Not free, what proof could they have giv'n sincere / Of true allegiance, constant Faith or Love . . .?" (3.103–04). The logic and theology of this are impeccable, but it's apt to give one at least a shadow of William Empson's reaction (in *Milton's God*): "I think the traditional God of Christianity very wicked, and have done since I was at school, where nearly all my little playmates thought the same."[20]

Under Johnson's eraser, the passage becomes a luminous picture of the earth as a garden, emptied of the promise of heaven or the threat of hell, where the humans being's only duties are artistic activity and mutual affection:

The radiant image

                                        the only
                                         Garden

On the bare outside of this World,

                    no bars of Hell, nor

            far off Heaven,

And Man there placed.

the sole command

create

or love (R 51)

To "create" and to "love," and to be in love with a visible creation, are the primary themes of *Radi os*, which plays itself out as a spiraling of ecstatic utterances repeatedly circling around the motifs of sun, of light, of the circle, and of the eye that beholds and creates it all.

Radi os was published by Sand Dollar Books in 1977, in a direct photoreproduction of the 1892 Milton Johnson used; on some pages, by looking closely you can see the lines where the book has been exacto-knifed apart and glued back down. The recent Flood Editions reissue of the poem is something of an aesthetic triumph. Designer Jeff Clark (himself a fine poet) has replaced the crunky turn-of-century fonts with a highly readable Bembo, retaining precisely Johnson's spacings, and has added page numbers, a godsend for the cross-referencing Johnson's work always provokes.

In *Radi os*, it seems to me that Johnson has done something undeniably new. Of course, there is nothing innovative about piggybacking one's poem upon an earlier work. The modernists made something of an industry out of refitting old vehicles out of the Order of Monuments car lot, from the wholesale overhauling of the *Odyssey* in Joyce's *Ulysses* to the junkyard cherry-picking of shiny chrome quotations that makes up so much of *The Cantos*. And there is Tom Phillips's *A Humument*, a little-known Victorian novel (*A Human Document*, by W. H. Mallock) whose pages Phillips has drawn and painted over repeatedly, leaving wee clusters of words to peek out meaningfully from the midst of visual displays that range from op- and pop-art to impressionistic pastiche.

It is Johnson's wise decision to leave Milton's words undisturbed, *where he found them*, so that each page of *Radi os* is both a labyrinth of meaning, inviting the reader to traverse the clusters of language in a variety of orders, and a visual display. It's unsurprising that *Radi os* follows close upon Johnson's experiments with "concrete" poetry, though to my ear (and eye) the Milton adaptation is far superior even to such lovely pieces as the first poem of *Songs of the Earth* (1970), in which one can distinguish, flickering in and out of focus, the resonant words *ear*, *earth*, *hear*, *heart*, *hearth*, and *art* (and the less resonant *the*):

earthearthearth
earthearthearth
earthearthearth
earthearthearth
earthearthearth
earthearthearth (TD 67)

There is a good deal of concrete poetry and other visual material in *ARK*, Johnson's long hymn of praise to natural process and the human eye that has evolved to wonder at it. Some of it is rather trifling, like the diagram of cell division in BEAM 25, *A Bicentennial Hymn*, or this bit of mechanical cuteness from BEAM 29: "no where / now here / no where / now here" (A 68, 79). Other seemingly tossed-off gestures have deeper implications. BEAM 15, for instance, is simply the print of Johnson's right hand—nothing at all like what we recognize as a poem, and barely qualifying as a piece of visual art (A 48). But it's a Duchamp-like gesture, more important for its idea than its execution: the poet is in the midst of a long poem celebrating the workings of nature, the way blind matter has evolved itself into a thinking being—the human—able to grasp and wonder at the process of his own evolution; what more concrete self-portrait of the poet as embodied consciousness could there be than a print of the lines and whorls of his composing hand?

In his Note at the end of *ARK*, Johnson acknowledges the "risks and shipwrecks" (A 311) of the American long poem before him—Pound's *Cantos*, Williams's *Paterson*, Zukofsky's *"A"*, Olson's *Maximus Poems*—all of them save *"A"* ending badly, trailing off into incompletion. The problem with these poems, Johnson came to believe, had to do with their investment in history. "The epic," Pound said, "is a long poem including history," and once a poem began including history, it had perforce to comment upon history, to take a stance, to become polemic.

Johnson's solution is to write a long poem *without* history: "If my confrères wanted to write a work with all history in its maw, I wished, from the beginning, to start all over again, attempting to know nothing but a will to create, and matter at hand." Unlike *The Cantos* or the modernist epics in its wake, *ARK* would be based not on a historical vision but upon a formal model: it would be "structure rather than diatribe, artifact rather than argument, a veritable shell of the chambered nautilus, sliced and polished, bound for Ararat unknown" (A 311–12).

ARK's structure is—another pun on the title—architectural. Its three books contain thirty-three "Beams" ("The Foundations"), thirty-three "Spires," and thirty-three "Arches" ("The Ramparts"). (At some point someone must have told Johnson that you couldn't very well place an arch atop a spire, so in his Note he writes of The Ramparts "rounding the periphery" of it all [A 312].) These three sections move in a roughly chronological progression, "The Foundations" lasting from dawn till noon, "The Spires" taking one to dusk, and "The Ramparts" occupying the night and culminating, one assumes, in the moment before a new dawn. Aside from BEAM 33's "High noon stands still as a just picked apple" (A 91) and the lovely dusk of *ARK* 66, *Finial for Ez*, in which the sun has fallen beneath the horizon and is visible only as reflection on the mountain peaks—"so Ossa / pale upon / Pelion" (204)—however, this time-sequence frankly isn't much in evidence. ("The Spires" include several fireworks poems, an entertainment not usually associated with the afternoon.)

Johnson's formal conceit in *ARK* is less a program to be followed than a numerical armature upon which he can hang his various approaches to his chosen subjects, most of which appear quite explicitly in "The Foundations." BEAM 4, BEAM 7, and BEAM 12, prose meditations on the eye, ear, and brain, respectively, lay out the poem's cosmology quite neatly:

> The human eye, a sphere of water and tissue, absorbs an energy that has come ninety-three million miles from another sphere, the sun. The eye may be said to be sun in another form . . . Mind & Eye are a logarithmic spiral coiled from periphery . . . After a long time of light, there began to be eyes, and light began looking with itself. (A 12–14)
>
> Matter delights in music, and became Bach. Its dreams are the abyss and the empyrean, and to that end, may move, in time, the stones themselves to sing. (A 23)
>
> Branches, from the top of its arch, network the light in our heads—out of a stuff of rays, partiples, and pulses: the artifice of reality . . . Thinking about thinking moves atoms—however mirrored: and so, as in a rainbow the architecture of light is revealed, mind is a revelation of matter . . . Both consciousness and the unconscious "collect." It is as if some eons-old mind (in a time when it could do these things) cast the future on its cold eye, saw Plato's cave, and became our brains. (A 34–35)

These are the themes upon which Johnson rings variations, an evolutionarily inflected version of Wordsworth's doctrine of the "fitting" of the universe and human mind, and *ARK* pursues the isomorphism of world and perceiver with a kind of relentless "Well gosh!" wonder. (I recall a video of Johnson reading BEAM 4—the one on the eye—and pausing between sentences to gush, "All these things are *facts*!") A number of other motifs weave their way through the book, perhaps most prominently the Orpheus and Oz myths. *ARK* 64, *Rungs III, The Lilac Tree* gives us a snapshot of Johnson's childhood Kansas, seen through the prism of the rainbow Dorothy wishes (in the movie) she might be over:

emerald, the front porch swing
down yellowbrick road
sun orange beyond the barn
—Tornado Rose—
beings stept forth in geode amethyst,
nor atom blue of dust lost
(A 200)

When Johnson writes "*o hoher Baum im Ohr!*" in BEAM 14, he's quoting the first of Rilke's *Sonnets to Orpheus* ("o high tree in the ear"), but he's surely also referring to L. Frank Baum (A 32). And in the final lines of *ARK* 45, *Spire of Limbs*—"As well you might / arch garland all the worlds"—it's difficult not to see a reference to Judy Garland, that cinematic Dorothy (A 136).

Oz (often embedded in "Zion" or even "Ozymandias") is a touchstone to which Johnson returns again and again, a comfortable and much-loved, talismanic tale, but he makes larger claims for the Orpheus story: "My central myth is that of Orpheus and Euridice [Johnson's own regular misspelling], the blessed argument between poet and muse, man and his anima" (A 313). But just as important to *ARK* is the myth of Theseus and the labyrinth, which here figures the poet's quest to unravel and understand the mazy connections of the mind and natural process. It's unfortunate for Johnson that Orpheus and Theseus were not a single myth: the poet-magician Orpheus, rather than descending into Hell to retrieve Eurydice in an awkwardly Jungian search for his own anima, should have navigated the treacherous labyrinth, a task instead parceled out by the ancients to the bully-boy warrior Theseus.

In a late statement of poetics, "Hurrah for Euphony," Johnson recounts his own working methods: "I wake every morning either with a song in my head, or a phrase. These I hum and ponder until they seem worked (or played) out. One morning it was 'riddle iota sublime.' Obviously meant as a direction for my next *Spire*, and I puzzled it out (one Anglo-Saxon word, one Greek, one Latin) an edict for either scientist or poet: render radiant sense from smallest thing. When you are thrown a line like that you've got to live up to it. So I added the lines 'and know no more / than when cast forth garden.' The rest came, night by night, via 'America the Beautiful,' to the end of bells from the Sunken Cathedral 'set in great hymnal font.'"[21]

You get the sense, reading *ARK*, that you've heard a great deal of the language before—and you have, for Johnson's magpie compositional aesthetic is still firmly in place, only now the individual quoted elements have become smaller and smaller. The quotational flair of Johnson's early poems has become in *ARK* a kind of composting, a shoveling in of words and phrases from every which direction. Johnson kept a notebook by him at all times in which to jot down words and phrases from whatever source caught his ear—his readings, conversation, even TV. I suspect I'm not the only one of Johnson's correspondents to have found phrases from one of my letters turning up in *ARK*.

Often, pages of Johnson's notebooks are taken up with anagrammatical permutations of words, fun little games that show up throughout *ARK*: *ARK* 61's "of pyramids, a / myriad afar"; BEAM 9's "Lave & Weave / Wave & Leave"; and (most egregiously) *ARK* 39's "stair squared air / mid violin, lens, loved line, dove, divers voids, lives lived, / of these, image a nation" (A 189, 29, 116). The delight Johnson takes in the isomorphism between mind and world, and in the patterns repeated within nature, is expressed most immediately as a delight in the pattern and permutations of language itself, the instrument human beings have evolved in order to make sense of one another and of the world in which they live.

At least I suppose, if pressed, Johnson would adduce something like that to explain the "theory" behind his language. On a more immediate level, he's simply having fun, shuffling letters and seeing what meanings come forth. At its worst, this poetics can produce lines and lines of overlush sound effects, echoing little beyond their own chiming—Dylan Thomas, or Turkish Delight. At its best, it issues forth a brittle euphony, somewhere between the music of Basil Bunting and Zukofsky's asperities. The sixty-six sections of "The Foundations" and "The Spires" are formally various and mostly high-spirited, though there a few moments of mourning—the tremendous *ARK* 34, *Spire on the Death of L.Z*—and thoughtful introspection, as in *ARK* 58, *Balloon on Being 50*:

a r o u n d a y e a r
t o d a y I s o u n d
f u t u r e a f a c e
r a f t e r o f a i r
h e a r t ' s f e a t s
f o u n d e d i f i c e
(A 182)

But for the most part the first two-thirds of *ARK* is a rich confusion of paeans to light, ecstatic dances (*ARK* 56, *The Balanchine Spire*), clusters of fireworks, and phallic herms and pillars.

The *Ramparts*, which occupied Johnson through the late 1980s, when the AIDS epidemic was ravaging his beloved San Francisco, are a rather more somber series of poems, "a night of the soul" (as he calls them in his Note [A 312–13]). The formal variety of *ARK*'s first two divisions has given way to a single form—each Arch is made up of eighteen three-line, center-justified stanzas. The reader flags, I fear, in this final stretch, as the poet seems to flag: the visual sameness of the Arches becomes a staging ground for a desperate struggle to maintain the mask of ecstasy in the face of hard events. But Johnson manages to keep it up, and winds up *ARK* 99, *Arches XXXIII* on a note of triumph:

as speech arc Simulacrum, 0
chorus us Homo Sapiens
in a major key!

tools, consonant & vowel
to fashion a voice
commensurate wheel of time

Origins great aorta
leaved from the wrist up, but
yet to attain the skies

all arrowed in a rainbow midair,
ad astra per aspera
countdown for Lift Off
(A 307)

That Latin tag—"to the stars through hardships"—is the Kansas state motto, linking Johnson back to his home state and commenting both on the travails of the ninety-nine-section poem now at an end and, more generally, the upward progress of Homo Sapiens as a whole. We may be "yet to attain the skies," but are in the process of counting down to some transcendent "Lift Off" to the stars. I'm afraid the Buck Rogers enthusiasm of those final lines feels a trifle forced, given the darkness of many of the Arches preceding them, and may be entirely unavailable to readers too young to recall the heady days of the moon shots and the early space shuttle launches.

ARK went out of print soon after its single-volume publication in 1996;

the arrival of a new (and corrected) edition from Flood Editions is very welcome indeed. One had to make do for some years with the generous selection of the poem Johnson's executor and editor Peter O'Leary provides in *To Do As Adam Did*. The book's a more than adequate introduction to Johnson's work as a whole, but I wish O'Leary had been allowed another fifty pages, both to give us a bit more of *ARK*, and to provide a taste of more of Johnson's post-*ARK* work—the longish travelogue "Road Side (Desert to Pairie)" or a few stanzas of his bleak monument to AIDS, "Blocks to Be Arranged as a Pyramid."

* * *

Johnson left the Bay area for good in 1995, and spent the last few years of his life—he died of a brain tumor in 1998—living with his father and working as a "handyman, gardener, and occasional cook" at Ward-Meade, a historic property in Topeka, Kansas.[22] One senses that over the years he had made his peace with his flat, monochrome homeland, much as Dorothy (at the end of the movie, at least) finds all of the colorful characters of Oz there among her townspeople. It was during this period that he wrote the approximately three hundred short poems that O'Leary edited down into *The Shrubberies*.

Joyce was still casting about for a new, post-*Wake* subject when he died in 1941, and death relieved Pound and Olson of the ugly burden of figuring out what to write next if they finished *The Cantos* and *The Maximus Poems*. But Johnson turned from the grand architecture of *ARK* to the tiny horticulturalisms of *The Shrubberies* with something like gusto. The clear parallel is to Zukofsky, whose book of eight-line flower poems, *80 Flowers*, was already well along in its planning stages when he finished *"A"*. The pensioner's stereotypical task, of course, is to tend his garden.

The poems of *80 Flowers* are tributes to late Zukofsky's single-minded anality: each of them focuses on a single flower or plant, collaging words and phrases—sometimes translated or transliterated—from Zukofsky's intensive reading in literature, philosophy, history, and horticultural lore. Johnson's *Shrubberies*, by contrast, are a far more relaxed set of garden poems, marveling and wondering at the order of it all within the confines of a single garden, sometimes a single parterre or a single plant:

catalpa with a skirt
of fluted ivory bloom

oblivious to dandelion
globe to reach stars

robin intent succulent
& loam-pulsing worm (S 15)

More often than not the poems of *The Shrubberies* are reflections on the act of gardening, of making and maintaining order in the natural world, and—in the manner of so much of *ARK*—expressions of wonder at the beautiful orders of mind and universe:

quincunx of succulents
subtle colors and forms
succinct in dust

appropriate the pot
assigned, set each
for spill into Other

always my core dream
winding a garden
secret in every sense (S 67)

("Succulent," with its play of "u" sounds, is a Turkish delight word for Johnson if ever there were one.) Here at the end of Johnson's writing career, the reader is struck by the continuity of his vision. "This is the Garden, where all is a poet's / topiary" (TD 3), he wrote in *A Line of Poetry, A Row of Trees*, and thirty years later, having passed through the splendid visionary architectures of *ARK*'s emerald city, he is back to "winding a garden / secret in every sense."

"Would God that all of the Lord's people were prophets," Moses fulminates in Numbers 11:29, a passage of which Blake was fond. I for one am glad that not all poets are visionaries of Ronald Johnson's stripe. His pitch of ecstasy, of marvel, is so relentless that after a while his wonders become cloying, even deadening: a twelve-course banquet, every dish of which is some variety of marzipan or peanut brittle. Taken in the right doses, however, his verse is a welcome and happy counterpoint to the gritty poetries of contemporaries more grounded in the pain, disappointment, and wastage of the social and personal world. It is a shiny reminder of the rainbow of beauties that persist around us, however obscured by the monochrome picture tubes of our daily lives.

[Two decades of talking about Ronald Johnson with Eric Murphy Selinger have left me unsure as to whom I should attribute any given Johnsonian insight. No doubt the good ones are Eric's.]

2. Notes and Numbers

I like to imagine Ronald Johnson, completing his bachelor's degree at Columbia University in the late 1950s, as being in good hands. His mentor and lover Jonathan Williams knew the ropes both of poetry and cuisine: Williams had studied with Charles Olson at Black Mountain—he was thoroughly up-to-date on developments in post-Poundian American poetry; he could provide Johnson with entrée into the circles and households of many of the most prominent poets and writers then working in and around New York, among them Allen Ginsberg, Gilbert Sorrentino, William Carlos Williams, and Edward Dahlberg. And, when it came to feeding the body as well as the poetic soul, Jonathan Williams knew a good Mexican restaurant to stop at on the way to a meal at Louis Zukofsky's Brooklyn apartment. The Zukofskys, Johnson would recall some three and a half decades later, were partial to the miniature: "you had thimblefuls of coffee or if it was a drink it was about a thimbleful, too. Everything was tiny." And then there was that Christmas dinner, where every dish was either green or red, from the canned ham to the creamed spinach to the green jello mold impregnated with crushed mints.[1] Johnson would come to be known as a writer of fine and original cookbooks, an expert on American cuisine; Zukofsky was famously indifferent to food. Guy Davenport recalls Zukofsky "dining on a half piece of toast, crumb by crumb."[2] His wife, Celia, asked to recall Zukofsky's favorite food, confessed that "he ate anything that you put down. Sometimes I think he wasn't even aware of what was on the plate."[3]

What the Zukofsky household lacked in culinary sophistication, however, it made up for in literary hospitality. Since the 1930s, when he had painstakingly blue-penciled the manuscripts of his friends Carl Rakosi, Lorine Niedecker, and William Carlos Williams, Zukofsky had grown used to poets bringing their nascent writings to his attention, pleading for advice, revisions, or—most probably—recognition. And then there were all those freshman themes from the would-be engineers of Brooklyn Polytechnic. Who knows how exhausted his stores of patience were when Jonathan Williams and Ron Johnson came around? But "Louis was wonderful," Johnson remembers. "And he was very patient with me. He didn't like my poems much."[4] Perhaps it was the somewhat hazy Emersonian Transcendentalism in Johnson's early work that put Zukofsky off; perhaps it was the Olson strain, the headlong "projective" thrust and the occasional humble references to the rector of Black Mountain College. After all, there were literary politics at work here: Olson's 1950 manifesto "Projective Verse," Zukofsky was convinced, was in large part a sloppy but energetic restating of his own 1931 "Sincerity and Objectification."[5]

Johnson's earliest poems, collected in *A Line of Poetry, a Row of Trees* (1964) and *Valley of the Many-Colored Grasses* (1969), were indeed written under Olson's sprawling shadow. *A Line of Poetry*, in fact, is dedicated to Olson (as an errata sheet in my copy reminds me), and culminates with a sequence entitled "Landscape with Bears, For Charles Olson."[6] But there was something very un-Olsonian even in Johnson's earliest work, a painstaking, Flaubertian, almost finical attention to the *mot juste* that bore far more resemblance to, say, the lyrics of Zukofsky's *Anew* than the fury of projectivist bombardment. The only poem that Johnson recalled Zukofsky's actually liking was "Of Circumstances, the Circum Stances" (later collected in *A Line of Poetry*) and that was, Johnson said, "the one that sounded most like his own."[7] ("Interview" 52). While the American setting and the attention to particulars in "Of Circumstances" are very Olsonian indeed, there is a strong sense of Zukofsky's characteristic care in the poem, almost a tip-toeing through the objects of the poet's attention, especially when that attention turns to a third American master, Charles Ives:

> . . . men, or elements may place
> objects in time
> as in a photograph of
>
> another composer,
> Charles Ives: a shelf over his music-room
> piano
>
> holds his father's Union Army cornet & a battered
> felt hat above
> a peeling black-and-white sign
>
> reading: BALLFIELD
>
>   with its arrow pointing
>   to some—it is now a forgotten—field
>   of the past.

That ballfield sign reappears a bit later in the poem:

> BALLFIELD –>
>
> There the poem should
> end, as poems must always, at the tip
> of an arrow (V 66–67)

This "BALLFIELD" with the right-pointing arrow following it isn't just a proto-concrete gesture on Johnson's part, forecasting his deep involvement in the concrete poetry movement of the 1970s. It is also an instance of active seeing, of collage: an exercise, one might argue, in objectivist "thinking with the things as they exist." Charles Ives's music room, the scene described in such detail in the poem, can be observed in a portfolio of photos included with Leonard Bernstein's 1958 Columbia Masterworks recording of Ives's Second Symphony, and I suspect this is where Johnson himself saw the music room. That portfolio includes two pictures of Ives's music room by the photographer Lee Friedlander, the second of which is a close-up of, as the caption describes it—and one can hear how Johnson has appropriated the caption's language—"An Ives composition in objects . . . a shelf above his music room piano with a characteristic clutter of cherished objects: the time-scarred sign from some now-unidentifiable 'Ball Field,' his father's Union Army cornet and a thoroughly battered felt hat, Ives' favorite headgear."[8]

"Of Circumstances, the Circum Stances" is a poem about origins: one which spans Johnson's childhood and ancestry in Ashland, Kansas, on the "horizontal prairie" (V 65) to evoke the Native Americans who inhabited the prairie before its settlement by whites. Olson might well approve. Yet, although their ancient handicrafts lend Johnson images for his own poetics, the more telling and predictive image offered by the poem comes in its invocations of twentieth-century American music, represented by Harry Partch and his custom-made instruments and by that "composition" of Ives memorabilia, complete with a "BALLFIELD" sign. For Ives, the lifelong baseball fan, the sign's arrow pointed toward some "forgotten . . . field / of the past." For Johnson, it points toward the future, toward the field poetics of his later long poem, *ARK*. In *ARK*, after all, the Olsonian or Duncanesque undefined field in which the poem takes its open-ended shape proves a less important model than the architectural and musical ideas of composition that Johnson learned not only from the musically obsessed Zukofsky, but also from Ives himself.

* * *

The long poem would seem to have always been in the cards for Johnson. His first volume to attract wide notice, *The Book of the Green Man*, was a book-length revision of English Romanticism, a young American's tour through the places and mythologies of English outdoor writing from Wordsworth through Selby (touching even, in its quaintly pedantic footnotes, on Tolkien). It's really a collection of visionary lyric poems, generously spiced with touchstone quotations from the English pastoral tradition and loosely organized by the places Johnson and Williams visited on their 1962–1963 walking tour and by the cycle of the seasons from winter to autumn. Like Robert Duncan, Johnson is an openly "derivative" poet in this book. The poems are as often as not mortared together out of quotations and allusions, and Johnson tries his hand several times at outright pastiche (most notably of Christopher Smart, who will reappear in the first section of *ARK*).

Of course, Johnson's real triumph in the long-poem genre is not the widely reviewed and praised *Book of the Green Man*, but *ARK*, the work he spent the decades of the 1970s and 1980s writing. The epic-length (or longer) poem has had a hypnotic and perhaps dangerous attraction for contemporary American poets working in the tradition of radical modernism, and Johnson—like Theodore Enslin, Ron Silliman, Frank Samperi, and a raft of others—must have begun his work with a worried backward glance at Pound's *Cantos*, Williams's *Paterson*, and Olson's *Maximus*. These were the looming achievements of the American nonnarrative long poem in the twentieth century, and all three of them had petered out into incompletion. Pound sank into depression and silence before he could figure out how to end his *Cantos*; Williams thought he'd finished *Paterson* with its fourth book, only to tack on a fifth seven years later and leave a handful of notes for a sixth at his death; and while Olson specified the one-line poem with which he wanted *The Maximus Poems* to end, the last volume of that work was largely reconstructed by his editors after his death.

Two things saved Johnson from the "risks and shipwrecks" of those coming before him. On the one hand, there was the architectural metaphor with which he conceived his poem—"a structure rather than diatribe, artifact rather than argument, a veritable shell of the chambered nautilus"[9]—and which he stuck to through thick and thin. And on the other, there was the example of Zukofsky's long poem *"A"*, which was half done when Johnson met him and was completely finished in 1974. While one could certainly make an argument for the importance to Johnson of Dante's *Divine Comedy* or L. Frank Baum's *Wizard of Oz*, in the long run, the architectures and articulations of Zukofsky's *"A"* are the most significant *literary* instigation for *ARK*.

"A" begins, to put it baldly, as a Marxist version of *The Cantos*, advancing a leftist critique of Depression-era American society through a poetics of juxtaposition. Beginning with its seventh movement, however—a sequence of seven sonnets—the poem increasingly leaves ideology behind and becomes a loosely articulated series of formal experiments, all disposed upon the "foreseen curve" of a twenty-four-section structure and the unfolding events of Zukofsky's own life. The problem of form in the long poem, Zukofsky came to realize midway through his labors, need not be a problem of ideology. One

does not need an "Aquinas-map" to show you where to go, how to get to the Paradiso at the end of the yellow brick road. The poet's life will provide the poem's subject matter: in his later years, Zukofsky took to calling *"A"* "a poem of a life." The poet's task in regard to form, then, is an *aesthetic* one, a matter of finding a beautiful, harmonic, resonant shape in which to dispose that subject matter. And once you have a general armature to build on—say, twenty-four movements—then the form of each of those movements opens up to possibility. You can write an evanescent four-word commentary on the civil-rights struggle ("A"-16); you can collage together quotations from your previous works to pay homage to William Carlos Williams ("A"-17); you can translate Plautus's *Rudens*, cramming each Latin hexameter line into five English words ("A"-21); you can—if you're as careful, cunning, and downright obsessive as Zukofsky—cram six thousand years of history into a thousand five-word lines (and you can do that one *twice*, in "A"-22 and -23). And as he shaped these disparate movements into a whole that somehow, amazingly, hangs together, Zukofsky taught the poets of a younger generation a home truth (or perhaps only reminded them of it) that might easily be lost in the barrages of significant data that make up *The Cantos*, *The Maximus Poems*, even *Paterson*: ultimately, the meaningful details that go into the long poem are only as luminous as the overall form in which they are embedded.

So when Ronald Johnson devises his "architectural" form for *ARK*—a form that owes less to Mies van der Rohe or Robert Adam than to a whole bevy of eccentric, self-taught visionaries from the projects of Los Angeles, to Washington, DC, to rural France—he has left the ideogrammic method of high modernism far behind. Left it behind, that is, after taking it as a self-evident starting point. The earliest poems he thought to preserve, Johnson recalled in 1974, were constellated out of others' words: "I saved boxes and boxes of words and phrases cut from newspapers and made collage poems from them—before I knew what collage was either."[10] In 1983, deep into the writing of *ARK*, Johnson describes a poetics crucially involved with the quotation. Unlike his modernist forebears, however, for whom the quotation as likely as not is a signpost to an extratextual cultural fact, for Johnson the quotation is semirandom, simply the right piece of language upon which the poet has happened. Simon Rodia (builder of the Watts Towers), James Hampton (the Washington janitor whose astounding *Throne of the Third Heaven of the Nations Millennium General Assembly* is now on display at the Smithsonian's Museum of American Art), and the Facteur Cheval (who built his *Palais Idéal* out of the stones, shells, and pieces of glass he stumbled upon on his daily rounds); all these men, Johnson writes, "worked from an armature to an outer encrustation of curious rocks, broken colorful tiles or bits of glass, gold and silver foil—anything they could get their hands on from detritus of a world which had not eyes to see. Just so, *ARK* composed itself from the everyday fragments of phrase, words plucked out of context, trouvailles to be worked and knitted and sawn or welded in."[11] When he looks to Rodia, Hampton, and the Facteur Cheval for inspiration in designing his long poem, then, Johnson reconceives the modernist poetics of juxtaposition and the "luminous detail," revising it downward, as it were, into the realm of folk culture and bricolage. Or, to put it in less portentous terms: in *ARK*, the fragment or quotation is no longer a cultural index, but merely a shiny bit of language that fits into some crucial point of the poem's mosaic.

Sometime in the late eighties, when I was in correspondence with Johnson, out of the blue, the mailman brought an envelope containing a page of his typescript, on which he was working out the lineation of three lines of one of the Arches. "Dear Scroggins," he had penned at the top, "this is *your Arch*, via yr. last letter / *scissored*."[12] And lo and behold, in "ARK 73, *Arches VII*" I found:

"never did eye see sun
unless it had become first sunlike" i.e.
an architecture, music frozen
(A 229)

The first two lines are a rearrangement of some Goethe I had quoted to Johnson in a letter, trying to track down an elusive phrase from *The Book of the Green Man*. The last, according to his scribble at the foot of his typescript, is "another Hydra quote!" A "hydra" quote, one assumes, because it springs up everywhere, but has no single determinate source. (For the record, when Goethe told Eckermann "Baukunst eine erstarrte Musik nenne," he seems to have been quoting Schelling's *Philosophy of Art*). But the point is that the words' source—for Johnson, and for the readers of *ARK—doesn't matter*. The words have gone in to make part of one of the tercets of an Arch, fitting in with the poem's intricate imagery of sound and architecture, and the original speaker no more matters than that the previous two lines, playing on *ARK*'s ongoing themes of light, eye, sun, and microcosm/macrocosm, come from somewhere in Goethe, weakly translated by a graduate student in upstate New York.

* * *

It's fairly easy to point out obvious debts Johnson's poetry owes to Zukofsky. *Radi os*, his "rewriting by excision" of *Paradise Lost*, the twelve-page reduction of the Psalms Johnson entitles "PALMS" (BEAMS 21, 22, 23), and the late sections of *ARK* that derive from single sources (Arches VIII from Thoreau's *Journals*, Arches XII–XIV from various Protestant hymnals), are all anticipated for instance in a section of "A"-14 (composed 1964), where Zukofsky boils some nine books of Milton's epic down to six pages of spare verse.[13] The cosmological obsessions of *ARK* have a counterpart in Zukofsky's continuing interest in such metaphysical texts as the *Rig-Veda*, his semiserious investment in numerology, and his semiscientific theory of the solid, liquid, and gaseous states of human language and culture. And the music of Zukofsky's verse is powerfully echoed in Johnson's. Echoed, that is, but transformed, for where Zukofsky's music over the course of his career approaches more and more a dry, elliptical atonality—the condition of Webern—Johnson's grows lusher and lusher, reveling in rhyme, off-rhyme, and an almost overripe alliteration.

It is structure with which I began, however, and it's with the question of structure that a bracketing of *"A"* and *ARK* must culminate. *"A"* began in the Poundian mode, weighing the historical and cultural forces of its day, holding out the promise of a poetic resolution that would somehow involve both history and culture. It was Zukofsky's initial decision (dating as far back as 1927) to write his poem in twenty-four sections that allowed him to abandon that early mode, to open his work to the exigencies of his own ongoing life. The second half of *"A"* is a treasure house of formal experiment, organized around two principles: the events of Zukofsky's life (which include his family, his reading, and the history through which he lives); and the numbers 12 through 24. In the course of completing his poem, Zukofsky offered Johnson a model of how the individual sections of a long poem could be articulated one with another, a model in which narrative, mythos, and ideological argument are all displaced by poetic form and the spectacle of language at play.

Johnson laid aside narrative and ideology at the outset. "*ARK*," he writes, "was conceived to be a poem *without* history . . . a poem which needs no reference except itself."[14] History intrudes, of course. Louis Zukofsky and Robert Duncan die, and are commemorated in "ARK 34" and "ARK 71." Johnson ages, and marks time with "ARK 58, *Balloon on Being 50*." And part of the darkness of The Ramparts, the poem's final section, can be traced to the AIDS epidemic devastating Johnson's beloved San Francisco through the 1980s. But mythos? Writing for his son in 1946, in the wake of Hiroshima and Nagasaki, Zukofsky could see no further point in the "mythic method" Eliot had praised in Joyce's *Ulysses*: "The poet wonders why so many have raised up the word 'myth,' finding the lack of so-called 'myths' in our time a crisis the poet must overcome or die from, as it were, having become too radioactive." The task of the contemporary epic poet, in a world laid waste by the pursuit of political myths, lies in a renewed attention to minute details of language, our shared human life-world: "instead a case can be made out for the poet giving some of his life to the use of the words *the* and *a:* both of which are weighted with as much epos and historical destiny as one man can perhaps resolve."[15] Johnson, with typical gusto, pronounces the "central myth" of *ARK* to be one of the oldest poetic *topoi* in the Western tradition, the story of Orpheus and Eurydice, "the blessed argument between poet and muse, man and his anima. Orpheus, who made the trees bend and animals one with his lyre. Orpheus, the beheaded voice floating downstream" (A 313).

What Johnson calls a "central myth," however, is far from a *structural* myth, like the story of Odysseus in *Ulysses* or the Grail legend in *The Waste Land.* It is instead one of a cluster of themes and stories Johnson alludes to and retreats from in the course of his poem. Others include the journey of Dorothy to the Emerald City of Oz, Noah and the deluge, and the more general scene of the writer as recipient of apocalyptic visions, from Jacob's Ladder to Revelation. The true structure of *ARK* is not based on a myth, nor is it based on an architecture, despite the poet's assertions, and the poem's tripartite division into Beams, Spires, and Arches.

ARK's structure is rather based on number, on the simple decision to write a poem in ninety-nine manageable segments. (Yes, there were originally to be one hundred sections, as in the *Divine Comedy*, with the completed *Radi os* forming a "Dymaxion Dome" over the whole. Johnson's decision to table that idea [sometime in the late eighties?] was aesthetically canny—the whole of a "ventilated" *Paradise Lost* would surely have both overbalanced and dispersed the energies of the rest of the poem.) Settling on a ninety-nine-section structure allowed him to work a theoretically infinite variety of word matter into a strictly finite series of forms, though the precise shape of each section could be decided on an ad hoc basis. In the Foundations and the Spires, this flexibility shows itself in a rich variety of forms: prose poems, pictures, the poet's handprint, a herm, and various "pillars." In the Arches, Johnson settles on a three-line stanza (echoing Dante's tercets) in groups of eighteen. (The late Zukofsky, addicted to gematria-like number-crunching, would have approved, breaking the eighteen down into further threes: 1 + 8 = 9, which is 3 x 3; 18 reversed is 81, or 3 x 3 x 3 x 3; each Arch contains 54 lines, and 5 + 4 = 9, another 3 x 3. And so forth; the draft materials for the later movements of "*A*" are full of such number games.) This three-line stanza, within which Johnson can name animals, call them into Noah's Ark, and celebrate the vision of an endlessly interwoven world, is his equivalent of the five-word line that served Zukofsky through the geological and literary histories of "A"-22 and -23 and through the horticultural labyrinths of *80 Flowers*.

This, I suppose, is the perennial function of form in poetry, to provide what Blake called a "wirey, bounding line" within whose boundaries the poet's imagination can weave, wind, bound, and leap.[16] Pound, Williams, and Olson, one might venture, all forgot this lesson, allowed the arguments and ideas of their evolving poems to overcome the formal sensibility that would allow them to complete those poems. Zukofsky took it to heart. Faced with the specter of the atomic bomb, the specter of a literally postapocalyptic history, he would turn from the conception of the epic as a "poem including history" to that of the epic as contained within the discrete materials of human language, the words through which we live both our private and public lives. Pound's goal of telling the "tale of the tribe" is replaced by Mallarmé's—to purify the tribe's language. And in this shift, Zukofsky learns where to stop. It is the poetics, perhaps, of a "diminished thing," but *"A"* is both a lived and a livable poetry. The formal and sonic beauties of *"A"* are ordinary beauties brought to light; the incandescence of Pound's "great ball of crystal" might dazzle, but one cannot lift it, and one might find oneself—"if you're a Jewish boy," as Zukofsky wrote in 1926—caught like a fly in its amber.[17]

* * *

Johnson follows Zukofsky, then, in conceiving the long poem as "structure rather than diatribe, artifact rather than argument" (A 312). His poem is an intensely various collocation of psychological and cosmological glitterings; new beauties and fascinations spring up at every turn of the page, all held together by the poem's elastic but ultimately coherent form. In a 1996 interview, Peter O'Leary asked Johnson about the presence of a second compositional model for the long poem, one equally open to quotation and formal invention: the *Universe Symphony* of Charles Ives.

> PO'L: In a letter you once sent me Charles Ives's notes for his Universe Symphony, which you called one of the models for *ARK*. In what ways does Ives play into the poem? . . . .
>
> RJ: Ives is not that different from the Watts Towers. He was like me—he knew a lot about music, but he wanted to appear a naif, to get back to where you don't know anything about art. And then you construct something. I was trying to forget about music and then start all over again. Try to remember everything. I think the structure of Ives's symphonies had been more of an influence on me than just about anything else.[18]

One is reminded of Davenport's introduction to *Valley of the Many-Colored Grasses*, which ends by grouping Johnson with Ives and Buckminster Fuller, "both of whom went back to the beginning of their arts as if time did not exist, and began anew" (V 14). This Ives—a faux naïf, a forgetter and then reinventor of his craft—is needless to say not the Ives of the musicologists, who are on the contrary anxious to emphasize the extent to which Ives had mastered the nineteenth-century classical tradition before putting his own American stamp upon it. But Davenport, if he has not described the Ives of the conservatories, has described *Johnson's* Ives, and Johnson's own construction of Ives—shall I venture, his "strong misreading" of Ives?—is a central influence on Johnson's poetics. In the music of Ives, and in Ives's own conception of what he was up to as a composer, Johnson finds models, both large scale and local, for the late modernist labyrinth of *ARK*.

The turn to music as a formal model is, of course, hardly unique to Johnson. Ezra Pound bequeaths it to twentieth-century poetics; the Provençal poems that so captured Pound's imagination were *songs* before they were texts; and Pound's conception of the melopœia of poetry, as well as his avowal that "poetry begins to atrophy when it gets too far from music,"[19] evoke at some remove Walter Pater's famous assertion in *The Renaissance* about all arts striving toward "the condition of music." Both Basil Bunting and Zukofsky—the two unlikely dedicatees of Pound's *Guide to Kulchur*—were likewise music-obsessed. Bunting called his long poems "sonatas," going to some trouble to show how their forms imitate those of Scarlatti and Johann Christian Bach. Much is made in *"A"*, Zukofsky's "poem of a life," about how the poet has adapted various baroque musical forms—the fugue in *"A"*'s early movements, the mass of "A"-10, the partita of "A"-13, the harpsichord pieces of Handel that make up one of the five "voices" (the other four speak Zukofsky's words) of "A"-24.

Johnson, however, had a certain advantage over his "mentor" Zukofsky, who was by some accounts practically tone-deaf, and whose appreciation of music was largely theoretical: Johnson could actually read music, had studied the piano from a very young age. He was not, however, a professional musician, nor did he approach Ives from the standpoint of a musicologist, but that of a poet. I imagine Johnson read everything by and about Ives that he could, but when he was writing his first Ives-influenced poems—around the early 1960s—there was precious little available: Ives's *Essays Before a Sonata*, Henry and Sidney Cowell's *Charles Ives and His Music*, and a handful of liner notes to various Ives recordings. I think Johnson would have been fascinated by some of the recent books on Ives—J. Peter Burkholder's *All Made of Tunes: Charles Ives and the Uses of Musical Borrowing*, or Stuart Feder's *Charles Ives, "My Father's Song": A Psychoanalytic Biography*[20]—but I can't say whether he read them; at any rate, the Ivesian poetic of *ARK* was already firmly in place before the real efflorescence of Ives criticism and commentary of the 1980s.

For Johnson, Ives was—alongside Pound, Zukofsky, and Williams—one of America's greatest modernist artists. In Ives's music he found a confirmation of the collage-based quotational poetics of *The Cantos*, *"A"*, and *Paterson*, married to a fundamentally American, even patriotic, sensibility.

Johnson's final "Note" to *ARK* cites Ives as a "major influence" on *ARK* in the way he uses previous material; Ives, Johnson writes, "wove patriotic anthem and church hymn into his work, like breathing" (A 313). Leonard Bernstein and David Johnson, in their liner notes to the Second Symphony, point out how much Ives quotes, both from himself and from others. The first movement is reworked from an organ sonata Ives wrote when he was a church organist during his Yale days; the symphony alludes to the "knocking" theme of Beethoven's Fifth, quotes a few bars from the slow movement of Brahms's First Symphony, and touches on Wagner, Bach, and Dvorák; more humbly, the symphony quotes—in addition to a number of college songs—Stephen Foster's "Camptown Races" and "Old Black Joe," the hymns "When I Survey the Wond'rous Cross" and "Bringing in the Sheaves," and the patriotic songs "America the Beautiful" and "Columbia the Gem of the Ocean."

In 1975, when *ARK* was in its early stages, Johnson published a brief piece entitled "Charles Ives: Two Eyes, Two Ears"; this construction—though it is in prose, one can hardly call it an essay—is patched together entirely of quotation: words from Ives, Henry David Thoreau, Louis Agassiz, John Ruskin, Isaac Newton, Webster, and "The Star-Spangled Banner."[21] *ARK*, of course, is woven largely of quoted language—phrases, words, whole passages from previous texts. But the quotations in *ARK* are not indices, hypertextual references to other texts—as are the quotations in *The Cantos* or *Maximus*—but rather the independent, fragmentary, melodic building blocks of a larger structure. They work, at least in part, as Henry and Sidney Cowell describe Ives's musical quotations working: "These snatches of hymns, minstrel songs, college songs, fiddle tunes, and so on, sewn through the fabric of his music, are never left as quotations only; certain fragments soon develop a life of their own, and some aspect of their musical structure is always made the basis of the piece's subsequent behavior."[22] While these bits of melody might bring up a "burden of nostalgic emotion" for the composer and listener, their primary function is as musical elements *within* the piece at hand.

Ives justified his own reliance on quotations, as David Michael Hertz has shown, not by pointing to high-modernist poetic practice or even by gesturing toward Dvorák's or Bartók's use of folk song, but by going back to Ralph Waldo Emerson. In his late essay "Quotation and Originality," Emerson profoundly destabilizes the ideology that would set the "original" apart from the writer who relies on quotation. "Every book," Emerson writes, "is a quotation, and every house is a quotation out of all forest and mines and stone-quarries; and every man is a quotation from all his ancestors."[23] In his own "Emerson" essay, Ives pokes holes in the notion of absolute originality. "If we would stop and attribute too much to genius, [Emerson] shows us that 'what is best written and done by genius in the world, was no one man's work, but came by wide social labor . . .' If we would stop and trust heavily on the harvest of originality, he shows us that this plant—this part of the garden—is but a relative thing. It is dependent also on the richness that ages have put into the soil. 'Every thinker is retrospective.'"[24] (In truly Johnsonian fashion, Ives's own quotations are more rough paraphrases than word-for-word repetitions of Emerson.)

Like Bartók, who adapted Hungarian folk songs, Ives's use of preexisting melodic material serves an agenda of cultural nationalism. The music that Ives quotes—hymns, minstrel song, popular song, collegiate song—is strikingly *American*, deeply rooted in American popular culture. The same can be said of many of the borrowings incorporated into Johnson's *ARK*. Like the *Concord Sonata* or the *Holidays Symphony*, *ARK* is a deeply *American* work. By "American" I don't mean something particularly profound, like a democratic ethos underlying the work—Whitman of course made such an argument for his own *Leaves of Grass*—but something rather more superficial: that Johnson's "matter at hand" (A 311) is as often as not homegrown and demotic, rather than highbrow or "literary." One could multiply examples: the "*whose bright stripes & broad stars*" of "BEAM 5," a quotation from the national anthem; the "till the cows come / purple home" of "ARK 34," which crosscuts Gelett Burgess's "I never saw a purple cow" with the demotic "till the cows come home"; the "coming for to carry us home" of "ARK 71, *Arches* V," borrowed from "Swing Low, Sweet Chariot" (A 16, 199, 221); and perhaps above all else, the pervasive references to L. Frank Baum's *The Wonderful Wizard of Oz* and its film version.

Johnson habitually evokes the imagery of American patriotism with a guileless affection upon which cynical postmodernity is likely to cast a cold eye. "BEAM 25," which quotes "The Star-Spangled Banner" and "The Battle Hymn of the Republic," is "*A Bicentennial Hymn*." "ARK 69," which alludes to Emma Lazarus's "The New Colossus," mimes the uplifted torch of the Statue of Liberty. *ARK* includes poems datelined "Memorial Day, 1981" ("ARK 47, *Plow Spire*") and "Memorial Day, 1990" ("ARK 90, *Arches XXIV*"). And the poem contains no fewer than three "Fireworks" Spires: Georg Frideric Handel is a reference, of course—"BEAM 25" cites "A / FIREWORKS MUSIC" (A 69)—but in America fireworks usually mean one holiday—the Fourth of July. Is this Charles Ives, or is it Currier & Ives? It is, of course, both. The most spirited movement of Ives's *Holidays Symphony*, *The Fourth of July* (ca. 1913–1919), "recalls the sounds of patriotic tunes, a fife-and-drum corps, and the fireworks exploding, the last using loud string glissandos, multiple chromatic figuration in the winds and brass, irregular rhythms in the percussion, and huge clusters played by the forearms on the piano."[25] Or, as Johnson describes it, "a fireworks of thirteen rhythmic patterns zigzagging through the winds and brasses, seven percussion lines criss-crossing these, the string divided in twenty-fours going up and down every-which-way—and all in FFFF" (A 22).

Johnson's optimism, not to mention his patriotism, is oddly out of step with the contemporary literary landscape. His poetry is consistently visionary, celebratory; elegiac, but not mournful; rueful, but never despairing. If Johnson is a contemporary Blake, he is a Blake without a Urizen. *ARK* may be "a mirror held / to the horror" (39), but it is a gesture not so much to reflect the world's horror in the poem—even inverted, as Eric Selinger argues[26]—as to admire the complex and beautiful metalwork of the mirror's reverse—the Shield of Achilles, as it were, with nothing but peaceful themes. (Or is this Perseus's mirrored breastplate, which protected him from the gorgon's gaze?) The America of Johnson's associates Robert Duncan, Allen Ginsberg, and Michael Palmer is more often than not an imperialistic, repressive, terrifying nightmare. For Johnson, as for Whitman, America is in itself "essentially the greatest poem," a political system and symbology that represents the human instantiation of freedom and heterogeneous oneness.[27]

Johnson's somewhat *corny* affection for the trappings of the red, white, and blue—and who could resist a glance back to "Mayse," and to his prairie upbringing?—is of a piece, however, not merely with Ives's patriotism, but with Ives's Transcendentalism, which is most thoroughly presented in his *Essays Before a Sonata*. The *Essays*, first published in 1920, are a set of rambling program notes to Ives's *Concord Sonata* (1909–1915), whose four movements give us musical portraits of the major mid-nineteenth-century literary personages of Concord, Massachusetts: Emerson, Hawthorne, the Alcotts, and Thoreau. Three of these—Emerson, Thoreau, and Bronson Alcott—are among the most prominent members of the Transcendentalist movement, a homegrown American version of Wordsworth and Coleridge's Kantian Romanticism. As Ives puts it, the *Concord Sonata* "is an attempt to present (one person's) impression of the spirit of Transcendentalism that is associated in the minds of many with Concord, Massachusetts, of over a half century ago."[28] What Ives sees in Transcendentalism (and this is a fairly canonical interpretation of these writers) includes a sense of the pervasiveness of spiritual forces throughout the human and natural worlds; the notion that the human and natural spheres are parts of a single continuum; and the idea of human perfectibility, both in the individual and in the mass: humanity, that is, is moving toward a higher state, both socially and spiritually. These ideas permeate the *Essays*, from Ives's evocation of Emerson's "spiritual message"—"the soul of humanity knocking at the door of the divine mysteries, radiant in the faith that it *will* be opened—and the human become the divine!"—to his description of Alcott's "common interest in common things and common men," to his closing evocation of the "stream of change [flowing] towards the eventual ocean of mankind's perfection."[29] Ives saw his own sonata as communicating these same ideas, and his long "Epilogue" is a sustained if idiosyncratic argument for the very communicability of ideas in a musical idiom.

Ives's most ambitious attempt to communicate Transcendentalist ideas in music, however, was his unfinished *Universe Symphony*. This is the work of Ives's, Johnson told O'Leary in a letter of February 8, 1993, that had most immediately served as a formal instigation for *ARK*. "The notes left for its architecture," Johnson wrote of the symphony, "were one of the earliest models for *ARK*."[30] The *Universe Symphony*, which Ives began in 1911 and worked at for the rest of his composing life, was to be in three parts: the Past ("formation of the waters and mountains"), the Present ("Earth, evolution in nature and humanity"), and the Future ("Heaven, rise of all to the spiritual").[31] One is immediately struck by the resemblance between this three-part structure and *ARK*'s division into "Foundations," "Spires," and "Ramparts." It is important to bear in mind, however, that the *Universe Symphony* is an *early* model for *ARK*, and that *ARK* is a poem that looks to a variety of different formal models and thematic scaffolds. Ives has clearly plotted his own thematic material over a very long temporal span—from creation to revelation, as it were—and this time span resembles more closely Zukofsky's two six-thousand-year histories in "A"-22 and -23 (which themselves echo the Biblical age of the earth, created, as Bishop Ussher calculated, in 4004 BC) than it does the essentially timeless parade of wonders presented in *ARK*. I suspect that more important for Johnson than the formal details of Ives's plan for the *Universe Symphony*, or even its temporal sweep, is its apocalyptic conclusion, a conclusion perfectly in accord with the Transcendentalist tenor of Johnson's own sensibility. "The goodness of Ronald Johnson," Davenport argues, "is in his having got the real Transcendentalism from the very start, the kind that served Ives and Buckminster Fuller" (V 14).

ARK opens with sunrise, with a visionary account of the physics underlying the sun's awakening of the earth: "then dot the plain / 186,282 cooped up angels tall as appletrees" (A 6). "The Foundations" concern themselves with such physical themes as the operations of the ear and the eyes; throughout is the underlying theme that the sensing human being is itself an integral "mode" of the breathtaking complex system it inhabits and senses: "After a long time of light, there began to be eyes, and light began looking with itself" (A 14). Here Johnson evokes one of the most famous (and derided) sentences of Ralph Waldo Emerson's *Nature* (1836), a moment of visionary oneness with nature during which, as Emerson rhapsodizes, "I become a transparent eye-ball; I am nothing; I see all; the currents of the Universal Being circulate through me; I am part and particle of God."[32] *Nature* as a whole is perhaps the best possible primer for the reader of *ARK*, for the poem is saturated with Emerson's vision of the interpenetration of spirit and matter, his version of the Kantian-Wordsworthian "fitting" of the objects of perception to the eye that perceives, and his boundless spiritual optimism.

That optimism, which reaches ecstatic heights in the speech of the "Orphic poet" in "Prospects," *Nature*'s final chapter, can be read as source both for the third movement of Ives's *Universe Symphony*—"Heaven, rise of all to the spiritual"—and the chastened but visionary conclusion of *ARK*. "As fast as you conform your life to the pure idea in your mind," says Emerson's Orphic poet, "that will unfold its great proportion. A correspondent revolution in things will attend the influx of the spirit . . . . The kingdom of man over nature, which cometh not with observation,—a dominion such as now is beyond his dreams of God,—he shall enter without more wonder than the blind man finds who is gradually restored to perfect sight."[33] "ARK 99," a hymn no less soaring, ends with a rocket-ship's takeoff, an apotheosis of the human will to aspire: "*ad astra per aspera* / countdown for Lift Off" (A 307).

Selinger has suggested that this ought to be not a spaceship but a balloon—like the balloon in which the Wizard leaves the Emerald City in *The Wonderful Wizard of Oz*, the moon-journeying balloon of Poe's "Hans Pfaall," or the playful balloon in Bergman's *Magic Flute*. But in cultural terms, in terms of the Transcendentalist legacy Johnson shares with and derives from Ives, this craft—whether phallic rocket or lighter-than-air inflatable—is the transformation of the human into the divine that Emerson predicts at the end of *Nature*, "The Divinity School Address," and so many other places. As Ives writes of his own sonata, "The strains of one man may fall below the course of those Phaetons of Concord . . . but the greater the distance his music falls away, the more reason that some greater man shall bring his nearer those higher spheres."[34]

"Charles Ives," Johnson writes, "heard the 19th century in one ear, and the 20th out the other, then commenced to make a single music of them" (A 24). Johnson himself was similarly listening both forward and backward, to Olson and Zukofsky, Wordsworth and Christopher Smart, Harry Partch and George Frideric Handel. Ives, however, was not merely one of many records on his turntable—or discs in his CD changer—but a pervasive soundtrack, a "major influence." Both his very particular version of modernist compositional methods, and in the visionary Transcendentalism that he inherited from his New England forebears and communicated through the challenging, overwhelmingly American collages of his music, Ives proved a central model for the works that assure Johnson a place both within the traditions of late modernism and American Romanticism.

3. Johnson's American England

From fall 1962 to summer 1963, the poet and publisher Jonathan Williams and his companion, the younger poet Ronald Johnson, made something of a grand tour of the sites of British cultural and literary history. Johnson's *The Book of the Green Man*, the long poem prompted by this visit, was published in 1967 by Longmans in England and W. W. Norton in the United States. The English poet Christopher Middleton, who by Williams's account had instigated the book's publication, contributed a dust-jacket note, complimenting this "young poet from Kansas" for having "unearthed an England which most people have forgotten." Johnson, according to Middleton, had depicted "sundry English scenes, with a vividness and strangeness beyond the reach of any English poet, and unknown, I venture to say, since the days of Blake, Calvert and Palmer."[1] (In all fairness, one must add that a significant section of *Green Man* takes place not in England at all, but in *Wales*.) Judging by the enthusiastic reviews the book received, many of its first readers agreed with Middleton.

The Book of the Green Man was a significant departure for Johnson, not least in its very subject matter. Ian Hamilton Finlay, the Scottish poet Williams, and Johnson had met in Edinburgh on their tour, had published Johnson's previous collection, the chapbook *Sports and Divertissements* (1965), which consisted of translations of the French composer Erik Satie's program notes for his music.[2] The poems of Johnson's first collection, *A Line of Poetry, a Row of Trees* (1964), while place-centered in a manner that foreshadowed *Green Man*, dealt with exclusively American landscapes.[3] In contrast, the subject matter of *Green Man* is overwhelmingly British: the poem essentially follows the itinerary of Johnson and Williams's walking tour of the isle, and the vast majority of the source texts Johnson cites in his four pages of closely printed notes are British.

What, then, is specifically American about *The Book of the Green Man*? In other words, why *couldn't* this poem, so concerned with "the matter of Britain," have been written by a British poet? And second, why is the poem—and it will be plain enough that I agree with Middleton's estimation—so successful? What specifically American baggage has Johnson brought on his British tour that has enabled him to produced a portrait of England and Wales as vivid and strange as those of William Blake and his disciples Edward Calvert and Samuel Palmer, the visionary group that called itself the "Ancients"?

The Book of the Green Man is a long poem in four sections, from "Winter" to "Autumn." It is, as Johnson writes in his introductory poem,

> Of the seasons,
> seamless, a garland.
>
> Solstice
> to equinox—
> days,
>
> measured a cock's stride,
> come full circle. (GM 11)

While the poem itself is structured around the seasons of a single year, however, it is by no means a simple record of Johnson and Williams's year-long tour of Britain. (The "Spring" section, it is true, is largely a journal of their walking tour of Wales, but in the other sections of the poem there are various—sometimes radical—dislocations of sequence from the tour that gave rise to the work.) Instead, Johnson uses the handy armature of the four seasons, a circular, endless progression, as a frame upon which to build a poem that exhibits a remarkable degree of rather old-fashioned closure and coherence—remarkable, that is, for a poet as saturated in Olson as Johnson was early in his career. Each section is built around a particular figure and locale: "Winter," the Lake District and Wordsworth; "Spring," the Wye River in Wales and Francis Kilvert; "Summer," Selborne and the recorder of its natural history, Gilbert White; and "Autumn," Shoreham in Kent and its most famous inhabitant, the painter Samuel Palmer, a disciple of William Blake. Each of these figures contributes the epigraph(s) to his section, passages that prove to be crucial keys to the poems that follow.

At the book's symbolic center is the overarching figure of the Green Man himself, a traditional English version of a broadly European nature deity. Johnson sees the Green Man, a human figure festooned with foliage, not merely in the carvings on countless English churches, but in Sir Gawain's Green Knight, in the Jack-in-the-Green, in Archimboldo's vegetable portraits, and in the mandrake, the plant thought to grow in the shape of a man. The Green Man will reappear throughout the poem as a figure for the interpenetration of the human and the natural, vegetative worlds. As Johnson writes, riffing on a passage of Whitman's *Song of Myself*,

My tongue assumes the apple's flesh
& my skin, the infinite spheres of the thistle's prickle. And as I
breathe

the wind has its billow—& all the grasses—

in a combing, mazy movement. (GM 38)

In many ways, *The Book of the Green Man* is a working-through of themes that Johnson will explore at much greater length in *ARK*, and there are passages of *Green Man* that directly prefigure *ARK*'s microcosm-macrocosm theme of light transmuting itself to matter, to life, and eventually to the human eye that beholds it. In a pastiche of Christopher Smart, for instance, Johnson writes, "*For the tree forms sun into leaves, & its branches & saps // are solid & liquid states of sun*" (GM 55). (Given Johnson's penchant for recycling his own work, I am surprised that these lines didn't find their way into *ARK*.) But while *ARK* makes free with the whole panoply of modern science—from evolution to chaos theory—within a poetic that eschews recognizable personal voice, that dislocates conventional syntax, and that pursues its moments of revelation within the interstices of a disarmingly lush verbal texture, *The Book of the Green Man*—in contrast—falls into far more recognizable categories of nature poetry and visionary poetry. That the visionary tradition is on Johnson's mind is clear from his citations of Blake, Christopher Smart, Jakob Boehme, and Samuel Palmer. Those figures, however, sit uncomfortably with the poet who dominates the first section of the poem—William Wordsworth.

Johnson, that is, is trying to marry two quite distinct strains of English poetic Romanticism: the ecstatic visionary strain exemplified in Blake and deriving ultimately from such prophetic and apocalyptic literature as the books of Ezekiel and Revelation, and a more serene tradition of, in M. H. Abrams's phrase, "natural supernaturalism," most famously found in Coleridge's "conversation poems" and in Wordsworth.[4] The two traditions don't exactly mix. In 1826, Blake went to the trouble of transcribing some lines from the 1814 preface to Wordsworth's *The Excursion*, lines that encapsulate much of *Green Man* and strikingly prefigure the themes of *ARK*: "How exquisitely the individual Mind . . . to the external world / Is fitted; and how exquisitely too . . . The external World is fitted to the Mind."[5] Wordsworth dominates the first ten pages of *The Book of the Green Man*, which begin at the poet's gravesite in Grasmere Churchyard, and it's clear that Johnson is deeply attracted to the vision of poet and nature advanced at greatest length in *The Prelude*. As Abrams shows, the Romantics—and here he means primarily Coleridge and Wordsworth, and later Keats and Shelley—transformed the ancient Christian notion of the *liber naturae*, the natural world as a book in which God's handiwork and will could be read, into a kind of natural supernaturalism, in which the poet, through his complex spiritual and sensory interactions with nature, comes to learn most of all about himself. Thus, the "exquisite fitting" between the "external World" and the "individual Mind."

Blake would have none of this. "You shall not bring me down to believe such fitting & fitted I know better & Please your Lordship," he scribbled in his copy of *The Excursion*.[6] For Blake, the bodily senses, and the whole vegetative world that they perceive, are but an impediment to the imagination, which alone can provide spiritual truth. "He who does not imagine in stronger and better lineaments, and in stronger and better light, than his perishing mortal eye can see," Blake wrote, "does not imagine at all."[7] Johnson, for his part, is deeply attracted to a Blakean poetics in which the poet writes visions beyond those of normal bodily sight. Blake's *Marriage of Heaven and Hell*, in which one allegorical vision is succeeded by another, is one model for *The Book of the Green Man*, which also traffics in visionary moments. That Johnson takes Blake *and* Wordsworth for two of his guiding lights, then, may simply show a salutary eclecticism in his influences, but are these two traditions, after all, compatible? Blake for his part certainly didn't think so.

Of course there are *two* Wordsworths in *Green Man*, not merely the poet William but also his sister, the journal writer Dorothy. They lie buried side by side in the Grasmere Churchyard where the poem's "Winter" section begins. William, Johnson comments, "could not see / daffodils / only // 'huge forms', *Presences* & earth 'working / like a sea'." It was Dorothy who "brought home // lichen & cushions of / moss" (GM 15–16), who was able to record the minute particularities of a landscape that for her brother merged into one giant, undifferentiated mirror of his own poetic nature. The poet Wordsworth is clearly a moving spirit behind *The Book of the Green Man*'s conception of the relationship between the poet and the landscape, but it is Dorothy Wordsworth who shows Johnson how to read that landscape, not at large, but in its minute particulars.

There is a whole pantheon of close observers in *Green Man*, from Francis Kilvert and Gilbert White, diarists and natural historians, to the painters Turner, Constable, and Stubbs. The latter is an unlikely group: Turner is usually held to be a precursor to Impressionism in his light-saturated seascapes, while Stubbs is known as the preeminent English painter of horses. But in his section "Turner, Constable & Stubbs," Johnson brackets them, through a single telling anecdote apiece, as painters who taught themselves, sometimes at great pains, "*To see*"—Turner, by having himself lashed Odysseus-like to the mast of a ship, Constable by sitting "still in the fields / till something came." And then there is Stubbs, who

> fixed an iron bar to the ceiling of his room, with hooks
> of various sizes & lengths, in order to suspend the body of a horse.
> The horse remained for six or seven weeks
> 'until no longer endurable'. (GM 57)

All this time, the painter was preserving the "form of muscles, blood vessels & nerves" "by tallow injections," dissecting the body to its bones, and "making full length drawings / & studies of the ear & nose." Johnson also cites various English writers who are no slouches at close observation. "Upon First Opening a Cuckoo" quotes John Ruskin's astonishing description of a bird as "*Little more than / a drift of air, brought // into form by plumes*" (GM 51), and Johnson buttresses his own description of clumps of moss by referring the reader to twentieth-century poet Geoffrey Grigson's *An English Farmhouse and Its Neighbourhood* (GM 87).

There's one figure I haven't yet mentioned in this roll call of *Green Man*'s inspirations, yet I believe that he's the key to Johnson's affectionate end run around the traditions of English Romanticism: Henry David Thoreau. Thoreau is perhaps the finest writer, and by far the most minute observer, among the Transcendentalists. The Transcendentalism sparked by Emerson and brought to fruition in Thoreau and Whitman is indeed a home-grown variety of European Romanticism, but Thoreau especially wears his Romanticism with a difference. Of course, the Transcendentalists were keen on the constant interchange, the isomorphism of nature and perceiver that they found in Coleridge and Wordsworth. Thoreau in particular stressed, however, in Guy Davenport's words, "that man must do his perceiving and his thinking for himself, and that he must learn how with much discipline and with constant awareness."[8]

Like *The Book of the Green Man*, Thoreau's *Walden; or, Life in the Woods* (1854) is organized around the cycle of the four seasons, and it's commonplace to note how Thoreau has compressed and rearranged his own two years at Walden Pond to produce the book's elegant one-year structure. With the availability of Thoreau's more than voluminous journals, one can also see how the moral, social, and metaphysical pronouncements of *Walden* have been distilled from multiple years' reading and concentrated observation. Johnson spent a good deal of time with Thoreau's journals—"I spent years reading in the two huge volumes of the Dover Edition," he comments in "Hurrah for Euphony"[9]—and it's Thoreau as journal writer that Johnson explicitly acknowledges in *Green Man*. Thoreau's entry for 16 March 1852, which Johnson reproduces at the head of his notes to the poem (though he misdates it to 1851), perfectly captures Johnson's sense of previous texts as "a rich silt of bibliography, books which lead to other books": "When I looked into Purchas's Pilgrims, it affected me like looking into an impassable swamp, ten feet deep with sphagnum. . . . Those old books suggested a certain fertility, an Ohio soil, as if they were making a humus for new literatures to spring in. I heard the bellowing of bullfrogs and the hum of mosquitoes reverberating through the thick embossed covers when I had closed the book. Decayed literature makes the richest of all soils" (GM 83). This isn't the Thoreau who's taught to thousands of undergraduates every year, or the Thoreau who's lent his considerable cultural cachet to the ecocriticism movement—*that* Thoreau is an eloquent wild man of the woods, a nineteenth-century Euell Gibbons demonstrating how one can live off of pine bark and snails. The Thoreau of Johnson's headnote is a protomodernist, a writer who cobbles his books together out of the phrases and aphorisms of the whole stock of human literature—a writer who bears a striking resemblance to Johnson himself. The modernists from whom Johnson derived his poetics clearly prepared him to see Thoreau as a member of that same quoting community. The Thoreau of *Green Man*, then, is prototype of the poet who has written *Green Man*: in this headnote, he provides a warrant for Johnson's own magpie collage poetics.

But Thoreau is important to Johnson as well at the points where he memorably encapsulates Romantic/Transcendentalist ideas about the relationship of the world and the observer, as in the spot where his journal appears as the source of a title that reiterates Johnson's fundamental microcosm-macrocosm theme, "*Unless the Humming of a Gnat is as the Music of the Spheres //* & the music of the spheres is as the humming / of a gnat" (GM 61). Most critical, however, are those moments where Thoreau tempers his more grandiloquent tendencies with a close observation of the world around him. Thoreau wrote, as Johnson quotes him in his notes (though he does not give the date of the journal entry), "So we went through the aspens at the base of the Cliffs, their round leaves reflecting the lingering twilight on the one side, the waxing moonlight on the other" (GM 87). This passage ends up in a section of *Green Man* Johnson entitles (alluding to a phrase of Samuel Palmer's) "*Of Certaine White Nights Wherein the / Darkes Doe Seem to Gette Up / & Walk & How Wee Saw Divers Wonders in Bothe / Earthe & Element*" (GM 70). (So far as I can tell, Palmer's own language is not marred with Ye Olde Englisshe Spellinge in which Johnson occasionally indulges.) This is a poem about a night walk in Palmer's Shoreham, and it is a visionary poem, shot through with blackbirds settling "as shapes of water on the land" and "a false / Aurora Borealis enfolding us as we came." And here's where Thoreau comes in:

> We also came upon one tree,
> out of those that abound here, whose leaves
> seemed brought into curious relief
> by the twilight being reflected upon one
> side, & a waxing moon,
> on the other—
>
> *it is thus our nights, everywhere,*
> *continued*
> *but dusks of daies.* (GM 70–71)

Johnson has transmuted Thoreau's matter-of-fact observation of aspens through lineation, some judicious rephrasing, and an utter recontextualization, into a singular visionary moment. At the same time, however, Johnson's note to the passage—quoting Thoreau's original words—grounds that visionary moment in an instance of careful naturalistic observation.

It is thus, I would argue, throughout *The Book of the Green Man*. Moments of Blake- or Smart-like visionary seeing are constantly grounded in Thoreauvian or Dorothy Wordsworth–like concrete observation. And this, precisely, is what makes *Green Man* a peculiarly *American* poem. Johnson has come to the British countryside, and the British literary tradition, with eyes trained not by Coleridge and William Wordsworth but by Thoreau and Whitman, Americans who married the metaphysics of English Romanticism to a delight in careful seeing and precise detail. He has also come to this countryside and this tradition with a poetics stemming from American modernism, and I suspect that Williams and Zukofsky taught him to *see* as much as anyone did. To what extent those writers can be read as by-blows of American Transcendentalism—I suspect very much indeed—is another argument.

Johnson ultimately has little patience with the *poetry* of natural supernaturalism (*The Prelude* alone appears in "Winter," and Coleridge and the rest are entirely absent): I imagine that poetry simply isn't radical enough to express his often-ecstatic vision of how the human and natural worlds interpenetrate. Smart, Blake, and the younger artists following Blake offer a wilder model, more visionary, more congenial. But Smart and Blake were both Christians, of however heretical a cast, and had hundreds of years of common faith in a supernatural reality—a deity, a "Heavenly host"—to underwrite their own visions. The Johnson of *Green Man* is no theist; he has only his visions of a *natural* reality "Most Rich, Most Glittering, Most Strange" (GM 67) and a conception of the interrelatedness of humanity and nature far more radical and fundamental than that of Coleridge and Wordsworth. He has grounded those visions, in best Thoreauvian fashion, in moments of vivid and precise natural perception (whether his own or that of the host of sources from whom he has borrowed), and in *The Book of the Green Man* has produced a vacation snapshot of Britain far stranger than that of Wordsworth and far more concrete than that of Blake.

4. A Note on Johnson's Anagrams

1] The anagram—a "name or phrase formed by rearranging the letters of another"—although a feat of undeniable ingenuity, has gotten little respect over the history of English poetry. In *The Arte of English Poesie* (1589), George Puttenham dismissed the anagram as "a thing if it be done for pastime and exercise of the wit without superstition commendable inough and mete study for Ladies, neither bringing them any great gayne nor any great losse unlesse it be of idle time." The anagram's "pleasure" lies in the "grateful newes or matter" that can be wrung from the transposition of the letters of one phrase into another: Pilate's question "Quid est veritas?" (*What is truth?*) can be answered "Est vir qui adest" (*It is the man who is here*); Puttenham's own happy anagrammatizing finds in "Elissabet Anglorum Regina" "Multa regnabis ense gloria" (*By thy sword shalt thou raigne in great renowne*) and "Multa regnabis sene gloria" (*Aged and in much glorie shall ye raigne*). "[B]icause there is much difficulty in it, and altogether standeth upon hap hazard," Puttenham concedes, the anagram "is compted for a courtly conceit no lesse than" the emblem.[1] A "courtly conceit," but something less than true poetry: Puttenham's discussions of both the emblem and the anagram were cancelled from most copies of *The Arte of English Poesie*.

2] How better to attack a poetaster than to accuse him of dithering with verbal toys? Dryden, scolding Thomas Shadwell in the 1684 *Mac Flecknoe*:

> Thy Genius calls thee not to purchase fame
> In keen Iambicks, but mild Anagram:
> Leave writing Plays, and choose for thy command
> Some peaceful Province in Acrostick Land.
> There thou maist wings display and Altars raise,
> And torture one poor word Ten thousand ways.[2]

3] A quarter-century later, Joseph Addison again brackets the anagram and the acrostic as equally trivial pursuits: "I do not speak this out of any Spirit of

Party. There is a most crying Dulness on both Sides. I have seen Tory *Acrosticks* and Whig *Anagrams*, and do not quarrel with either of them, because they are *Whigs* or *Tories*, but because they are *Anagrams* and *Acrosticks*."[3] For Addison, the anagram is a species of "false wit": "As *true Wit* generally consists in this Resemblance and Congruity of Ideas, *false Wit* chiefly consists in the Resemblance and Congruity sometimes of single Letters, as in Anagrams, Chronograms, Lipograms, and Acrosticks: Sometimes of Syllables, as in Ecchos and Doggerel Rhymes: Sometimes of Words, as in Punns, and Quibbles; and sometimes of whole Sentences of Poems, cast into the Figures of *Eggs*, *Axes* or *Altars*."[4]

4] Ronald Johnson's *ARK* contains great chunks of poetry that seem generated by anagrammatic manipulation of words' letters; it also contains varieties of acrostics and puns and quibbles aplenty. And while Dryden and Addison's scorn for poems in the form of wings, eggs, or altars would seem to be intended for George Herbert, Johnson was famously and deeply invested in precisely the concrete poetry of which Herbert's work is an ancestor.

5] For Puttenham, for Dryden, and for Addison, the anagram is a subpoetic toy, a species of "false wit," a "mete study for Ladies," because it represents the manipulation of the *forms*, the *dress* of thought—of "true wit," the "Resemblance and Congruity of Ideas." True wit, true poetic imagination, finds connections among and juxtaposes ideas, images, and concepts: the language in which those ideas, images, and concepts are expressed is no more than instrumental, a phonemic and graphemic shorthand for the ideas held within the poet's head and shared among the heads of his readers. It is bad enough to manipulate words—the sound-shapes that point toward mental concepts—it is downright scandalous, downright silly to play with the graphic symbols in which those words are written down.

6] The anagram is a scandal—synecdoche for the scandal of poetic language in general, the scandal of the materiality of the signifier. If the critical tradition running through Puttenham, Dryden, and Addison rejects the anagram as an illicit, playful, but ultimately harmless distraction from the "real" business of connecting *ideas* rather than graphemes, the tradition of Saussurean and post-Saussurean linguistics would found a similar rejection on Saussure's first and fundamental principle: that "*the linguistic sign is arbitrary*." The phonemic signifier, and even more so its graphemic written record, is linked to the conceptual signified only by convention: the signifier, in short, is *unmotivated*, unmoored to the mental world it maps and the outside world to which it points by anything stronger than the socially shared code of differences that is a language as a whole.[5]

7] It is paradoxical that Saussure, who so strenuously and influentially insisted on the arbitrary nature of the signifier, would spend so many of his late years detecting anagrams in the work of Latin poets and agonizing over whether those anagrams were *accidental*, the inevitable by-product of manipulating a finite number of graphic and phonemic elements, or were somehow part of a submerged poetics of repetition.[6] To my knowledge, the only scholar to take Saussure's anagrams seriously and to explore them as a compositional principle in Classical poetry is Frederick Ahl.[7] I am told by one scholar that Ahl's work is viewed among Classicists—predictably—as "eccentric."

8] But as scandalous, as trivial as it may seem, the anagram—much like rhyme itself, the coincidence of sound—entices, particularly at those moments when it touches upon a coincidence of meaning: in this sublunary world, all too often *the law* equals *wealth*; to *listen*, one must perforce be *silent*. We know that *hate* is often felt as a *heat* in one's vitals, that Adam and Eve found the *Garden* to be a place of *danger*, and that *love* sometimes manifests itself in one's innards as a burrowing, gnawing rodent—a *vole*. What is *evil* is often, indeed, *vile*. *Ronald Wilson Reagan*, to some, was an *insane Anglo warlord*. It is in such moments that we catch flashes, intimations, of a *motivated* relationship between language and the world. "The scandal of the pun," Jonathan Culler writes—and he might as well be writing of the anagram—"is that it treats a supposedly accidental and contingent relationship between signifiers (say *history* and *his story* or *write* and *right* as if it were a conceptual relationship"[8]).

9] In a 1985 notebook, Ronald Johnson jots down the following:

in *earnest*, a word which
    ~~ear nest~~
    ~~earn nest~~
    includes star, seen, ear
    nearest, and earn-nest
    as I hear it.
[stern, steer, rest, tease, aster
    trees][9]

He is doodling here, I take it, extracting words from a word, playing scales as it were: but he is also very much *in earnest*, for such games will not merely supply him with much of the material of *ARK*, but will be embedded in the very texture of the poem.

10] A few examples, for the most part at random:

Lave & Weave
Wave & Leave[10]

It is lucid as Euclid. (A 61)

words sword the swallow
from falling
(A 59)[11]

bent ambient
(A 70)

and a resonant gnomon before it will stretch regions of signalling
gnat-like resiliencies
(A 84)

violet eyelets in olive
(A 110)

mid violin, lens, loved line, dove, divers voids, lines lived
(A 166)

anemone mnemonic
(A 125)

lost lilac, lit shellac
(A 149)

arose a battleground:
rows on rows of roses
wound round and around
(A 185)

11] So, one asks, is Johnson merely playing here, pushing his words through hoops and flipping them off of trapezes like the animals and acrobats in a circus? Verbal playfulness is not the least amiable trait to find in a writer: Gertrude Stein, James Joyce, Vladimir Nabokov, and James Merrill, one might argue, built whole poetics out of the pun. Most of us simply delight in those puns; others, more dour, allow the writers their puns as an adjunct or ornament to the emotional depths of the works. But Johnson, I repeat, anagrammatizes *in earnest*.

12] It seems to me that one can push discussion of the anagram—and of the material signifier in general—in two different directions. On the one hand (a hard-nosed and no-nonsense critical hand), one can read the manipulation of letters within words, as well as the manipulation of the physical shapes of words in concrete poetry, as an attempt precisely to *motivate* the signifier, to make words mimetically conform to the systems of correspondences that one perceives in the world. Like all such attempts to undermine the fundamental arbitrariness of the signifier, Saussure would argue (he has specifically dismissed both onamatopoeia and exclamations), this is no more than wishful thinking: a toy, a "conceit."

13] Opposed to such critical dismissal, however, is an ancient, even mystical organicism of language, which insists on the *motivated*, even *spiritually* motivated connection between words and things. In Genesis, there is a connection between word and thing—stemming no doubt from the deity's primary act of creation, the *speaking* of being out of chaos—that transcends the merely arbitrary. *Adam* is so named because he was made of the clay, *adamah*; the critical moment of Jacob's life comes in the aftermath of his wrestle with the angel, when his name Yaakov ("heel-grabber") is replaced with Yisrael ("God-struggler"). One finds the faith in a motivated language, a lexis in which meaning inheres in every grapheme, in full flower in Gematria, the manipulation of the numerical equivalencies of Hebrew letters to find meaningful equivalencies and hidden messages. The pawky rabbis of the Talmud generally were sparing with *gematriot*, deploying them largely as mnemonic devices, rarely using a gematria to discover a meaning not already implicit in the text. Such Kabbalists as Jacob ben Jacob ha-Kohen and Abraham Abulafia were more extravagant in their explorations: the *Sefer ha-Zoref* of Heshel Zoref of Vilna and Cracow consists entirely of gematriatic elaborations of the *Shema Yisrael*.[12] Kabbalistic gematria, in full flower, traces the correspondences between the twenty-two letters of the Hebrew alphabet and ten *Sephirot* through which *Ain Soph* manifests himself in the universe.

14] But *my* Ronald Johnson is neither a hard-nosed rationalist nor a mystic (despite his fondness for the work of poetic mystics from Christopher Smart and William Blake to Robert Duncan). His work is suffused with the language of spiritual traditions, but I find little evidence in it of an actual belief in the numinous, in a supernatural reality to which one gains access through some devotional, mystical, or even pharmacological derangement of the senses. There is more than enough to wonder at, for Johnson, in the world as we see it and as it is revealed and analyzed in contemporary science. If labels were necessary, I would call him an exponent of "Transcendental Naturalism."

15] For the Transcendental Naturalist, the founding scripture on language is of course Emerson's *Nature* (1836), which asserts an original motivation in even the most abstract of words: "Every word which is used to express a moral or intellectual fact, if traced to its root, is found to be borrowed from some material appearance. *Right* means *straight*; *wrong* means *twisted*. *Spirit* means primarily *wind*; *transgression*, the crossing of a *line* . . . . Most of the process by which this transformation is made, is hidden from us in the remote time when language was framed."[13] Behind Emerson's thinking here is of course are some of the arguments in Plato's *Cratylus*, one of the earliest meditations on the question of whether the linguistic sign is arbitrary or motivated, a meditation in which the final position at which Sokrates and his interlocutors arrive is not at all clear.[14]

16] But what interests me most about the Emerson text—though one could have chosen any number of others, from Plato or Leibniz to some scattered passages in Saussure himself—is Emerson's emphasis on the passage of time, on our distance from "the remote time when language was framed." In order to present the linguistic sign as fundamentally arbitrary, to rule out a motivated relationship between word and world, Saussure confines linguistics to the study of language as a system *at a particular moment*—a "synchronic" standpoint. Ruled out of court—relegated to the realms of etymology or philology—is the study of language as it changes and evolves *over time*, from a "diachronic" standpoint.[15]

17] And time is of the essence for Johnson. For Johnson, as Transcendental Naturalist, language indeed "fits" the world, has a motivated connection thereto. (We ought not to forget his most blatant anagram-like permutation, the unsubtle working title for *ARK*: "Wor(l)ds." Those who would argue for a theistic Johnson will no doubt point out that the parenthetical "l" sounds the Hebrew word for God.) But that motivated connection is neither the trace of an originary, God-given ur-language nor a mystical set of correspondences, but an entirely natural phenomenon, part of the ongoing process of human evolution leading us toward some vaguely defined "Lift Off" (A 307). Human language, that is, should be viewed not as a tool or a technology—a prosthetic mediator between consciousness and its objects—but as a wholly *organic* and highly evolved constituent of the human being: as much an *organ* as the ear or the eye.

18] "The eye," Johnson writes in BEAM 4, "may be said to be sun in other form. . . . After a long time of light, there began to be eyes, and light began looking with itself." "Matter delights in music, and became Bach," he writes in BEAM 7 (A 12–14, 23)—and as matter was evolving its highest exponent of patterned sound, it was simultaneously evolving the complex organic machinery of mind and ear that would receive, process, and delight in that patterned music. Language, in both its phonemic and graphemic forms, has evolved right along with the human eye, ear, and brain; and the grammatical and lexical structures of language, its sonic shapes, even its graphic traces have evolved in tandem with our experience of the world, itself a dynamic process of which we are no more or less than a self-conscious development.

19] What then of those anagrams? On a most basic level, Johnson would let striking and shiny combinations of words be his *trouvées*, would set them down and follow where they led, building the poem around the unwinding of their implications. And of course Johnson was *playing* as he unpacked and rearranged the letters of words (perhaps sitting in front of the TV): but his play was *in earnest*. The *nest* of the brain and the labyrinth of the *ear*—and the organ of language, in its aural and written form, which buzzes between the two—have evolved in tandem with the world itself; is it any wonder then that unraveling the arcane connections of the constituents of language might yield us an *earnest* of truths about the universe, a universe in which language itself is perhaps the most sophisticated, self-conscious mirror?

Notes

Section 1

1. Ronald Johnson, *The American Table: More Than 400 Recipes That Make Accessible for the First Time the Full Richness of American Regional Cooking* (New York: William Morrow, 1984) 357.

2. Ronald Johnson, *To Do As Adam Did: Selected Poems*, ed. Peter O'Leary (Jersey City, NJ: Talisman House, 2000) 20; hereafter cited parenthetically in text as TD.

3. Ronald Johnson, *ARK* (1996; Chicago: Flood Editions, 2013) 190; hereafter cited parenthetically in text as A.

4. Ezra Pound, *Poems and Translations*, ed. Richard Sieburth (New York: Library of America, 2003) 1108.

5. Ronald Johnson, *A Line of Poetry, a Row of Trees* (Highlands, NC: Jargon, 1964. A solid overview of Johnson's life and career is Dirk Stratton, *Ronald Johnson*, Western Writers Series 122 (Boise, ID: Boise State UP, 1996), and there is much biographical information in *Ronald Johnson: Life and Works*, ed. Eric Murphy Selinger and Joel Bettridge (Orono, ME: National Poetry Foundation, 2008).

6. Andrew Marvell, "The Mower Against Gardens," *The Complete Poems*, ed. Elizabeth Story Donno (Harmondsworth, Eng.: Penguin, 1972) 105.

7. Elizabeth Sewell, *The Orphic Voice: Poetry and Natural History* (1960; New York: Harper, 1971) 39.

8. Sewell, *The Orphic Voice* 41.

9. Ronald Johnson, *The Book of the Green Man* (New York: Norton, 1967) 17–18; hereafter cited parenthetically in text as GM. (The full text of *Green Man* is available online at http://www.thing.net/~grist/ld/rjohnson/rj-gm-1.)

10. William Wordsworth, *Poetical Works*, ed. Thomas Hutchinson, rev. Ernest de Selincourt (Oxford: Oxford UP, 1969) 590.

11. William Blake, *The Complete Poetry and Prose*, ed. David V. Erdman (Garden City, NY: Doubleday, 1982) 667.

12. Blake, *Complete Poetry and Prose* 541.

13. Ronald Johnson, *Valley of the Many-Colored Grasses* (New York: Norton, 1969).

14. Blake, *Complete Poetry and Prose* 565–66.

15. Barry Alpert, "Ronald Johnson—An Interview (1974)," *Ronald Johnson: Life and Works* 550.

16. Ronald Johnson, *Radi os* (1977; Chicago: Flood Editions, 2005) ix; hereafter cited parenthetically in text as R.

17. This according to Peter Ackroyd, *Blake: A Biography* (New York: Knopf, 1996) 112–13; G. E. Bentley, Jr., *The Stranger from Paradise: A Biography of William Blake* (New Haven, CT: Yale UP, 2001) 102, identifies Blake's drawing medium as "probably a variant of the ordinary engravers stopping-out varnish, chiefly 'pitch diluted with Terps.'"

18. Blake, *Complete Poetry and Prose* 39.

19. *Paradise Lost* text quoted here and hereafter from *The Riverside Milton*, ed. Roy Flannagan (Boston: Houghton Mifflin, 1998), and cited by book and line number.

20. William Empson, *Milton's God* (1961; Cambridge: Cambridge UP, 1981) 10.

21. Ronald Johnson, "Hurrah for Euphony: Dedicated to Young Poets," *The Cultural Society*, http://www.culturalsociety.org/texts/prose/hurrah-for-euphony-dedicated-to-young-poets/.

22. Peter O'Leary, afterword to Ronald Johnson, *The Shrubberies*, ed. Peter O'Leary (Chicago: Flood Editions, 2001) 127; hereafter cited parenthetically in text as S.

Section 2

1. Peter O'Leary, "An Interview with Ronald Johnson (1995)," *Ronald Johnson: Life and Works*, ed. Joel Bettridge and Eric Murphy Selinger (Orono, ME: National Poetry Foundation, 2008) 584.

2. Guy Davenport, *The Geography of the Imagination: Forty Essays* (San Francisco: North Point, 1981) 348.

3. Carroll F. Terrell, "Louis Zukofsky: An Eccentric Profile," *Louis Zukofsky: Man and Poet*, ed. Terrell (Orono, ME: National Poetry Foundation, 1979) 70.

4. O'Leary, "An Interview" 584.

5. Terrell, "Louis Zukofsky" 73.

6. Ronald Johnson, *A Line of Poetry, a Row of Trees* (Highlands, NC: Jargon, 1964) and *Valley of the Many-Colored Grasses* (New York: Norton, 1969); hereafter cited parenthetically in text as V.

7. O'Leary, "An Interview" 584.

8. Liner notes by Leonard Bernstein and David Johnson to Charles Ives, *Symphony No. 2*, New York Philharmonic, cond. Leonard Bernstein (Columbia Masterworks KL 5489, n.d.).

9. Ronald Johnson, *ARK* (1996; Chicago: Flood Editions, 2013) 311–12; hereafter cited parenthetically in text as A.

10. Barry Alpert, "Ronald Johnson—An Interview (1974)," *Ronald Johnson: Life and Works* 546.

11. Ronald Johnson, "Planting the Rod of Aaron," *Northern Lights* 2 (1985–1986) 2.

12. Ronald Johnson, undated letter (ca. 1987–1988) to author.

13. Louis Zukofsky, *"A"* (1978; New York: New Directions, 2011) 319–25.

14. Johnson, "Planting" 2.

15. Louis Zukofsky, *Prepositions+: The Collected Critical Essays* (Hanover, NH: Wesleyan UP, 2000) 10.

16. William Blake, *The Complete Poetry and Prose*, ed. David V. Erdman (Garden City, NY: Anchor, 1982) 550.

17. Ezra Pound, *The Cantos* (New York: New Directions, 1995) 815; Louis Zukofsky, *Anew: Complete Shorter Poems* (New York: New Directions, 2011) 15.

18. O'Leary, "An Interview" 579–80.

19. Ezra Pound, *ABC of Reading* (New York: New Directions, 1960) 14.

20. Stuart Feder, *Charles Ives, "My Father's Song": A Psychoanalytic Biography* (New Haven: Yale UP, 1992); J. Peter Burkholder, *All Made of Tunes: Charles Ives and the Uses of Musical Borrowing* (New Haven: Yale UP, 1995).

21. Ronald Johnson, "Charles Ives: Two Eyes, Two Ears," *Parnassus: Poetry in Review* 3.2 (1975): 345–49.

22. Henry and Sidney Cowell, *Charles Ives and His World* (New York: Oxford UP, 1955) 147.

23. Qtd. in David Michael Hertz, "Ives's *Concord Sonata* and the Texture of Music," *Charles Ives and His World*, ed. J. Peter Burkholder (Princeton, NJ: Princeton UP, 1996) 80.

24. Charles Ives, *Essays Before a Sonata, The Majority, and Other Writings*, ed. Howard Boatwright (New York: Norton, 1962) 15.

25. J. Peter Burkholder, "Ives and the Four Musical Traditions," *Charles Ives and His World* 23.

26. Eric Murphy Selinger, "*ARK* as a Garden of Revelation," *Ronald Johnson: Life and Works* 339.

27. Walt Whitman, *Complete Poetry and Collected Prose*, ed. Justin Kaplan (New York: Library of America, 1982) 5.

28. Ives, *Essays* xxv.

29. Ives, *Essays* 36, 47, 73.

30. Peter O'Leary, "Gilding the Buddha: My Apprenticeship with Ronald Johnson," *Ronald Johnson: Life and Works* 610.

31. Charles Ives, *Memos*, ed. John Kirkpatrick (New York: Norton, 1972) 106.

32. Ralph Waldo Emerson, *Essays and Lectures*, ed. Joel Porte (New York: Library of America, 1983) 10.

33. Emerson, *Essays and Lectures* 48–49.

34. Ives, *Essays* 102.

Section 3

1. Christopher Middleton, jacket copy to Ronald Johnson, *The Book of the Green Man* (New York: Norton, 1967); hereafter cited parenthetically in text as GM.

2. Ronald Johnson, *Sports and Divertissments* (Dunsyre, Scotland: Wild Hawthorn, 1965).

3. Ronald Johnson, *A Line of Poetry, a Row of Trees* (Highlands, NC: Jargon, 1964).

4. M. H. Abrams, *Natural Supernaturalism: Tradition and Revolution in Romantic Literature* (New York: Norton, 1971).

5. William Wordsworth, *Poetical Works*, ed. Thomas Hutchinson, rev. Ernest de Selincourt (Oxford: Oxford UP, 1969) 590.

6. William Blake, *The Complete Poetry and Prose*, ed. David V. Erdman (Garden City, NY: Anchor, 1982) 666–67.

7. Blake, *Complete Poetry and Prose* 541.

8. Guy Davenport, *The Geography of the Imagination: Forty Essays* (San Francisco: North Point, 1981) 194.

9. Ronald Johnson, "Hurrah for Euphony: Dedicated to Young Poets," *The Cultural Society*, http://www.culturalsociety.org/texts/prose/hurrah-for-euphony-dedicated-to

-young-poets/; *The Journal of Henry David Thoreau*, two vols., ed. Bradford Torrey and Francis H. Allen (1906; New York: Dover, 1962).

Section 4

1. George Puttenham, *The Arte of English Poesie* (1589; facsimile repr., Kent, OH: Kent State UP, 1970) 121–23.

2. ll. 203–08.

3. *Spectator* #61 (Thursday, 10 May 1711) [False wit; punning]; Richard Steele and Joseph Addison, *Selections from the Tatler and the Spectator*, ed. Angus Ross (Harmondsworth: Penguin, 1982) 343.

4. *Spectator* #62 (Friday, 11 May 1711) [True, false and mixed wit]; *Selections* 345.

5. Ferdinand de Saussure, *Course in General Linguistics*, ed. Charles Bally and Albert Schehaye, trans. Roy Harris (La Salle, IL: Open Court, 1983) 67–69.

6. Jean Starobinski, *Words upon Words: The Anagrams of Ferdinand de Saussure* (New Haven: Yale UP, 1979) and Jonathan Culler, *Ferdinand de Saussure* (rev. ed. Ithaca: Cornell UP, 1986) 123–34.

7. Frederick Ahl, *Metaformations: Wordplay and Soundplay in Ovid and other Classical Poets* (Ithaca: Cornell UP, 1985) and "Ars Est Caelare Artem (Art in Puns and Anagrams Engraved)," *On Puns: The Foundation of Letters*, ed. Jonathan Culler (Oxford: Blackwell, 1988) 17–43.

8. Culler, *Ferdinand de Saussure* 129.

9. Ronald Johnson, "From the Notebooks," ed. Peter O'Leary, *Facture* 1 (2000) 75.

10. Ronald Johnson, *ARK* (1996; Chicago: Flood Editions, 2013) 29; hereafter cited parenthetically in text as A.

11. In this particular passage, from the "PALMS" section of the *The Song of Orpheus*, we see a *found* anagram, since Johnson has taken his words from the book of Psalms.

12. Gershom Scholem, *Kabbalah* (1974; New York: Dorset, 1987) 337–43.

13. Ralph Waldo Emerson, *Essays and Lectures*, ed. Joel Porte (New York: Library of America, 1983) 20.

14. See David Sedley's excellent analysis of the dialogue at the online Stanford Encyclopedia of Philosophy, http://plato.stanford.edu/entries/plato-cratylus/.

15. On Saussure and the limitations of establishing the arbitrariness of the sign from a purely synchronic standpoint, I've been deeply influenced by my colleague John Leeds's "From the Ground Up: Matter, Spirit, and the Linguistic Sign in John Lesley's Chronicles of Stewart Scotland," *Renaissance Syntax and Subjectivity: Ideological Contents of Latin and the Vernacular in Scottish Prose Chronicles* (Farnham, Eng.: Ashgate, 2010) 81–146. On Saussure and arbitrariness more generally, see J. H. Prynne, *Stars, Tigers and the Shape of Words* (London: Birkbeck College, 1993).

One Last Modernist

Guy Davenport

The vast sums of money that the art critic John Ruskin disbursed in the second half of his life—buying mineral specimens, paintings, and illuminated missals, improving a road on the outskirts of Oxford; funding the systematic sweeping of a stretch of Church Lane, St. Giles's, London; subsidizing a no-frills tea shop; and generally attempting to reform the entire social, intellectual, and moral life of Victorian England—were accumulated by his father's sherry-importing firm, Ruskin, Telford and Domecq. Pedro Domecq, Spanish-born but Paris-based, owned the Spanish estates on which the sherry was made, and was the firm's overseas partner. (At seventeen, Ruskin would fall in love, tragically, with his daughter Adèle.) John James Ruskin, a canny Scotsman, was the heart of the enterprise, responsible for the sales and marketing of what was considered the finest sherry available. As for Henry Telford, he did little more than oversee the firm's books during the midsummer holidays. And yet, however unknowingly, he set the course of the younger Ruskin's life. Telford gave the boy a copy of Samuel Rogers's long poem *Italy,* with engravings from drawings by J. M. W. Turner for his thirteenth birthday. "This book was the first means I had of looking carefully at Turner's work," Ruskin recalls in his luminous autobiography *Praeterita.* "I might, not without some appearance of reason, attribute to the gift the entire direction of my life's energies."[1] At all of sixteen, Ruskin wrote a passionate (though unpublished) defense of late Turner against his critics, a defense that later fed into the five volumes of *Modern Painters,* which in turn fed into *The Seven Lamps of Architecture, The Stones of Venice,* and the whole of Ruskin's nine-million-word body of writing.

On a far more modest scale, I could attribute much of my own life's direction to the moment in Blacksburg, Virginia, about a quarter-century ago when my professor Tom Gardner, who was supervising my independent reading of Ezra Pound, hauled Guy Davenport's *The Geography of the Imagination: Forty*

Essays down from his office bookshelf and handed it to me with the remark, "I think you'll be interested in some of these essays."

What he meant was that I'd probably be interested in Davenport's essays on Pound. But I suspect Tom had some inkling of the other riches and provocations that the book would offer me. For better or worse, I've spent much of the decades since treating it as a kind of reading list, an enormous hodgepodge of tantalizing suggestions about people to look into. Louis Zukofsky, Charles Olson, Ronald Johnson, Edward Dahlberg, Jonathan Williams, Ian Hamilton Finlay, Paul Metcalf, Pavel Tchelichew, Robert Kelly, Ralph Eugene Meatyard, Stan Brakhage, and so forth: *The Geography of the Imagination* offered an entire curriculum in twentieth-century authors, painters, and artists of whom I'd never heard, and who are still for the most part only rarely mentioned in college classrooms.

I wouldn't have cared one way or another about the unfamiliar names Davenport's essays dangled before me if I hadn't been irretrievably hooked by his prose. Back then I didn't *consciously* know good writing from bad. I read criticism first and foremost for information, and paid little attention to the shapes and sounds of the sentences in which that information was packaged. But there was something new in Davenport's writing: not merely a wealth of fact and anecdote and connection, but an electric punchiness and grace. Here's the bravura opening of his essay on Olson: "It is now almost seven years since the enormous presence of Charles Olson arrived rumpled and wild upon the yellow distances of the Plain of Elysion, on the outermost ring of the circle river Okeanos, estate of heroes and poets, where he would have had to bend deeply to embrace his beloved Keats, twenty-one inches shorter than Olson, who in his stocking feet was taller by half again than Alexander the Great."[2] And here's Davenport commenting acidly on *Time* magazine's naming of Robert Lowell as America's most significant poet in 1967: "Mr. Lowell has, indeed, worked hard at being a poet. He has been severe in his output, and knows, with Brahms, that writing is all too easy. What's hard is to throw most of what you've written in the trash-basket. He has been smart and modern in metric and diction. And he has been bleak, agonized, and serious, terribly serious. He seems to have always had a headache" (GI 133). Often, when I find my attention wandering from a piece of earnest, laborious, and indecently *dull* literary scholarship, I wonder how the author himself stayed awake to write such stuff. Davenport's essays are almost never like that: they rarely reek of the seminar room (though I confess there are some mighty tedious passages in "Ishmael's Double," a dutiful essay on Melville), and never of the tenure clock. "It is my hope never to be mealy-mouthed," Davenport remarks in a letter to Jonathan Williams. "There is no point to any criticism except to jog awake the sleeping and the dull."[3] I imagine Davenport's essays owe part of their freshness to their occasionality, springing into existence as they did in response to an editor's request for a review, an introduction, a contribution to a discussion on a given subject. In his introduction to *The Hunter Gracchus and Other Papers on Literature and Art* (1996), Davenport calls the collection a "miscellany," a fine old genre too rarely seen these days. But when he notes that his "gathering of studies, reviews, essays, and commentaries has for a semblance of unity only their being written on the same typewriter," we should interpret "being written on the same typewriter" as "having arisen out of the same alert, foraging sensibility."[4]

Aside from their consistently alert style—Davenport loathes an inert sentence the way my kids loathe unfamiliar vegetables—what most distinguishes these essays is their abundance of rich and strange detail. Here's Davenport on the composition of *Paradise Lost* (the passage is from his afterword to Ronald Johnson's *Radi os*): "While [Milton] dictated, the long rule of Louis XIV began, no rain fell in India for three whole years, Velazquez painted the Spanish court and Vermeer Dutch housewives pouring milk, the Turks cut their way through Hungary and Transylvania toward Vienna, and certain children were born and baptized Daniel Defoe, Henry Purcell, Matthew Prior. In the American colonies Michael Wigglesworth published *The Day of Doom*, which sold more copies than any book of poetry ever published in this country" (GI 200). There are offhand observations and factoids in Davenport essays that I have remembered—and repeated—for decades: "Like the gentle Anton Bruckner, who counted leaves on trees to while away a Sunday afternoon, Ludwig Wittgenstein in odd moments calculated the height of trees by pacing off from the trunk the base of a right triangle, wheeling around and sighting along his walking stick (up the hypotenuse) to the tree's top, invoking then the majestic theorem of Pythagoras" (GI 331).

Sometimes, as in the Milton passage above, the proliferation of detail is more ornamental than directly relevant (Indian drought and *Paradise Lost*?). More often, Davenport, who has no truck with the academic practice of context-free "close reading," hedges his subjects about with detailed description, exposition, and rumination. To truly read Johnson's *Radi os*, that extraordinary revision-by-excision of *Paradise Lost*, one ought—it seems—to know about the modernists' penchant for rewriting the *Odyssey*, William Blake's contrarian rewritings of Milton (*The Four Zoas* and *Milton*), and the coterie of "Ancients" who gathered around Blake in his old age—Edward Calvert, John Linnell, Samuel Palmer.

Davenport had a particular fondness for anecdotes. In his review of Donald Hall's *Remembering Poets*, he writes that the anecdote "is the folklore that plays around a high seriousness, the saints' legends of a religion, and usually has the truth of myth rather than fact" (GI 136). (I'm reminded of James Laughlin telling Davenport that even though Allen Ginsberg had denied leaving his early poems "under the milk bottles" on William Carlos Williams's kitchen stoop, "I'll continue to tell that one because I know it is TRUE. I'm positive. It is what should have happened."[5]) Davenport's anecdotes are almost always delicious, and sometimes pointed. Consider these two:

> Sir Walter Scott's son grew up in ignorance that his father was a novelist, and remarked as a lad in his teens when he was among men discussing Scott's genius, "Aye, it's commonly him is first to see the hare." (GI 337)

> Lincoln on horseback tipped his hat to [Whitman] one day, a gazing stranger who Lincoln must have supposed was some office seeker or underling in one of the departments, perhaps a geologist with that grizzled a beard. It was the republican equivalent of Napoleon looking in on Goethe to talk history and poetry. (GI 69)

Alas, some of Davenport's best anecdotes are demonstrably false. "Ruskin and Turner never dined together," he tells us in "The Anthropology of Table Manners from Geophagy Onward." "Turner knew his manners weren't up to those of the refined Ruskins, and said so, explaining graphically that, being toothless, he sucked his meat" (GI 347). The more detailed Ruskin biographies, however, mention numerous Ruskin-Turner meals. Of Charles Olson, we learn that "He once ate an oil rag" (GI 81) (an outlandish factoid repeated verbatim in Michael Schmidt's *Lives of the Poets*[6]). Well, no—Olson *dreamed* of eating a polishing rag, and worked the dream into a *Maximus* poem.[7] And I'd always relished the story (from, again, the afterword to *Radi os*) that Cromwell's cannons were inscribed "God Is Love" (GI 200). Its source, it turns out, is one of the bigotedly anti-English characters in the "Cyclops" chapter of *Ulysses*; Joyce scholars tell us the story is apocryphal.[8]

But anecdotes are only the surface spicing of Davenport's critical enterprise, whose deeper goal is neither to provide close readings of texts—like his friend Hugh Kenner, he somehow managed to avoid all contamination by New Criticism, even as he came of age in its heyday—nor to "deconstruct" them. Rather, Davenport is out to trace connections, to show how the most vital modernist and contemporary writing and art is embedded within a complex web of symbols and motifs that dates back to the archaic—a web that, in the final analysis, *is* civilization. The high modernists, Pound especially, were entirely conscious of their place within the ongoing orders of Western culture, and made the recovery of archaic and forgotten energies a primary task of their works. Pound forged a whole poetics out of fragments like the Sappho scrap he translated in "Papyrus"; Picasso looked for inspiration to African masks and the Lascaux cave paintings; the thin-lipped and impeccably civilized T. S. Eliot traced the "mind of Europe" back to "the rock drawing of the Magdalenian draughtsman."[9] Later writers like Olson, Zukofsky, and Johnson continued such archaeological labors in more complicated and idiosyncratic modes. Even the ostensibly "realist" Eudora Welty, Davenport shows in "That Faire Field of Enna," recapitulated a series of Greek mythological motifs in her stories and novels (GI 250–71).

As when he points out in "The Geography of the Imagination" that the pose of the farmer in Grant Wood's "American Gothic" duplicates that of "the Egyptian prince Rahotep, holding the flail of Osiris, beside his wife Nufrit" (GI 13), Davenport delights in reading the survivals of archaic culture in the seemingly most homegrown American products. He reads O. Henry's story "The Church with the Overshot Wheel," for instance, as a perhaps unconscious retelling of the Persephone myth; it is "a detail in the structure of a culture of strong vitality which decided on the expressiveness of certain symbols five thousand years ago, and finds them undiminished arid still full of human significance" (GI 11). In "Persephone's Ezra," he tracks that myth back to modernism's Victorian forebears: "Like Sappho and Chaucer, Ruskin wrote about girls as if they were flowers, about flowers as if they were girls (so that his botanical treatise called *Proserpina* has more of an archaic Greek flavour than any of the period's translations), and Lewis Carroll's Alice is a kind of Persephone. There is Tennyson's somber, Vergilian 'Demeter and Persephone,' Swinburne's 'The Garden of Proserpine' and 'Hymn to Proserpine.' Pound grew up in an ambiance congenial to myth" (GI 146–47). Even if O. Henry had never read his Ovid, it's not a matter of the writer happening upon some Jungian archetype, some story mystically embedded in the collective unconscious; rather, he is repeating a tale that has been common property of the tribe, told and retold until its origins are forgotten.

The tracing of such symbols and lines of descent is the central act of Davenport's criticism. (Its precise counterpart in art criticism is the iconography of Erwin Panofsky, as in his essay "The Ideological Antecedents of the Rolls-Royce Radiator," which winds through the history of English architecture, landscape design, and neo-Classicism before ending up at that iconic auto part.[10]) In *The Geography of the Imagination,* Davenport is much fascinated with tales—like that of Persephone—collected by Ovid. In the pieces gathered in *Every Force Evolves a Form* and *The Hunter Gracchus,* he returns again and again to the Greek concept of the *daimon*, the spirit messenger embodied in a bird (the mockingbird in Whitman's "Out of the Cradle," Poe's raven, Wordsworth's red-breast, Hopkins's windhover) or a mysterious little boy (the various children in Kafka, the three boys in *The Magic Flute*). When we follow such symbols, Davenport tells us, we are tracing "modulations in a long tradition, a dance of forms to a perennial spiritual force."[11]

There's a great pleasure in accompanying Davenport's Holmeslike pursuit of cultural forms, even when one begins to suspect that he's taking his analogies a bit too far. Or, more seriously, that he misrepresents the works in question. Take Davenport's reading of a few talismanic sentences from *Walden* in his essay-story-collage "The Concord Sonata." Thoreau writes: "I long ago lost a hound, a bay horse, and a turtledove, and am still on their trail. Many are the travellers I have spoken concerning them, describing their tracks and what calls they answered to. I have met one or two who had heard the hound, and the tramp of the horse, and even seen the dove disappear behind a cloud, and they seemed as anxious to recover them as if they had lost them themselves."[12] What to make of this passage? Davenport quotes the naturalist John Burroughs, who finds in it Thoreau's quest for "the transcendental, the unfindable, the wild that will not be caught," and the philosopher Stanley Cavell, who writes in *The Senses of Walden*: "I have no new proposal to offer about the literary or biographical source of these symbols in perhaps his most famously cryptic passage. But the very fact that they are symbols, and function within a little myth, seems to me to tell us what we need to know. The writer comes to us from a sense of loss; the myth does not contain more than symbols because it is no set of desired things he has lost, but a connection with things, the track of desire itself" (TGF 78). But it turns out that Burroughs and Cavell are merely straw men. In preparation for knocking them down, Davenport quotes a passage from *A Week on the Concord and Merrimac Rivers* where Thoreau in turn quotes the Chinese philosopher Mencius: "If one loses a fowl or a dog, he knows well how to seek them again; if one loses the sentiments of his heart, he does not know how to seek them again . . . . The duties of all practical philosophy consist only in seeking after the sentiments of the heart which we have lost; that is all" (TGF 79). The dove, Davenport reminds us, is familiar from scripture: Noah had a dove, a dove was present at the baptism of Christ, Jonah's name means "dove." It is as well Aphrodite's totem animal, and Christopher Columbus's family name. It is a universal symbol of peace. As for the horse, it represents, "the body, its stamina, health, and skills," while the hound "is faith and loyalty." "Mencius's Chinese cock," Davenport writes, and unimaginable Chinese dog have become under Concord skies a biblical dove, a Rover, and a bay horse. The one is a pet, one is a friend, one is a fellow worker.

We lose not our innocence or our youth or opportunity but our nature itself, atom by atom, helplessly, unless we are kept in possession of it by the spirit of a culture passed down the generations as tradition, the great hearsay of the past.

"Symbols," Davenport gravely cautions those who would embrace Cavell's and Burroughs's readings, "are not sense but signs" (TGF 83): Thoreau's dove, hound, and horse must be read within the wider cultural matrix, and so read they will unlock a very particular meaning. Cavell and Burroughs, Davenport insists, have not only misread Thoreau but, in doing so, exemplified the danger of which he warns. But I can't help feeling that Thoreau's enigmatic passage, respected as such by Burroughs and Cavell, has become in Davenport's hands rather less a Thoreauvian parable than another statement of his own convictions, derived ultimately from a Poundian version of Confucius.

* * *

We're all more or less partial to the first book we've read and loved by an author, but I don't think it's partiality telling me that Davenport's two later collections of essays, *Every Force Evolves a Form* and *The Hunter Gracchus,* have neither the range nor the depth of *Geography of the Imagination.* Both books have extraordinary moments, but also a number of essays and reviews that seem to be going through the motions, trying to float a series of commonplaces on the pontoons of Davenport's stylistic brio. I didn't much mind the disappointment of *Every Force,* however, for by the time I read it I was immersed in Davenport's other writings—his fiction, translations, and poetry.

By the time of his death in 2005, Davenport was probably best known, aside from his essays, for his short stories and novellas. But he came to fiction relatively late, in his forties. Early on he aspired to be a poet. In the 1960s, he published a number of fine poems; one of his first books was a long poem, *Flowers and Leaves,* published in 1966 by Jonathan Williams's Jargon Society; and among his most rewarding writings are the translations of archaic poets collected in *7 Greeks* (1995).

Flowers and Leaves is a full-blown Poundian pastiche. Of all the writers educated at the Ezuversity, whether in Rapallo or St. Elizabeths, Davenport studied hardest and most took to heart the master's teachings and techniques. He first read *The Cantos* on a walking tour of Italy and France, and even without understanding the poem took it as instigation: "My Pound was first of all a man who had written a rich, barely comprehensible poem, a man whose portrait bust had been chiselled by Gaudier. My first response was to learn Italian and Provençal, and to paint in the quattrocento manner. All real education is such unconscious seduction" (GI 174). Whatever posterity's final verdict on Pound, he will be remembered as one of his century's great *influences*. "I have seen students learn Chinese because of him," writes Davenport in an obituary tribute, "or take up mediaeval studies, learn Greek, Latin, music" (GI 176).

To trace the rhizomatic course of Davenport's reading, one should begin with the barrage of unfamiliar names that constituted Pound's syllabus. It's striking—or perhaps simply irritating—how many of Pound's central themes reappear in Davenport's work: "the renaissance of the archaic"; the lingering presence of numinous forces that the ancients identified with deities; the inextricability of sexual desire and learning; the centrality of translation to poetry.

Davenport also shares Pound's frustration with contemporary cultural, social, and economic life. It is, ultimately, a nineteenthcentury frustration, visible, for instance, in *Fors Clavigera,* where Ruskin fulminates at great length against the sin of usury. Davenport remarks: "How strange [Pound's] condemnation of usury sounded to a world that had forgotten the rage of Ruskin against the shrinking of all values into the shilling, the passionate voices of Fourier, Thoreau, and Marx that men were becoming the slaves of factories and banks" (GI 172). But unlike certain others who visited Pound at St. Elizabeths—there are a number of eye-widening passages in Hugh Kenner's *The Pound Era* that amount to a defense of Pound's economic theories and, by implication, his fascism—Davenport holds no brief for the more unhinged reaches of Pound's thought. One day Davenport showed me a copy of Leo Frobenius's *Kulturgeschichte Afrikas* that Pound had given him in St. Elizabeths—first reversing the dust jacket so that Jewish agents wouldn't spot it on the train. Pound's anti-Semitism "made no sense that I could see," Davenport writes. "I had paid attention to the war, I knew refugees, I understood Treblinka and Buchenwald, I had seen Europe in ruins" (GI 174).

But Pound is for Davenport first and foremost a writer who set out a range of new voices and forms to be explored. Davenport's *Flowers and Leaves* (subtitled *Poema vel Sonata: Carmina Autumni Primaeque Veris Transformationum*) is a late flowering of Poundian forms and motifs, a celebration of natural process, sexuality, and the web of culture that imbues it all with sacred power. As Davenport described it to Jonathan Williams, the poem is "long, metaphoric, mythological, parodistic, inept, elegiac, sexual, Ivesian, Poundian, Stevensish, Orffische, Christian, pagan, Brakhagean, and simple-minded" (GCP 30). Not many readers would endorse that last adjective. Like *The Cantos, Flowers and Leaves* is dense with references and spangled with foreign words—indeed, there are whole stanzas in French, Provençal, Latin, and Classical Greek. The poem has passages of great beauty, such as this one about Persephone:

> She was gillyflower, leaf and frond,
> Pale where not pink, cinnamon and wild rose,
> Still playing with her kitty and her barley doll,
> Little Persephatta, millet topped, mama's *cara*,
> The holm wood's Cora in her tucked yellow dress.[13]

It also has passages of delicious, none-too-delicate lubricity:

> The transparence in which they lay together,
> Persistent light upon the inviolably forever other,
> Folded inward with them, salacious silver of his eyes,
> Her face all mischief, roguish, and mouth drinking air,
> Thrust beyond the blind world in a rush of breath,
> Deep her socket's quick as long strokes touched plumb,
> The warped cone olive-rose in the fire of her shiver,
> Blunt on its resolute vein-wound stiff shaft,
> Heart dark, that gripped slide, lavish as their eyes,
>
> Boy impacted in girl, slow haste in their fastness. (FL 22)

And it has great stretches in the quatrain form of Pound's *Hugh Selwyn Mauberley* (or Eliot's quatrain poems), all too often parroting *Mauberley's* cultural pessimism:

> All made things engineered not to last;
> Styles hold a fortnight, words a month;
> Self expression, or whatever, has passed
> For verse, for song; all senses altered
>
> To fatten every taste. *D' essere senza*
> Eyes, glans, or tongue, serves
> To blunt even expectation. *Senza coglione*
> We greet the light with wounded nerves.

Or:

Holbein's Henry is reproduced nowadays
From the navel up; the brain,
In disrepute anyway (his testoons
Sold to India after his reign) . . . (FL 38–39)

Flowers and Leaves is the work of a young poet besotted with high modernism, echoes of which reverberate throughout the poem, from the hidden children of Eliot's *Burnt Norton*, to Poundian imitations of Arnaut, to a kind of Charles Ivesian phantasmagoria (Ives is the poem's dedicatee) that sets the Civil War, Whitman, Rimbaud, Ty Cobb, and Henri Rousseau within the frame of "The Star-Spangled Banner"—which, Davenport reminds us, should be recognized as a classic *alba,* or morning song.

Davenport would later remark that *Flowers and Leaves* convinced him he wasn't a poet. I'm not sure what exalted conception of poetic identity would exclude the author of that poem's best lines, or of the wonderful bagatelle "The Resurrection in Cookham Churchyard," published in *Poetry* in 1967. This latter poem plays off of one of the English artist Stanley Spencer's visionary paintings, and depicts in well-turned tetrameter couplets the bodily resurrection of seemingly every semi-obscure figure Davenport has ever taken an interest in:

Sir Edward Coke in rotten lace
Sits up with wonder on his face.
Michael Ventris surfaces near
The round and pious Edward Lear.
Theda Pigbone with the stick-pin
Finery she was buried in,
All cackle, warts, and raddled gums,
From tumbled earth triumphant comes.[14]

The final passage, in which God himself speaks in the accents of Blake, Ruskin, and the author of Job, is tremendous:

Zophar, Bildad, did you expect
The burning tiger's architect,
Quaternion, stone-hearted men,
Never to wake his own again?
Entuthon Benython break out,

Light from the quick of carbon spout.
Let beryl Golgonooza burn,
Loom and furnace and man return
Within my bowels' very life:
Jerusalem shall be his wife.[15]

Though "The Resurrection in Cookham Churchyard" could also be called pastiche (of what I'm not sure), in another sense it's Davenport's last substantial original poem—from the late 1960s on he produced only occasional squibs (encomia for Basil Bunting and Jonathan Williams, for instance) and translations.

* * *

"English literature lives on translation, it is fed by translations," Pound wrote, "every new exuberance, every new heave is stimulated by translations."[16] Yet he wasn't saying anything new, only reasserting a truth that English-language poets are sometimes inclined to forget. In his forties, with the major achievements of *Lycidas* and *Comus* behind him, Milton turned his hand to translating the Psalms. Marlowe translated Ovid, Pope Homer, Longfellow Dante, Rossetti a great deal of early Italian poetry.

The oldest Greek poetry is at the very base of our literary tradition: that's part of what Pound was getting at when he began *The Cantos* with a translation of the *nekuia* (the descent into the underworld) from Book XI of the *Odyssey,* a passage he believed predated the rest of the poem. But for an audience without Greek, the Classical poets need to be translated anew for each generation. Reviewing Richmond Lattimore's version of the *Odyssey,* Davenport writes, "This is a *new Odyssey*. . . . There it sits, beside many *Odysseys* obviously less competent and in various Wardour Street and Walter Scott styles; and beside burly, noble Chapman; beside good old leafy William Cullen Bryant; beside the graceful and inventive Robert Fitzgerald." Lattimore's version is sound and serviceable, but alas less than inspiring: "Ours, [Lattimore] sighs, is not a heroic culture. So he feels he must make do with a diction all but featureless, all but denatured. Yet this is the age of Eliot and Pound and Joyce" (GI 42).

Davenport's own translations of the Greek poets are very much products of "the age of Eliot and Pound and Joyce," not least in his refusal of Victorian padding. If, in Davenport's account, one of the virtues of the modernists was their recognition of the freshness of the archaic (as much in Lascaux as in Homer), another was their recognition that it survives largely in fragments, and that there is something compelling about this fragmentation. The bulk of

Davenport's translations of Archilochos, Sappho, Alkman, and Anakreon—collected in *7 Greeks* along with his renderings of Herakleitos, Diogenes, and Herondas—consists of bits and pieces preserved as quotations in grammatical treatises, in palimpsests, and on scraps of paper used to wrap Egyptian mummies. His version of Sappho 60 reads in full as follows, with brackets indicating lacunae:

> Rose
> [ ]
> Speak
> [ ]
> Yearning
> [ ]
> Sweat. [17]

Here's Sappho 89:

> [ ]
> not even
> lovely
> [ ]
> flower
> longing
> pleased
> [ ]. (SG 93)

There are scores of fragments in Davenport's Sappho, Archilochos, and Anakreon (not, he is careful to tell us, the familiar poet of the "Anacreontics," who is the product of a group of admiring Byzantine imitators) that consist of single words or phrases, entirely free of syntax or context. These are chips of language that have been preserved by pure chance, or by some grammarian's desire to illustrate a particular dialect's constructions. But for Davenport they cast a light back upon the very springtime of human culture. As he remarked in a letter to James Laughlin, what the poems of *7 Greeks* "have in common is their age—and in the Poundian sense that caused me to do them, their *firstness*" (GD/JL 170).

In his translations of the more complete poems, Davenport is conscious that translation cannot deliver anything close to the experience of the poem's first readers—or hearers, rather, since archaic poetry was performed. As a kind of compensation, he sometimes provides more than one version. Alkman's "Hymn to Artemis of the Strict Observance" he translates no fewer than four times: in a fairly literal version that indicates the manuscript's elisions; in tetrameter couplets; in hexameters; and finally in a spare, "aerated" version reminiscent of the William Carlos Williams of *Spring and All.*

At their best, Davenport's translations vividly capture recognizable moments of emotion as expressed by deeply foreign sensibilities. The mercenary Archilochos, for instance:

> Some Saian mountaineer
> Struts today with my shield.
> I threw it down by a bush and ran
> When the fighting got hot.
> Life seemed somehow more precious.
> It was a beautiful shield.
> I know where I can buy another
> Exactly like it, just as round. (SG 39)

The passion-struck Sappho:

> Percussion, salt and honey,
> A quivering in the thighs;
> He shakes me all over again,
> Eros who cannot be thrown,
> Who stalks on all fours
> Like a beast.

Or, alternately:

> Eros makes me shiver again
> Strengthless in the knees,
> Eros gall and honey,
> Snake-sly, invincible. (SG 87–88)

("Sexual frenzy," Davenport comments, "was as respectable a passion to Sappho as rapacious selfishness to an American" [SG 9].) And the self-satisfied, lyrical Alkman:

> This is the music Alkman made
> From partridge dance and partridge song
> With his fluttering partridge tongue. (SG 135)

As Davenport is at pains to detail in his introduction to *7 Greeks,* the seventh century BC is an unimaginable distance from us, a world "half oriental, half Viking." Its inhabitants "dressed like Samurai; all was bronze, terra cotta, painted marble, dyed wool, and banquets. Of the Arcadian Greece of Winckelmann and Walter Pater they were as ignorant as we of the ebony cities of Yoruba and Benin" (SG 1). Davenport's versions of these poets give us a picture of the ancient world—colorful, smelly, sweaty with passions, and shot through with alien pieties—far removed from the pristine Classicism of Flaxman or Poussin.

* * *

One Saturday in my last year as an undergraduate, I made a road trip to Charlottesville to buy books with my history professor Charlie Reed, a Classicist and expert on Greek coinage. I found a copy of Davenport's *Archilochos, Sappho, Alkman: Three Lyric Poets of the Seventh Century BC* (1984), and on the drive back to Blacksburg, Charlie regaled me with his appreciation of Davenport's version of Sappho's "Poikilothron' athanat' Aphrodita": this was not merely a poet blundering his way through a half-understood tongue but the real thing.[18]

By that time Davenport had captured my imagination, and I was writing a thesis on the Poundian ideogram that dealt in part with Davenport's fiction. Having found his address in some writers' directory, I sent him a list of no doubt obvious questions, couched in what was surely the worst adolescent fan-mail obsequiousness. (Thank heavens I no longer have a copy of that letter.) To my surprise, he replied practically by return mail, answering my questions patiently and encouraging me in a way that seemed wholly disproportionate to the merits of my work. After that we exchanged letters for some fifteen years, maybe a half-dozen a year. A letter from Guy (for he shifted us to a first-name basis early on) was always an event, something to set me thinking and reading and, likely as not, running off to the library. I understand that he carried on scores of such correspondences, and everyone I know who had letters from him praised them as models of wit and information.

There must be many thousands of Davenport letters in libraries and private collections around the world. They make fascinating reading, at least those in the three selections that have been published over the past five years: Davenport's early correspondence with Jonathan Williams, his late exchanges with James Laughlin, and his late 1970s–early 1980s letters to the poet, artist, mystery novelist, and Italian translator Nicholas Kilmer.[19] The letters to Kilmer, carefully culled and annotated by their addressee, present Davenport in mid-career, writing genially as man of letters to man of letters. Kilmer, the grandson of poet Joyce Kilmer, initiated the correspondence after reading Davenport's little *New York Times* essay on his grandfather's poem "Trees": "there is a silvery, spare beauty about [the poem] that has not dated. Its six couplets have an inexplicable integrity, and a pleasant, old-fashioned music. It soothes, and it seems to speak of verities" (GI 178).

The letters Davenport and Jonathan Williams exchanged between 1964 and 1968 are something else altogether, full of enthusiasms and discoveries, spiced with personal disclosure and literary gossip.[20] Davenport had just moved from Haverford College to the University of Kentucky when he and Williams began corresponding: "Haverford finally decided that I didn't fit into their studied nonconformity, so I'm in exile: I chose the remotest offer with the best pay" (GCP 15). In the second half of the sixties, he hadn't yet found his precise niche as a writer: he was working hard on his poetry (Williams would publish *Flowers and Leaves* in 1966); he had translated Archilochos and Herakleitos, and had begun his complete Sappho; and he was publishing essays and reviews in a wide variety of periodicals, perhaps most notably William F. Buckley's *National Review,* to which he had gained entrée through Hugh Kenner, a close friend of Buckley.

Williams, by contrast, was fully established in his career as poetpublisher and all-round cheerleader for culture, crisscrossing the country in his blue Volkswagen bus to do readings and show slides, continually snapping up residencies and visiting gigs. If Davenport was settling into his role as the hermit of Lexington, walled up among his pictures and books, Williams was constantly on the move, in his own words "flitting around like a half-frigged fly (as the Brits say), hardly in the same place for two letters in a row" (GCP 12). The two men quickly became "cousins" (drawing on their shared Carolina backgrounds). But Davenport found himself drawn all too soon into an avuncular role, counseling Williams on his volatile relationship with the poet Ronald Johnson, urging the (slightly) younger poet to rein in his enthusiasm for new entanglements.

Perhaps what is most touching about their correspondence is the kinship these two deeply unlike men—Davenport, shy, scholarly, and Spartan; Williams, the consummate party animal and sybarite, always on the alert for the next fine meal, the next fine wine, the next well-turned poem or young man's thigh—found in their common love of word-craft. "Jonathan has yet to read *War and Peace,*" Davenport writes in the preface to *A Garden Carried in a Pocket*, "and I have yet to read [A. Merritt's] *The Moon Pool.* Our tastes in music, philosophy, film, politics, clothes and people could not be more different if we inhabited different planets. Add food and drink. What keeps our conversation going is writing itself, the art of arranging words on a page" (GCP 10).

The correspondence of Davenport and James Laughlin, the founder of New Directions, is no less a meeting of disparities. Laughlin, over a decade older than Davenport, was also a disciple of Pound—he had visited him in Italy beginning in 1933, had published his books since 1938, and had even offered to pay for Pound's defense at his treason arraignment in 1945. Laughlin followed Pound in more than aesthetic matters: his letters to Davenport are spotted with approving references to Social Credit, Pound's favorite economic panacea.

Just as Ruskin, Telford and Domecq's sherry revenues underwrote John Ruskin's Guild of St. George, New Directions was largely funded by Laughlin's considerable family fortune; his great-grandfather had founded the Jones and Laughlin Steel Company in Pittsburgh in the mid-nineteenth century. Laughlin's personal wealth sometimes lent an air of dilettantism to his literary interests: there seemed to be no rare book he could not afford. (At one point, Laughlin tells Davenport the hair-raising story of having his briefcase stolen in a Penn Station restroom: it contained his much-annotated copy of *The Cantos,* along with an original copy of Andreas Divus's 1533 Latin translation of Homer—the source for Canto I [GD/JL 29].)

Unlike Pound, who had told Laughlin early on that there was no future for him in poetry and that he should turn his energies to publishing, Davenport took Laughlin's epigrammatic, sometimes breezy, and often salacious poetry quite seriously. Laughlin sent him poems throughout their correspondence, both in print and in typescript, and Davenport's responses were almost always generous, even enthusiastic. Though Davenport uniformly addresses Laughlin with a playfully respectful "Mr. Laughlin," theirs is clearly a correspondence of student and teacher, Davenport pointing the older poet toward things he ought to read, correcting his Greek, and sometimes gently attempting to fix Laughlin's more wayward compositions: "I find the narrative technique full of untied shoestrings," he writes of one section of *Byways,* Laughlin's verse autobiography. "Your style, however, is such that I can't see how to tie them and keep your distinctive voice. . . . I feel like an unforgiveable smart aleck tampering with your Roman verses" (GD/JL 141).

When North Point Press, Davenport's principal publisher, went belly-up in 1990, Laughlin was swift to offer Davenport a publishing home at New Directions. For his part, Davenport was delighted: "I am inordinately proud to be accepted by a publisher whose books have been the best part of my education (without Pound and WCW I would have been somebody else), and to whose list I never dared hope to be added" (GD/JL 86). New Directions would go on to publish five Davenport volumes between 1993 and 1996: three volumes of stories (including a reprint of *Da Vinci's Bicycle*), *7 Greeks*, and Erik Anderson Reece's *A Balance of Quinces: The Paintings and Drawings of Guy Davenport.* (Davenport had no shortage of publishers in the 1990s: even as New Directions was publishing his fiction and translations, North Point founder Jack Shoemaker had established a new imprint, Counterpoint, that was publishing his essays and lectures—*The Hunter Gracchus, Objects on a Table: Harmonious Disarray in Art and Literature*—and, with Benjamin Urrutia, *The Logia of Yeshua,* a collection of the sayings of Jesus.)

If the narrative curve of *A Garden Carried in a Pocket* follows the youthful flowering of friendship, punctuated by the crises of Williams's erotic life, the Davenport-Laughlin letters chronicle, painfully, the slow winding down of Laughlin's life. Among the literary conversations, the reminiscences of Pound, the excited reports of discoveries of new authors, runs an undercurrent of pain and diminution, Davenport consoling Laughlin upon his son's suicide, his wife's illness, a fire in his library, his strokes and falls and sometimes debilitating depression.

By the time he and Davenport began corresponding in earnest, Laughlin had already begun handing over much of the daily business of New Directions to his staff. The firm's publishing Davenport, it is clear, was something of a rare personal project for him, a momentary return to the small-press ethos of the early days of New Directions, when a book was taken on because it *ought* to be published, whether or not it had any potential to make a profit. This is most evident in Laughlin's acquisition of *A Balance of Quinces,* which led to protracted negotiations over the length of Reece's text and the best methods of color-plate reproduction. I'm glad the two men stood firm against the cost-cutting counsels of the New Directions staff, for *A Balance of Quinces* is a fine and fascinating tribute to Davenport's visual imagination.[21] His drawings, meticulous networks of crow-quill cross-hatching, present copies of photographs in intricate and meaningful juxtaposition. His painting is at its best when he eschews realism and deploys bold colors in strong contrastive masses—Davenport the painter is something like the love child of Mondrian and Stuart Davis.

* * *

Davenport was a widely published author of fiction when New Directions accepted *A Table of Green Fields* in 1992. But he was also a late starter. He had taken a class in creative writing as an undergraduate at Duke (William Styron and Mac Hyman of *No Time for Sergeants* were classmates), but the experience had "paralyzed" him, and he did not return to writing fiction until he was forty-three (GD/JL 96). The first story he wrote, "The Aeroplanes at Brescia," was collected in *Tatlin!* (1974), and seven further books of stories followed. (His last, *The Death of Picasso,* presents a selection of both stories and essays, some of them previously uncollected.)[22]

I tend, perhaps unfairly, to bung Davenport's fictions into two rough-and-ready categories: those that recreate the lives and milieus of historical figures (artists, writers, philosophers), and those that revolve around the sexual awakening of young boys. The stories in the former category are of a piece with Davenport's essays: they represent his attempts to inhabit the sensibilities of people who have conceived the world in extraordinary ways, seeing further or more clearly than those around them. No fewer than five feature Franz Kafka, such as "The Aeroplanes," in which Kafka and Max Brod visit an air show in Italy; Kafka muses on a castle on a distant mountain (Brunnenberg, where Pound would spend some of his later years) and becomes fascinated by a curly-haired, intense Austrian in the crowd, who turns out to be Ludwig Wittgenstein. "Tatlin!" concerns the maverick Russian architect and artist Vladimir Tatlin, while "1830" (*Tatlin!*) is narrated by Edgar Allan Poe, who inhabits a fantasy world, half St. Petersburg and half Classical Greece, that is radically unlike his own hardscrabble American-Grub-Street reality. As in Pound's early poems, where we hear the voices of Bertran de Born, Arnaut, or Simon Zelotes, in Davenport's stories we hear Santayana (in "Dinner at the Bank of England," *The Cardiff Team*), Kierkegaard (in "Mr Churchyard and the Troll," *A Table of Green Fields*) and Victor Hugo (in "John Charles Tapner," *Da Vinci's Bicycle*). "I don't think I have an ego," Davenport once admitted to Laughlin. "That is, I have nothing to say for myself, or as from myself" (GD/JL 97). Davenport's fiction is precisely *not* an exploration of the self but rather, in the best modernist tradition, a *made* thing, a fashioned artifact.

But then there are those mutually masturbating boys, whole Dutch pornographic libraries of them, who dominate Davenport's later collections. In story after story, young boys begin tentative physical relationships, go hiking and camping, and are taken under the wing of wise, learned, handsome men who teach them to appreciate the delights of their own and each others' bodies. Davenport sets these stories for the most part in Holland or Denmark, but their true setting is Utopia: his sexually awakening boys—tousle-haired "spadgers" and "nippers"—inhabit a kind of imaginary space in which eros, companionship, and affection can flourish untrammelled. Their world is a playing-out of the ideal of Charles-Marie Fourier's "phalansteries," utopian communities in which provision was to be made for every human proclivity, in which "body is not bruised to pleasure soul." In Davenport's fiction, sexual exploration is part and parcel of a holistic process of *learning,* of finding one's physical and spiritual place in the world. His prepubescent boys are as anxious to tackle calculus, astronomy, and Greek aorist verbs as they are to discover the workings of each other's anatomy.

It's a brave and in many ways charming vision, and I appreciate the deftness with which Davenport explores the varieties and vagaries of affection across social strata and generations; but in the end it all gets a little *dull,* I'm afraid. The utopian bracketing of Davenport's little Fourieran wonderlands is manifest: this is, after all, not to be confused with the real world, where sexual relations are always power relations, where, as Angela Carter puts it, sex is "the most self-conscious of all human relationships, a direct confrontation of two beings whose actions in the bed are directly determined by their acts when they are out of it."[23] But utopian fantasies have an uncomfortable way of bleeding into the world outside of the page. I'm told that it's not uncommon to meet the odd white supremacist at Pound conferences, convinced that the poet is the great unrecognized laureate of the Aryan cause. Similarly, Davenport's fictions have a kind of icky currency among the more literary of the "man-boy love" crowd.

* * *

At its best, Davenport's fiction is a triumph of what he calls, in "The House that Jack Built" (an essay on Ruskin and modernism), "Daedalian art": "Between Ruskin and Browning, Pound's first master, we can see the invention of Daedalian art in literature: the discovery that only in that intricacy which the Greeks called *poikilia*—cunning craftsmanship—can complexities of meaning beyond inherited styles of narrative and poetry be summoned into play" (GI 48). In Daedalian art, linear storytelling (X happens, then Y), familiar to us from Daniel Defoe to Jonathan Franzen, is displaced by the juxtaposition of images, as in a Brakhage film or a modernist poem; causal relationships (X makes Y happen) are set aside in favor of relationships of coincident or contrastive form. The "cunning" craftsman is one who weaves these images, forms, and verbal coincidences into complex patterns—prose analogues, almost, of the Celtic knotwork on the initial pages of the Book of Kells. "Au Tombeau de Charles Fourier" (*Da Vinci's Bicycle*) is exemplary in this regard, a tightly knit story that brings together Gertrude Stein, Picasso, the Wright brothers, Fourierian utopianism, Davenport's 1974 conversation with Samuel Beckett, wasps, and the incredibly complex cosmology of the Dogon people of Mali, all of these forged into a single emblem for the perennial urge to forage and discover.

Andre Furlani's *Guy Davenport: Postmodern and After* is a careful, even exhaustive exploration of Davenport's aesthetic, with special attention to his essays and fiction.[24] Furlani really can't be beaten for close readings of the stories, but he makes rather heavy weather of periodizing Davenport as a modernist rather than a postmodernist. In this he follows Davenport himself: "I come too late as a Modernist and too early for the dissonances that go by the name of Postmodernism," he writes in the postscript to *Twelve Stories*.[25] If one views modernism as a quest for the continuities underlying the apparently discontinuous, and postmodernism as the renunciation of that quest, then there's no arguing with Davenport. But Furlani won't settle for calling Davenport a modernist outright, nor will he allow him to be a "late modernist"; instead he coins the awkward term "metamodernist," which both acknowledges Davenport's modernist affinities and asserts a kind of "afterness" to his work not to be confused with the unmoored experimentation of postmodernism. I'm unconvinced, and not merely because when it comes to terminology I took Occam's razor to heart decades ago. Davenport was quite happy to be considered a modernist pure and simple, and wore his "belatedness" as a kind of badge of honor. Indeed, his accounts of Joyce, Pound, and David Jones suggest that a sense of belatedness—of having come *after*, of being at a distance from the originary springs of culture—is intrinsic to modernism itself.

The past spreads itself out in a vast panorama before us, but much of it is fragmentary—bits and pieces of Sappho, the ruins of Knossos, the photographs of Tatlin's destroyed sculptures. Davenport's self-appointed task was not so much to recreate the wholeness from which those fragments came as to tease out the affinities among them, and to make their constellated arrangement gesture back to a remote past that, through the continuity of culture, is still alive to us. As he has the second-century traveller Pausanias remark in "The Antiquities of Elis," "How old the world!"[26]

* * *

In my early years of reading Davenport, I was tantalized by the fact that the man himself lived in Lexington, not far from my Tennessee hometown. At the time, living in Lexington seemed to me an eminently reasonable thing to do. Both my parents had grown up in western Kentucky; my uncles subscribed to the Louisville *Courier-Journal,* not because it was better than the Murray or Paducah papers, but so they could follow the University of Kentucky Wildcats in more detail. But I soon figured out that in both the academy and the literary world of writers, Davenport's choice was seen as something of a perverse self-exile, like living in a Merlin's hermitage tucked in an out-of-the-way corner of an eighteenth-century formal landscape, or a stint at Yaddo that had become nightmarishly permanent. Why not New York or San Francisco? Why didn't he teach at the University of Chicago, or Yale, or, like Kenner, Johns Hopkins?

When I knew I was going to be in Louisville, a mere hour's drive from Lexington, for a conference one February, I plucked up my courage and asked Davenport if I might visit. By all means, he replied, though my visit would come perilously close to that of a David Jones biographer. So one evening, I navigated the achingly beautiful hillscape between the two Kentucky metropolises, found my way to Sayre Avenue, sat fidgeting in the car for a few minutes, and finally walked onto the front porch and rang the doorbell. It was to be the first of maybe a dozen visits, all of them scheduled around that same Louisville conference, except for one time when I visited to interview Davenport for my Louis Zukofsky biography.

As I discovered that first evening, Guy was graying, paunchy, and far more Southern in accent and manner than his prose had given me to expect. His house was an unremarkable two-story affair. What struck me most was its cavelike aspect. There were bookcases everywhere, and every flat surface was stacked with papers and more books. The bits of wall not obscured by bookshelves were crowded with photographs, drawings, and paintings. There was no television. The detached garage had been converted into a painting studio that was a marvel of clean wood and bright colors, all Mondrian and aseptic Scandinavian lines. Out there he proudly showed me Zukofsky's tiny, fragile, rush-bottomed chair ("that's the chair in which he wrote *'A'*!"), rescued by a friend from a Long Island dump after it had been damaged in a flood and discarded. Back in the house, there was a worktable modeled on the one Pound made for his Kensington apartment.

Guy's front room was designed for the *tête-à-tête.* Before the fireplace, where he would begin the visit by ceremoniously "laying" a fire, two leather recliners with ottomans faced each other. One sat, ashtray and coffee at hand, and one talked. Or rather, since one's interlocutor was Guy Davenport, one mostly listened. Often Guy would talk about what he'd been reading. The canonical went without saying—he knew his Shakespeare, his Dickens, his Shelley and Coleridge. He had worked his way through all thirty-nine volumes of Ruskin's works, and had spent a summer with Sir Walter Scott's twenty-seven Waverley novels. One time he lamented that he might not get around to reading all of Bulwer-Lytton. He hated, however, the notion of "erudition." "How can I shake and dispel the awful reputation of being an 'erudite' writer?," Guy wrote Nicholas Kilmer in 1979; "I'm about as erudite as a traffic cop. I like to know things; what's so two-headed peculiar about that?"[27]

"Erudition" was the armor of the half-educated. I recall vividly his snort of disgust at Edward Dahlberg's reference to "Diodorus Siculus, the Sicilian"—"Doesn't he know that 'Siculus' *means* 'from Sicily'?"

If anecdotes dotted Guy's essays like currants in a pudding, they dominated his conversation. It was in talking with Guy that I came to realize the value such brief stories held for him: they were not merely diverting tales, but "luminous details" that (in Pound's words) give "sudden insight into circumjacent conditions, into their causes, their effects, into sequence, and law."[28] That's perhaps a bit highfalutin—but an eyewitness story, Guy felt, could sometimes offer something unobtainable from books. Often I found his own accounts shifting my sense of things. For instance, he once brought up Richard Avedon's 1958 photograph of Pound, in which the poet's face is screwed up into a knot of seeming pain, and which has been taken for evidence of his regret. Nothing of the sort: "He's looking for a word," Guy said. "That's the face he would make when he couldn't get the word to come. I saw it a thousand times at St. Elizabeths." (Guy had a similar word-searching face, usually accompanied by a hand pressed to the side of his head, as if he could squeeze the elusive name or title from his brain to his lips.)

Despite his reputation as a hermit, I gathered from Guy's conversation that he had a pretty constant flow of visitors. (His letters to Kilmer and Laughlin confirm this.) One evening he told me, with some pride, of an Orthodox Jewish correspondent who wanted to drop by, but whose only free day in Lexington fell on *Shabbat.* The visitor talked it over with his rabbi, describing Guy's writings, artworks, and general view of the world, and they agreed that the interdict on Sabbath travel could be waived just this once: after all, it was obvious that this Davenport was a true *tzadik.*

* * *

For all the range and allusiveness of Davenport's writings, he saw himself as a rather simple human being, motivated by straightforward urges that he discusses in three of his rare "personal" essays: "Finding" (in *The Geography of the Imagination*), "On Reading" (*The Hunter Gracchus*), and "II Timothy" (ditto). "On Reading" traces his love of books back to its primordial sources: his Aunt Mae, caretaker of the "small library of my uncle Eugene, a soldier in World War I, buried in France a decade before my birth," and Mrs. Cora Shiflett, a neighbor in Anderson, South Carolina, who lent the young Guy a Tarzan novel that belonged to her son Clyde, serving a decade "in the penitencher." "I was thought to be retarded as a child, and all the evidence indicates that I was," Davenport writes. "No teacher in grammar or high school ever so much as hinted that reading was a normal activity, and I had to accept it, as my family did, as part of my affliction as a retarded person" (HG 20–21).

If Davenport's reading life began with that Tarzan novel, Antonia Vallentin's *Leonardo da Vinci* (borrowed from a pious neighbor who chose the volume from the Book-of-the-Month Club on the strength of *The Last Supper*) taught him "that what I liked in reading was to learn things I didn't know." He was never one to read what one "ought to be reading," or to take a teacher's word for what to value or ignore: "In truth, my education was a systematic misleading. Ruskin was dismissed as a dull, preacherly old fart who wrote purple prose. In a decent society the teacher who led me to believe this would be tried, found guilty, and hanged by the thumbs while being pelted with old eggs and cabbage stalks. I heard in a class at Duke that Joyce's *Ulysses* was a tedious account of the death of Molly Bloom. An Oxford don assured me that Edmund Wilson is an astute critic. Around what barriers did I have to force my way to get to Pound, to Joyce, to William Carlos Williams?" (HG 24) What is remarkable is not merely the stubborness with which he followed the impulse "to learn things I didn't know" despite institutional discouragement, but the contagious excitement with which he presents his findings: how many people have read *Fors Clavigera,* Doughty's *Dawn in Britain,* and Marcel Griaule's accounts of Dogon cosmology, and managed to convince readers that all three are indispensable?

"II Timothy" represents Davenport's attempt to come to terms with his upbringing in the Baptist Church, where the gospel was anything but "good news": "It was bad news, dreary and dull all the way. With adolescence came a questioning of it all. To identify bigotry and narrowmindedness in a Southern Baptist congregation is no great feat. Our church was for white people only; some members of it belonged also to the Ku Klux Klan. Miss Lottie Estes told us in Sunday School that Jesus' nudity on the cross was far more painful to him than the nails in his hands and feet" (HG 66). With his mature reading of the Bible, however, Davenport came to recognize some of the virtues of Christianity: "What Jesus had done was to cancel the classical idea of fate, to silence the oracles, to unify the human spirit under one dominion, which each of us is to find in our heart. Others were to be another self, treated as such. The bond would be love, respect, loyalty, a kinship for which the metaphor would be that we are all children of one father. So redeemed, Cain would embrace Abel rather than kill him" (69–70). In an interpretation of the New Testament familiar from Emerson down through Liberation Theology, Davenport goes on to declare that Jesus's message was perverted by Paul ("a bald and seriously bearded official, born to administrate"), who "inadvertantly divided us all again" and "made Christianity a preparation for fullest life, rather than the fullest life itself" (HG 67, 70).

Happily, the Sundays of Davenport's youth were not entirely devoted to "the tediousness of Sunday School and the appalling boredom of church" (GI 359). After dinner, the entire family would pile into the car and drive through the countryside to look for Indian artifacts. Davenport recalls those quasi-archaeological excursions in "Finding," perhaps the most conventionally "personal" of his essays. The act of searching, of wandering through fields with concentrated, downcast eyes, was simultaneously communal and private: "'I've found one!' the cry would go up from the slope of a knoll, from the reaches of a plowed field, a gully. One never ran over; that was bad form. One kept looking with feigned nonchalance, and if one's search drew nigh the finder, it was permissible to ask to see. Daddy never looked at what other people found until we were back at the car. 'Nice,' he would say, or 'That's really something'" (GI 360). Worthless finds were unceremoniously chucked out the car window. But it's clear that precisely *what* one found was less important than the searching itself, participating as an independent member in a shared family enterprise.

Davenport knew nobody else who spent Sunday afternoons as he did. The unspoken eccentricity of the family's outings—they were never mentioned to his grandmother, for "the thought that her daughter, son-in-law, and their children walked all over fields and meadows in public would have sent Granny Fant to her bed with a vinegar rag across her forehead" (GI 363)—taught him something about how the various provinces of one's life are sequestered from each other, without implicit criticism. "My family, praises be unto the gods, never inspected anything *we* enjoyed doing . . . . Consequently I spent my childhood drawing, building things, writing, reading, playing, dreaming out loud, without the least comment from anybody." The outings also trained him in the art of looking, and of "foraging, that prehistoric urge still not bred out of man" (GI 366–67).

Given this quirk in his upbringing, it's not surprising that so many of Davenport's poems, essays, and fictions dramatize the process of foraging, or take as their heroes artists, thinkers, and makers driven by a thirst to learn things they don't know, and to share those things with others in relationships of loving mutual discovery. In the third volume of *Modern Painters,* Ruskin states his own ethics of looking and writing in phrases that—minus the hyperbole—encapsulate Davenport's ethos: "The greatest thing a human soul ever does in this world is to *see* something, and tell what it saw in a plain way. Hundreds of people can talk for one who can think, but thousands can think for one who can see. To see clearly is poetry, prophecy and religion,—all in one."[29]

Another point of affinity between Davenport and Ruskin is their Ludditism. Ruskin's was of a piece with his pastoral medievalism, and expressed itself in particular as a revulsion against the railway—he was horrified at seeing the countryside despoiled by bridges and embankments that facilitated the meaningless movement of people who ought to be satisfied with their surroundings ("now, every fool in Buxton can be at Bakewell in half-an-hour, and every fool in Bakewell at Buxton"[30]). Davenport's *bête noire* was the automobile, "the mechanical cockroach that has eaten our cities" (GI 78). (He never learned to drive.) In the view of both writers, the increasing pace of modernity has undermined the communities that make possible the creation and transmission of culture. Where Ruskin lamented how modernity has laid waste the single-minded faith and aesthetic simplicity of the Middle Ages, Davenport takes the Spenglerian position—he read Spengler early on, and was strongly influenced by him—that we live in the declining days of the West.

But decline and doom were never his preoccupations. Like his modernist forebears, Davenport had his eyes firmly fixed on the past, forever seeking out its gleaming shards. There is perhaps too little of the *future* in his vision, aside from a Utopia of childhood. All of his works are founded on a few deeply pursued insights, a limited gamut of themes rehashed in dozens of variations—but that could be said of Beckett's, of Zukofsky's, of Joyce's works as well. What makes Davenport's essays, poems, and fictions enthralling, ultimately, is their coruscating richness of detail, their precision of language, and their almost evangelical enthusiasm.

Notes

1. John Ruskin, *Works*, 39 vols., ed. E. T. Cook and Alexander Wedderburn (London: George Allen, 1903–1912) 35, 29.

2. Guy Davenport, *The Geography of the Imagination: Forty Essays* (San Francisco: North Point, 1981) 80; hereafter cited parenthetically in the text as GI.

3. Guy Davenport and Jonathan Williams, *A Garden Carried in a Pocket: Letters 1964–1968*, ed. Thomas Meyer (Haverford, CT: Green Shade, 2004) 125; hereafter cited parenthetically in text as GCP.

4. Guy Davenport, *The Hunter Gracchus and Other Papers on Literature and Art* (Washington, DC: Counterpoint, 1996) ix; hereafter cited parenthetically in text as HG.

5. Guy Davenport and James Laughlin, *Selected Letters*, ed. W. C. Bamberger (New York: Norton, 2007) 18; hereafter cited parenthetically in text as GD/JL.

6. Michael Schmidt, *Lives of the Poets* (London: Weidenfeld and Nicolson, 1998) 740.

7. Charles Olson, *The Maximus Poems*, ed. George F. Butterick (Berkeley: U of California P, 1983) 100.

8. James Joyce, *Ulysses: The Corrected Text*, ed. Hans Walter Gabler et al. (New York: Random House, 1986) 273–74; Don Gifford with Robert J. Seidman, *Ulysses Annotated: Notes for James Joyce's Ulysses*, rev. and expanded ed. (Berkeley: U of California P, 1988) 365.

9. T. S. Eliot, "Tradition and the Individual Talent," *The Sacred Wood: Essays on Poetry and Criticism* (1920; London: Methuen, 1960) 51.

10. Erwin Panofsky, *Three Essays on Style*, ed. Irving Lavin (Cambridge, MA: MIT P, 1995) 127–64.

11. Guy Davenport, *Every Force Evolves a Form: Twenty Essays* (San Francisco: North Point, 1987) 155.

12. Qtd. in Guy Davenport, *A Table of Green Fields: Ten Stories* (New York: New Directions, 1993) 77; hereafter cited parenthetically in text as TGF.

13. Guy Davenport, *Flowers and Leaves: Poema vel Sonata: Carmina Autumni Primaeque Veris Transformationum* (1966; Flint, MI: Bamberger Books, 1991) 10; hereafter cited parenthetically in text as FL.

14. Guy Davenport, *Thasos and Ohio: Poems and Translations 1950–1980* (San Francisco: North Point, 1986) 9.

15. Davenport, *Thasos and Ohio* 13–14.

16. Ezra Pound, "How to Read," *Literary Essays*, ed. T. S. Eliot (1935; New York: New Directions, 1968) 34–35.

17. Guy Davenport, *7 Greeks* (New York: New Directions, 1995) 85–86; hereafter cited parenthetically in text as SG.

18. Guy Davenport, *Archilochos, Sappho, Alkman: Three Lyric Poets of the Seventh Century B.C.* (Berkeley: U of California P, 1984) 79; Davenport's later, to my mind inferior, rendering of the lyric can be found in *7 Greeks* 69.

19. Guy Davenport, "Fragments from a Correspondence," ed. Nicholas Kilmer, *Arion* 13.3 (Winter 2006): 89–130.

20. Rather too much personal disclosure: the published version of *A Garden Carried in a Pocket* included material that Davenport had specifically insisted be omitted; its inclusion led to a final break between Davenport and Williams (GD/JL 139n.).

21. Erik Anderson Reece, *A Balance of Quinces: The Paintings and Drawings of Guy Davenport* (New York: New Directions, 1996).

22. Guy Davenport, *Tatlin!* (New York: Scribner's, 1974), *Da Vinci's Bicycle* (Baltimore: Johns Hopkins UP, 1979), *Eclogues* (San Francisco: North Point, 1981), *Apples and Pears* (San Francisco: North Point, 1984), *The Jules Verne Steam Balloon* (San Francisco: North Point, 1987), *The Drummer of the Eleventh North Devonshire Fusiliers* (San Francisco: North Point, 1990), *A Table of Green Fields*, *The Cardiff Team* (New York:

New Directions, 1996), and *The Death of Picasso: New and Selected Writing* (Washington, DC: Shoemaker & Hoard, 2003). A full description of most of Davenport's writing can be found in Joan Crane, *Guy Davenport: A Descriptive Bibliography 1947–1995* (Haverford, CT: Green Shade, 1996).

23. Angela Carter, *The Sadeian Woman and the Ideology of Pornography* (New York: Pantheon, 1979) 9.

24. André Furlani, *Guy Davenport: Postmodern and After* (Evanston, IL: Northwestern UP, 2007).

25. Guy Davenport, *Twelve Stories* (Washington, DC: Counterpoint, 1997) 236.

26. Davenport, *Da Vinci's Bicycle* 138.

27. Davenport, "Fragments from a Correspondence" 100.

28. Ezra Pound, "I Gather the Limbs of Osiris," *Selected Prose, 1909–1965*, ed. William Cookson (New York: New Directions, 1973) 22.

29. Ruskin, *Works* 5.333.

30. Ruskin, *Works* 27.86

II
Shorter Takes

The Piety of Terror

Ian Hamilton Finlay

In 1943, the Scottish poet Hugh MacDiarmid wrote John Lehmann, editor of *New Writing*, in order to introduce the eighteen-year-old Ian Hamilton Finlay, whom he described as "A very delightful and most personable young fellow, extremely well read and with excellently developed interests in literature and the arts."[1] It was an auspicious beginning for a literary relationship that would over the next two decades turn quite sour indeed. Finlay too was a poet, but one who had little patience either for MacDiarmid's devout socialism or for the "synthetic Scots" literary language that the older poet had pioneered in the early decades of the century. Finlay's first volume of poems, *The Dancers Inherit the Party* (1960), was written for the most part in English, with occasional gestures toward the Orkney dialect with which Finlay had grown up (it includes, as one of its "Orkney Lyrics," "Mansie Considers the Sea in the Manner of Hugh MacDiarmid," a blunt swipe at MacDiarmid's tendency to refer all matters to Marx). His second volume, however, *Glasgow Beasts, an a Burd* (1961), was a series of animal metamorphosis poems cast in an almost impenetrable working-class Glaswegian dialect. In this volume, Finlay's poetry was already beginning actively to intersect with the visual—specifically, a series of papercuts by John Picking and Pete McGinn. *Glasgow Beasts*, along with *The Dancers,* brought Finlay to the attention of a number of American poets, including Roberts Creeley and Duncan, Louis Zukofsky, and Lorine Niedecker; and his editing of the periodical *Poor. Old. Tired. Horse.* and of the Wild Hawthorn Press cemented that transatlantic connection, giving those same Americans a Scottish publication venue.

But MacDiarmid, by this point in his career at that awkward juncture where *enfant terrible* becomes elder statesman of Scottish letters, vehemently rejected Finlay's Glaswegian poetry—not on account of its failure *as* poetry, but because it was written in a Scots vernacular he considered inherently unsuitable *for* poetry: as he wrote in 1970, contemporary urban Scots "is not the kind of Scots in which high poetry can be written, and what can be done in it . . . is qualitatively little, if at all, above Kailyard level."[2] When in the mid-sixties Finlay, following tendencies already evident in his work, turned from poetry in conventional typography to more cross-generic modes of concrete poetry and multimedia, MacDiarmid denied the younger poet's works the status of poetry altogether: in a 1965 letter to Tom Scott regarding the *Oxford Book of Scottish Verse*, which Scott was then editing, MacDiarmid wrote that Finlay's work "has nothing in common with what down the centuries, despite all changes, has been termed 'poetry'. . . I am utterly unwilling to have any poems of mine included in an anthology in which any of Finlay's productions are also included."[3]

In the very public conflict between these two poets,[4] high modernism—the poetic revolution represented in England and America by Eliot, Pound, Moore—comes face to face with a late modernism that presents itself as nemesis or critique, rather than as fulfillment or continuation. That MacDiarmid, a modernist poet of the stature of an Eliot or a Pound—not to mention the unquestioned progenitor of Scots poetry in the twentieth century—would completely bar Finlay's work from the very category of poetry, is indicative of the extent to which Anglo-American (though *not* French or Russian) literary modernism, even as it blurs the generic borders between prose and poetry, fiction and nonfiction, nonetheless jealously guards the boundaries between the literary and the visual arts. The visual arts, far from being the favored site of cross-generic experimentation, as they are for such continental poets as Apollinaire, represent for MacDiarmid and other Anglophone modernists a transgression beyond the limits of the literary, beyond the bounds of a "tradition" which, however it might be altered and expanded, remains a fundamentally *verbal* one.

But Finlay's work is more than a digression from the mainstream of Anglophone modernist poetry; its particular late modernism (a term which Finlay, I am sure, would vehemently reject, preferring to categorize his art as "neoclassical") represents a sustained "revolutionary" critique of the whole project of Enlightenment and post-Enlightenment Western thought, including the literary ideologies of both Romanticism and high modernism. MacDiarmid's attack on Finlay is an episode in literary politics, a falling-out motivated by both personal and aesthetic considerations: but it is oddly proleptic on MacDiarmid's part, for Finlay's work has in the last two decades proven to be a singularly compelling assault on the fundamental tenets of the rationalist modernity with which MacDiarmid so strongly identifies.

* * *

The extent to which important Anglophone modernist writers have attempted to break down the boundaries between the verbal and the visual was for many years a well-kept secret in canonical histories of poetic modernism, and in perpetuating this misrepresentation—this repression—literary critics were simply following the lead of the poetic-critical establishment nominally headed by T. S. Eliot. Eliot, as evidenced best in his "Burnt Norton," is consumingly interested in the Word made flesh—but only in the flesh of divine incarnation: his orthodoxy does not stretch to encompass the word made flesh in visual and material shapes. For poetry criticism after Eliot (and indeed until recently),[5] the American concrete poet Bob Brown does not exist; Blake and David Jones, despite the evidence of their incomparable composite arts, are primarily verbal artists; and if such poets as Charles Olson and Susan Howe disrupt and deform the conventions of typography, such deformations are mere disturbing static, and do not really nudge these writers' poetry from the realm of the verbal into some more ambiguous space.

MacDiarmid, of course, subscribes wholly to the ideology I perhaps parody here. While even Pound, in the decorated capitals of the first publications of his early Cantos, ventured into the ambiguous space between visual and verbal representation, MacDiarmid's work early and late is irreducibly linguistic, with no tincture of the visual, plastic, or musical arts. I would imagine that MacDiarmid's critique of Finlay's later work, if perhaps a trifle outraged, is essentially identical to what Eliot or Pound would have offered, given the extent to which Finlay has ruptured with traditional modes of poem-making, both modernist and earlier. In sharp contrast to most of the British poets of his generation, Finlay has in the decades since his break with MacDiarmid pursued a complex and both aesthetically and ethically difficult course, navigating between the realms of poetry, the plastic arts, gardening, and cultural criticism. Since his turn from strictly verbal to more concrete modes of poetry, he has created "poems" in a variety of media: stone, plaster, bronze, neon, embroidery, and, most ambitiously, the medium of a full-scale garden, his Little Sparta, in progress since 1967. These poems, especially to the extent that they situate the semantic properties of their words within a visual and conceptual field, thereby displacing the purely verbal, simultaneously return poetry to its etymological roots as *poeisis*—"making"—and propose a radical redefinition of the relationship of reader to poem, a radical renegotiation of the meaning-making contract implied in the poetic act: the act of reading a poem is no longer a matter of making sense of a given string of verbal signifiers, but now includes more importantly the puzzling out of the relationship among a given set of words (sometimes, a single word), the medium in which it is instantiated, and the surroundings that form its context.

One key to the complex balance of verbal and extraverbal elements that makes up Finlay's work, and perhaps a indication of why MacDiarmid rejected that work so aggressively, lies in the notion of the textual fragment, both as it is originally theorized by the Romantics, and as it is appropriated and altered by the high modernists. It doesn't do to monolithize either of these groups, but it's worth comparing Finlay's use of ostensibly fragmentary linguistic structures to what I see as representative fragments, and thinking about fragments, by poets before him. The continuities and contrasts cast light on Finlay's overall project and on the relationship of that project—critical, destructive, and simultaneously retrospective—to earlier cultural projects. The fragment, which is so often fetishized and nearly glorified in Romantic and modernist practice, becomes a crucial index of the distance between Finlay's late modernism/neo-Classicism and the cultural moments upon which his own poetic practice is built.

Consider for instance Finlay's proposed inscription for a tree-seat, in his 1979 *Monteviot Proposal*, a two-line "poem" that reads "of flutes / & wild roses." In the first place, this "Proposal" as a whole seems a somewhat anomalous project for a late twentieth-century poet, modeled as it is upon the eighteenth-century English garden designer Humphry Repton's "Red Books," "in which he proposed 'improvements' to the country estates of his clients."[6] For what it's worth, the relationship Finlay is proposing between the artwork and its audience, or between the artwork and its patron, is radically different from the somewhat unreflective post-Whitmanian democracy the typical American verbal poet takes for granted. The apparatus accompanying the *Proposal* notes with regard to the tree-seat inscription (and it is unclear to me to what extent this text is by Finlay's collaborator Nicholas Sloan and to what extent by the poet himself), "Clearly this inscription is not a 'poem' as we know it, but equally short fragments appear in recent translations of Archilocus, Alkman & Sappho" (VP 123). The writer here clearly has in mind Guy Davenport's translations of these three archaic Greek poets; Davenport translates every extant syllable of these poets' work; in contrast however to translators who would fill out these fragmentary texts into "complete" poems, he declines to speculate what words might have intervened between the meager scraps that remain to us of many of, say, Sappho's poems. Two of his translations, chosen pretty much at random from his Sappho, read "[ ] / around / you, Atthis / clouds / [ ]" (104), and "] him [/ [ ] /] becomes [."[7] Behind these translations lies the complex history of the modernist appropriation of the fragment, outlined in detail in Hugh Kenner's *The Pound Era*.[8] Kenner dates the modernist renaissance of the fragment to such works as Pound's "Papyrus" (1916), where the poet, instead of worrying over what might be missing from the poem at hand (a mere three words, a few stray letters, and three lines from a parchment published in Berlin in 1902), translates and presents the scrap as it stands, asserting the status of the poetic, not merely for the poem itself, but for the fragment of the poem.

It is just as useful in approaching Finlay, however—who is nothing if not a backward-looking artist—to look not only to high modernism, but also to the dawn of European Romanticism: the Jena *Athenaeum* group and its leader, Friedrich Schlegel, who himself theorized and perfected the fragment *as* literary form. In his *Athenaeum Fragments*, Schlegel notes, "Many of the works of the ancients have become fragments. Many modern works are fragments as soon as they are written."[9] This dictum makes a crucial distinction between the work that time or mischance has made a fragment, and the work composed *as* fragment. As Davenport puts it in the introduction to his translations from the Greek, "Many of [these] fragments are mere words and phrases, but they were once a poem, and, like broken statuary, are strangely articulate in their ruin,"[10] such a fragment, then, is much like the "colossal Wreck" of Shelley's "Ozymandias," the eloquent but fundamentally incomplete remainder of a "shattered" whole. (The implied equation of fragment and ruin is not coincidental here; as Philippe Lacoue-Labarthe and Jean-Luc Nancy point out in their study of the *Athenaeum* group, "The philological fragment, especially in the tradition of Diderot, takes on the value of the ruin."[11])

Schlegel's own fragments, however, are not the result of time and decay, but a purposeful gesture toward a new conception of genre, of the literary itself. Schlegel describes his conception of the literary fragment: "A fragment, like a miniature work of art, has to be entirely isolated from the surrounding world and be complete in itself like a porcupine."[12] As Lacoue-Labarthe and Nancy comment, "The detachment or isolation of framentation is understood to correspond exactly to completion and totality."[13] On the one hand, Romanticism's reading of the historical fragment or ruin works forcefully to suggest a lost totality; the fragment gestures back toward Coleridge's "pleasure dome," or Goethe's "Land wo die Zitronen blühn." At the same time, however, the Romantic fragment *per se*—that is, the work composed *as* fragment, rather than the abandoned or defaced work—is intended to be paradoxically both self-contained, autonomous—and, simultaneously, patently fragmentary. This is again in line with Schlegel, who characterizes Romantic poetry as essentially incomplete: "It should forever be becoming and never be perfected."[14]

But what are we to make of Finlay, and his purportedly fragmentary inscription? The text of *The Monteviot Proposal* quotes Robert Kennedy, who claims that Finlay "creates poetry by providing words with a rigorously controlled & potently significant environment" (VP 123). It is in Finlay's manipulation of words' environments, or contextual frames, that he breaks with the traditions of both the Romantic and the modernist fragment. The Romantic fragment is a world unto itself, "isolated from the surrounding world," but simultaneously the indicator of a desired but unreachable ideal wholeness; the modernist fragment—Davenport's Sappho, Pound's "Papyrus"—like the Romantic ruin, is an index that points back toward a lost *historical* totality. Finlay's tree-seat inscription occurs in a proposal for an entire garden, and its brief text—"of flutes / & wild roses"—, rather than standing alone, refers outward to a number of other elements of the garden. "Flutes," for example, is to be associated with the fluted columns that Finlay would place at intervals in the garden, with the pan-pipes of Mallarmé's "L'Après-midi d'un faune," whose first line—"Ces nymphes, je les veux perpétuer"—appears in the garden, and with "the sound of the breeze" (VP 123). The "wild roses" are real wild roses, planted throughout the garden, twining around the columns. The Mallarmé line—in English, "These nymphs, I would perpetuate them"—refers to the trees planted in the garden: "the nymphs are to be understood as the trees, and the need to 'perpetuate' them is explained by the setting of the inscription—on a felled or fallen tree."

The inscription on the tree-seat, then—"of flutes / & wild roses"—is a fragment in neither the Romantic nor the modernist sense: it serves neither as the occasion to meditate on a lost spiritual whole, nor as the surviving index of a historical moment now fallen into desuetude. Formally speaking, it is in no way detachable from its context, "complete in itself like a porcupine." Rather, the tree-seat "poem" is an element of the larger garden as a whole. It is a syntagm in the larger signifying complex of the entire piece, and seems fragmentary and abbreviated only when read out of context. When read *in* context, either in the garden itself or in the voluminous documentation and commentary of Finlay and Sloan's proposal for the garden, the inscription becomes replete with meaning, replete with resonances and echoes both to earlier texts—literary, visual, historical—and to other elements in the garden itself. Finlay regards such documentation and commentary, by the way, as an essential element of his work; they serve the necessary purpose of "connect[ing] the reader with the tissue of tradition" (VP 192) out of which the works proceed: such citational practice, one might argue, is akin to Pound's deployment of textual fragments, "luminous details," in *The Cantos*. But Finlay's aim, unlike Pound's, is not to gesture back toward a lost historical unity, or some previous state of wholeness before the intervention of philistinism, or usura, or whatever: it is rather literally to *create* that scene of aesthetic and moral plenitude, to reinstate for the garden's "reader" the classical wholeness toward which Keats's "Ode on a Grecian Urn," for instance, looks backward.

What such the quest for such Classical—or, more accurately, neo-Classical—wholeness would indicate is that there is in Finlay's work an ethical element which can be obscured by no amount of postmodernist irony. His restless experimentation in form and media, his avant-gardism, coexists with a severe, almost puritanical Classicism and a moral traditionalism: This is clearest in his decades-long and consistent championing, against the grain of much contemporary poetry and art, of the aesthetic—the beautiful—as the aim of the artist/poet. *The Monteviot Proposal*, for instance, clearly aims to create a garden that is *beautiful* in the balance of its proportions, the harmony of its elements—beautiful in a quite traditionally Classical sense. Finlay is thoroughly aware that he can no longer be a Classical artist; but being a neo-Classical artist, however fraught with postmodernist doubt and ironizing self-division that position might be, is a stance no less morally responsible. Indeed, neo-Classicism, given the catastrophic history that has intervened between the ancients and ourselves, is if anything a position of greater ethical weight than the painfully sincere moralism of such modernists as Pound and MacDiarmid. As Finlay writes, "Neo-classicism emulates the classical while at the same time withholding itself. Classicism aims at Beauty, neo-classicism at Virtue."[15]

Finlay, as the sternness of these aphorisms might imply, is also a poet of the sublime, the aesthetic that terrifies or transfixes; he is concerned, not merely with reinstantiating a Classical aethetic and moral order, but with uncovering a set of paradoxes at the heart of Western enlightenment, oppositions that he places under the sign of *terror*. This is clearest when he deploys the visual iconography of the French Revolution. Finlay is intensely attracted to the neo-Classicism of Revolutionary imagery, the manner in which French artists and intelligentsia, like the Americans before them, adopted the slogans, images, and characters of the Roman Republic to represent their own enterprise[16]; and even as Finlay evidences considerable fascination with (and, it seems at times, admiration for) the terrorism of Robespierre and Saint-Just, he makes clear that the worship of nature and the Utopianism of such pre-Revolutionary *philosophes* as Rousseau and Diderot cannot be extricated from the violence of the axe and the guillotine. His deployment of the image of the guillotine is clearest evidence of this, especially in the 1984 "Terror/Virtue" medal, on one face a guillotine with the inscription "Terror," on the other a visual "rhyme," a pair of corinthian columns with the inscription "Virtue" (VP 259). Note as well the 1989 print "Two Landscapes of the Sublime," which "rhymes" a guillotine and a waterfall (VP 273), and the 1987 "Both the garden style . . .": the latter print pictures a guillotine overgrown with blooming honeysuckle, and has as text, "Both the garden style called 'sentimental', and the French Revolution, grew from Rousseau. The garden trellis, and the guillotine are alike entwined with the honeysuckle of the new 'sensibility'" (VP 275).

But one cannot emphasize too much that Finlay's recognition of the symbiosis of terror and virtue is no facile deconstruction, no predictable New Historicist archaeology of the entertwined roots of the political and the aesthetic. As Finlay's keenest commentator Stephen Bann notes, "Nothing could be further from the truth . . . Finlay is concerned, on the contrary, to place as much emphasis as he can on the didactic aspect of the neoclassical reference [in the "Terror/Virtue" medal]. With regard to the present-day ideology which would like to dispense at one and the same time with Terror and Virtue, Finlay affirms their interdependence. They are two sides of the same medal."[17] Nor, despite the irony that pervades Finlay's work, is it a variation on familiar postmodern motifs of incongruity. Rather, Finlay would have us recognize, as did the ancients who saw their most pastoral scenes inhabited by deities capable of stunning violence and capricious cruelty, that any experience of nature, Rousseauvian, Romantic, or otherwise, must include a recognition of that violence that makes such peace possible. Where Poussin placed a skull in his grove—"Et in Arcadia Ego"—Finlay, neo-Classically, finds there a camouflaged Nazi tank.

Finlay's more recent fascination with the iconography and architecture of Nazi Germany is simply a further exploration of the dual nature of the project of Enlightenment rationality. In the 1970s, Finlay carried on a correspondence with Albert Speer, Hitler's foremost architect, imprisoned since the Nuremberg Trials. The result was Finlay's 1979 series of watercolors, *A Walled Garden*, based on the garden that Speer cultivated within the walls of Spandau Prison in Berlin. Finlay's 1982 project, "The Third Reich Revisited," is based on the grandiose neo-Classical construction projects that the Nazi architects were never able to bring to completion, and acts as ironic commentary upon the pallid public art and architecture that postwar European democracies have produced. As Finlay comments, "It was—is—an attempt to raise (in a necessarily round-about way) the questions which our culture does not want to put in idea-form" (VP 141). Finlay's 1987 work *Osso*, which raised a firestorm of protest when it was first exhibited in Paris, interpolates the Runic lightning bolts of the Nazi SS into the Italian word "bone," emphasizing how the horror of the Third Reich has, in our century, insinuated itself into the most fundamental of natural substances. Nature has lost its innocence; we can no longer confront any element of our phenomenological world without acknowledging that the irrationality of Nazism has always already been there.

Like Pound, with his physiocratic faith in the agricultural basis of wealth,

MacDiarmid, a perennial believer in the efficacy of the scientific method and the inevitable dictatorship of the proletariat, is as clear an uncritical child of the Enlightenment as one could ask for; one can only note that his rejection of Finlay's work, though certainly unsustainable on aesthetic grounds, seems uncommonly prescient with regard to the implications of that work for his own cherished shibboleths. Finlay's tutelary deity is both Classical Greek and Jacobin, "*Apollon Terroriste*"—depicted in a bronzed bust that is itself a visual poem, the name engraved on the figure's forehead—and Finlay's poetry is essentially a terrorist act: in the first place, as it breaks down the boundaries between the verbal and the visual in a manner that Anglo-American modernism had proved far too timid to essay; and, perhaps more importantly, as it uncovers and lays bare the foundations of rational modernity, foundations laid in terror and arbitrary violence. Finlay's generic transgressions, ostensibly Classical in their ordered restraint, mime the violence (however deceptively restrained) that lies at the heart of that order. What is sublime in his work—both terrifying and beautiful—is the manner in which Finlay accepts the necessity of that violence, accepting as well the moral responsibility implicit in the adoption of a virtue whose obverse is necessarily terror, an Apollo whose profession is "terrorist." Finlay is fond of the aphorism of Saint-Just's "Terror is the Piety of the Revolution": in Finlay's poetry of the verbal, visual, concrete, and conceptual, Terror and Piety are ultimately inextricable, and ultimately point toward Revolution.[18]

Notes

1. Hugh MacDiarmid, *Letters*, ed. Alan Bold (Athens: U of Georgia P, 1984) 596.

2. MacDiarmid, *Letters* 687. The late-nineteenth century "kailyard" (cabbage-yard) school in Scottish literature represented a kind of sentimentalized ruralism that MacDiarmid had vehemently repudiated.

3. MacDiarmid, *Letters* 703.

4. One can see the transatlantic repercussions of the clash in Lorine Niedecker's correspondence with Louis Zukofsky; in 1962, she transcribes a letter from Finlay in which he recounts MacDiarmid's attack on Finlay's periodical *Poor. Old. Tired. Horse*; see *Niedecker and the Correspondence with Zukofsky, 1931–1970*, ed. Jenny Penberthy (Cambridge: Cambridge UP, 1993) 313. See also Penberthy, "A Posse of Two: Lorine Niedecker and Ian Hamilton Finlay," *Chapman 78–79* (1994): 17–22.

5. One sees the beginning of a shift in the late 1980s and early 1990s, when Jerome McGann, in *Black Riders: The Visible Language of Modernism* (Princeton, NJ: Princeton UP, 1993), and Cary Nelson, in *Repression and Recovery: Modern American Poetry and the Politics of Cultural Memory 1910–1945* (Madison: U of Wisconsin P,

1989), drew attention to the works of Bob Brown, and McGann, in *The Textual Condition* (Princeton, NJ: Princeton UP, 1991), and Lawrence Rainey, in *Ezra Pound and the Monument of Culture: Text, History and the Malatesta Cantos* (Chicago: U of Chicago P, 1991), examined the hitherto ignored visual dimensions of the early publications of Pound's *Cantos*.

6. Yves Abrioux, *Ian Hamilton Finlay: A Visual Primer* (Cambridge, MA: MIT P, 1992) 121; hereafter cited parenthetically in text as VP.

7. Guy Davenport, *Archilochus, Sappho, Alkman: Three Lyric Poets of the Seventh Century B. C.* (Berkeley: U of California P, 1980) 116.

8. Hugh Kenner, *The Pound Era* (Berkeley: U of California P, 1971) 54–75.

9. Friedrich Schlegel, *Philosophical Fragments*, trans. Peter Firchow (Minneapolis: U of Minnesota P, 1991) 21.

10. Davenport, *Archilochus, Sappho, Alkman* 14.

11. Philippe Lacoue-Labarthe and Jean-Luc Nancy, *The Literary Absolute: The Theory of Literature in German Romanticism*, trans. Philip Barnard and Cheryl Lester (Albany: State U of New York P, 1988) 42.

12. Schlegel, *Philosophical Fragments* 45.

13. Lacoue-Labarthe and Nancy, *The Literary Absolute* 43.

14. Schlegel, *Philosophical Fragments* 32. On fragmentation and ruin in Romantic thought, see Thomas McFarland, *Romanticism and the Forms of Ruin: Wordsworth, Coleridge, and Modalities of Fragmentation* (Princeton, NJ: Princeton UP, 1981) 3–55.

15. Ian Hamilton Finlay, *Inter Artes et Naturam* (Paris: ARC, 1987) n. pag.

16. Robert Rosenblum's *Transformations in Late Eighteenth Century Art* (Princeton, NJ: Princeton UP, 1967) is the single most complete examination of the manner in which the French Revolution adopts neo-Classical imagery and techniques. A useful study of Revolutionary neo-Classicism as it impinges upon Romanticism is Jean Starobinski, *1789: The Emblems of Reason*, trans. Barbara Bray (Charlottesville: U of Virginia P, 1982).

17. Finlay, *Inter Artes et Naturam* n. pag.

18. Since this essay was composed, there has been a real efflorescence of writing on Finlay, including the collections *Wood Notes Wild: Essays on the Poetry and Art of Ian Hamilton Finlay*, ed. Alec Finlay (Edinburgh: Polygon, 1995) and *The Present Order: Writings on the Work of Ian Hamilton Finlay*, ed. Caitlin Murray and Tim Johnson (Marfa, TX: Marfa Book Co., 2010). Little Sparta has been examined at length in John Dixon Hunt, *Nature Over Again: The Garden Art of Ian Hamilton Finlay* (London: Reaktion, 2008), and lavishly illustrated in Jessie Sheeler, *Little Sparta: The Garden of Ian Hamilton Finlay*, photographs by Andrew Lawson (London: Frances Lincoln, 2003). Most important, however, has been the publication in the "Poets for the Millennium" series of Ian Hamilton Finlay, *Selections*, ed. Alec Finlay (Berkeley: U of California P, 2012).

Mules and Drugs and R&B

Harryette Mullen

The title of Harryette Mullen's fourth book, *Muse & Drudge*, names two roles women have assumed in Western poetry: ethereal, idealized aesthetic prompter, and manual laborer.[1] Before each great male poet stands a beautiful, inspiring muse; behind him, sweeping up the crumpled drafts and scrubbing the spilled ink, crouches a drudge—all too often, as in Milton's case, his own wife or daughter. But Mullen's title consists as well of two verbs, processes with which every poet is familiar: the protracted, wool-gathering musing that precedes actual composition, and the endless drudgery of whipping that composition into shape. One of the great joys of this book is how Mullen makes it all seem so easy: the language here dances, shakes, and splits itself into puns, allusion, and double-entendre, all the while maintaining a jaunty funkiness that can encompass both the joyful depression of lovelorn blues—"she wants to know is it a men thing / or a him thing" (149)—and the marriage of sorrow and joy that Du Bois analyzed in the African American spiritual—"Jesus is my airplane / I shall feel no turbulence / though I fly in a squall / through the spleen of Satan" (174). *Muse & Drudge* is a unrelentingly energetic poem, marrying the earthiest of African American vernaculars with a sophisticated lyrical sensibility, a complexly ironical social critique, and a moving emotional substructure: as the book describes it, this is a "slave-made artifact / your salt-glazed poetry / mammy manufacture / jig-rig nitty gritty"; or, four lines later and more simply, a "last chance apocalypso" (163).

Trimmings and *S*PeRM**K*T*, Mullen's two most recent books, were virtuoso exercises in prose poetry, merging Gwendolyn Brooks's high-spirited vernacular with the polysemic new sentence of Gertrude Stein's *Tender Buttons*. *Trimmings* played lovely and salacious riffs on the ways that women dress themselves and are in turn dressed (and undressed) by society; it wove its sixty brief swatches out of yarns of feminine sexuality and feminine adornment, dwelling especially on the implications of the West's "feminine" colors—white and pink—for a woman whose skin is emphatically brown. *S*PeRM**K*T*

(I don't need to emphasize the title's double significance) overlaid the realms of the bedroom and the supermarket, braiding and entwining the vocabularies of eating and making love, and—more darkly—noting how often sex, like grocery shopping, seems to wind up at the cash register, how the libidinous gaze reduces the beloved's body to a piece of meat—weighed, shrink-wrapped, and priced.

Muse & Drudge is also a sexy poem, but in this book Mullen has cast her conceptual net into historical and musical waters, in the process drawing in any number of remarkably odd fish. Mullen herself refers to the book as "Mules and Drugs," and that particular pun—which appears only in passing in the poem itself (172), but which Mullen emphasizes in a note on the book[2]—puts us firmly in the realm of the African American experience, yesterday and today: from the promised (and withheld) forty acres and a mule to the crack cocaine of the 1980s and 1990s urban scene. The first three quatrains introduce us to some of Mullen's obsessions:

Sapphire's lyre styles
plucked eyebrows
bow lips and legs
whose lives are lonely too

my last nerve's lucid music
sure chewed up the juicy fruit
you must don't like my peaches
there's some left on the tree

you've had my thrills
a reefer a tub of gin
don't mess with me I'm evil
I'm in your sin (99)

There is music here: the lovely assimilation of bluesy Sapphire and amorous Sappho, whose lyre has become some sort of coiffure device; there is love, sexuality, and bereavement: the proffered but untouched "peaches," straight out of the vocabulary of the blues; there is the artificial paradise of drugs and the intangible paradise of faith, here conflated in the "reefer," "gin," "evil," and "sin" of the third quatrain.

I am of course gesturing toward images and themes, but it's far more difficult to pinpoint what the poem is "saying" at any given point. You can do that fairly readily with many poets, from Shakespeare down to Allen Ginsberg. Mullen's technique, however, resists paraphrase pretty much completely, and one learns to take delight in the way words' and phrases' meanings shift, morph from line to line and even within a single line. "Styles" in "lyre styles" sounds like a noun, but the next line's "plucked eyebrows" makes it a verb as well. "Bow" could be the bow of a stringed instrument (noun), but even as a single adjective its implications in "bow lips" and "bow legs" are radically different. There is an exhilarating jumping between levels of diction: "lucid music" sounds like the painstaking lyrical structures of Zukofsky or Creeley, only to shift into the pop culture of Juicy Fruit Gum, which in turn becomes assimilated both to the "peaches" of the blues lyric and the Forbidden Fruit of the Garden of Eden.

Mullen delights in gesturing at but narrowly missing the expected phrase. One looks twice at "you've had my thrills" to make sure she hasn't written the lifeless "you've had *your* thrills," and the book as a whole is packed with such deflected clichés. "Up from slobbery," she writes, "the soles of black feet / beat down back streets" (144); "if you can't stand / sit in your soul kitsch" (105). And, coldly, "you have the girl you paid for / now lie on her" (120). Standing in the bulky and poker-faced shadow of Samuel Johnson, we've come to deplore the pun as the lowest form of humor; but the Renaissance playwrights certainly didn't think so, nor do most poststructuralist critics, for whom puns seem to be the driving force of many analyses of poetry. I'm not giving anything away by mentioning that Mullen is a lively and theoretically sophisticated cultural critic, well versed in all manner of French double-talk. As one might expect however from the author of *Trimmings*, whose title conflates adornment, pruning, and an African American term for the vagina, she wears her theory refreshingly lightly. While one can read *Muse & Drudge* as a poem that is deeply engaged with current theories of poetic language and subject-formation, it demonstrates that engagement precisely through its revisions of and variations on the spoken language. "Write on the vagina / of virgin lamb paper / mother times mirror / divided by daughter" (112) riffs on Jacques Lacan and various post-Lacanian French feminists, but it does so protected by a lambskin condom. The Mirror Stage here becomes both a newspaper and an element in a familial equation, and even the act of writing—horrors!—is subsumed in a hearty "right on!" The revered Saussurean signifier is conflated with signifying, both in the Shakespearean—"signifying nothing"—and the African American senses, and the deconstructive impossibility of determinate meaning finds its objective correlative in "your arms too short to box with God": "everlasting arms / too short for boxers / leaning meaning / signifying say what" (131). (And of course, one can't overlook that Everlast is a brand of boxing gear, boxers a type of underwear. Whenever one tries to paraphrase this work, one's left with what I suppose Derrida would call a "supplement"—"say what" indeed!)

The overwhelming exuberance and multiplicity of Mullen's language—its "leaning meaning" quotient—prevent her poem from becoming a tract, though it deals with matters of deep seriousness. *Muse & Drudge* has hard words for the industries of skin lightening and hair straightening and the color divisions within the African American community: "what we sell is enlightenment / nothing less than beauty itself / since when can be seen in the dark / what shines hidden in dirt" (132); "mellow elbow lengthy / fading cream and peaches / bleach burn lovingly / because she's worth it" (141); "pass the paperbag / whether vein tests / the wild blue / blood to the bone" (140). History has indeed, as Mullen writes, been "written with whitening" (143). There's a great preoccupation here with the outward signs of blackness, the specifically African American adornments of the Jheri Curl, the conk, and the ironed hair: "dippy tresses bagged / in plastic do-rag" (157); "my head ain't fried / just fresh rough dried / ain't got to cook / nor iron it neither" (145). But there's also a profound and tragic awareness of Black American history, of the legacies of slavery and racism that have shaped African American artistic expression. The plastic bag of the Jheri Curl shifts here into Aunt Jemima's headrag, just as Hamlet's desire for self-extinction evokes (by way of a jazz title) the slaves' longing for Africa: "the folks shuffle off / this mortal coffle and / bamboula back to / the motherland" (129).

In contrast to the prose poems of her earlier volumes, *Muse & Drudge* is written in what the eye registers as a fairly regular form, four quatrains to each of its eighty pages, "using," as Mullen puts it, "rhyme and rhythm inconsistently and, I hope, unpredictably."[3] The blues lyric of course can be lineated in quatrains, as is the ballad form that Dickinson makes such varied use of. Mullen gestures toward each of these "conventional" forms (as well as toward rap, the dozens, and the most hackneyed of all contemporary modes, free verse), but manages to keep her readers consistently off balance, surprised by rhyme or disappointed at its absence. Just as she plays high-velocity chicken with verbal clichés, Mullen avoids, often by a hair's breadth, the form or formlessness that she leads us to expect.

In other words, this poem is the work of a highly intelligent and resourceful lyric talent. This is evident, not merely in the way the quatrains hang together, but in the sonic dance the individual words play with one another. Mullen is especially fond of the aural chiasmus, the "crossing" of sounds (compare Keats's "truth is beauty, beauty truth"). Note how, in "a voyeur leers / at X-rated reels" (162), the "leers" flip-flops its consonants into "reels." The poem's first line is an especially compacted example: "Sapphire's lyre styles" shifts the initial "s" sound of "Sapphire" to the line-end position of "styles," while repeating the "ire" in "lyre"; in a second chiasmus, the "ly" of "lyre" flips into the "yl" of "styles." Out of such minute machining of language—what a more hasty poet might dismiss as simple drudgery—Mullen makes an echoing and ingenious music.

This is a poem with scores of subtexts and a whole passel of referents, "the songs of allusion," as Mullen puts it at one point. A poem with a cast of thousands: Mullen has worked to make *Muse & Drudge* speak in the voice, not merely of one poet, or of the Black woman in general, but of the entire African American tradition, from the Malian Dogon people—"I wouldn't be long gone / I'd be Dogon"(109)—to the Black Arts Movement's Larry Neal—"on the other side of far" (138)—and everything in between (and far beyond). It's not a poem weighed down by its forebears, however; like Ishmael Reed's *Mumbo Jumbo*, *Muse & Drudge* aims to joyously and jazzily "update old records / tune around the verses / fast time and swing out / head set in a groove" (125).

In the end, there is a deep sadness to *Muse & Drudge* that is largely absent from *Trimmings* and *S*PeRM**K*T*. This might be described most simply (too simply) as the legacy of the blues. In her note "Telegraphs from a Distracted Sibyl," Mullen quotes an old bluesman: "If it wasn't for women, we wouldn't have the blues."[4] Perhaps the hardest, most deeply realized strand of *Muse & Drudge* is that of disappointed love, the bereavement and unfaithfulness that fuel so many blues lyrics. That such loss is articulated in the voice of the black woman emphasizes to what degree the social and spiritual hardships of the African American experience have fallen upon her shoulders. She has been both muse and drudge, and now, a "men harnessed mule," has been (like the horse in my mother's aphorism) "rode hard put away wet" (123). "Was I hungry sleepy horny or sad," the poem wonders, "on that particular occasion" (171); whichever it may be, "dead on arrival / overdosed on whatever / excess of hate and love / I sleep alone" (122).

But this strain of loss—this lament, if you will, for the losses of Everywoman—cannot obscure the complex joy and high spirits of the poem as a whole. Mullen, despite—or perhaps because of—her repeated disavowal of the poetry workshop's personal "voice," has achieved a powerful voice in her poems, a voice that draws from the whole spectrum of African American experience to create, in the face of the tragic and tangled litany of losses that experience represents, a dense, important, and fundamentally triumphant poetic object. The poem's ending, fittingly, begins with a hymn and ends with an injunction:

just as I am I come
knees bent and body bowed
this here's sorrow's home
my body's southern song

cram all you can
into jelly jam
preserve a feeling
keep it sweet . . .

proceed with abandon
finding yourself where you are
and who you're playing for what stray companion (178)

And so should we all.[5]

Notes

1. Harryette Mullen, *Muse & Drudge* (Philadelphia: Singing Horse, 1995). Mullen's previous books are *Tree Tall Woman* (Galveston, TX: Energy Earth Communications, 1980), *Trimmings* (New York: Tender Buttons, 1991), and *S*PeRM**K*T* (Philadelphia: Singing Horse, 1992). I will cite *Muse & Drudge* parenthetically from its most recent publication as part of *Recyclopedia: Trimmings, S*PeRM**K*T, and Muse & Drudge* (St. Paul, MN: Graywolf, 2006).

2. Harryette Mullen, "Telegraphs from a Distracted Sibyl," *American Book Review* 17.3 (February–March 1996) 5.

3. Mullen, "Telegraphs from a Distracted Sibyl" 5.

4. Mullen, "Telegraphs from a Distracted Sibyl" 5.

5. Since this essay was written, Mullen has published two other books of poems, *Sleeping with the Dictionary* (Berkeley: U of California P, 2002) and *Urban Tumbleweed: Notes from a Tanka Diary* (St. Paul, MN: Graywolf P, 2013); *Tree Tall Woman* and other early works have been reprinted in *Blues Baby: Early Poems* (Lewisburg, PA: Bucknell UP, 2002).

Woodpaths, Obscure

Norman Finkelstein

Some seven centuries ago, a Florentine poet began his long poem in the midst of a dark wood, having gone astray from the straight path. Dante's *selva oscura* is a forest, Norman Finkelstein implies, in which we still wander. But is there a track through these woods, or is the forest a "collage," "an endless expanse of commentary"?

> The collage is the only version
> the only version of the forest
> in which there is no repetition
>
> but an endless expanse of commentary
> Listen carefully
> as something disappears.[1]

Track is trackless. This volume, the first installment of an open-ended project whose title brings to mind Robert Duncan's "Passages," is a single poem—or a series of poems—invoking the obliquities of Dickinson's fascicles or Kafka's parables. Unlike those parables, however, these lines disclaim realistic portraiture or singular "motif":

> In these operations
> no single motif
> or portrait
>
> called Emily or K
> so long as the letters
> arrive to be destroyed. (13)

This is an epistolary poem, one suspects, a series of letters—and this becomes explicit further on in the book, where lines begin "Dear J," "Dearest K," "Dear

M"—in which the condition of the dead letter office has become the state of all correspondence.

But even "series" is wrong for the elements of this poem, implying a sequence in which one statement, one image follows another in some logical progression. Instead, the fragments that make up *Track* constitute a collection of paths, of *Holzwege* through a dark, trackless wood that which gives way to no comedy, divine or otherwise. The book is a "track," but to what end? Martin Heidegger entitled one of his essay collections *Holzwege*—literally "wood-paths"—, a title rendered by his French translators *Chemins qui mènent nulle part*, "paths which lead nowhere." It's not that the poetry of *Track* leads nowhere, precisely, but that each of the various movements—or segments, or sections, or what have you—constitutes a new approach, a new track into a labyrinthine forest: a forest, one ultimately realizes, of language.

The ultimate source of such a poiesis, of course, is Biblical: the Torah, that primal, most familiar, and radically *strange* book; and the multiple layerings of commentary and interpretations that make up the Jewish textual tradition. "One thinks of the decalogue . . . Here the lines intersect / Here the lines are parallel / Thou shalt not thou shalt" (42). Like endlessly multiplying midrashim, the poems of *Track* both promise and withhold closure, seem to point in determinate directions but then veer off in others:

> This history
> this biography
>
> A frenzy
> of interpretation
>
> Suppose
> it were to lead elsewhere
>
> No inscriptions
> or erasures. (44)

But this is only supposition—"Suppose," as well, "there were only numbers" (45), a phrase that gestures toward the kabbalistic practice of *gematria*, or number-divination. (Each of the letters of the Hebrew alphabet has a numerical value; according to the Jewish mystical tradition, then, "words or phrases whose letters are equal are at some level meaningfully connected."[2]) But only *gestures:* "so much for rules / / about words or numbers."

> So much repetition
> in the beckoning depths
> it cannot be encompassed

by parts of speech
so that everything connects
or nothing does. (14)

Finkelstein is too serious, too *Western* a poet literally to base his practice on the shuffling of the numerical values attached to letters. Or rather—for *gematria* can be an endlessly subtle and engrossing practice—he hasn't quite the faith in the numinous qualities of letter and number that would allow him wholeheartedly to count: "everything connects / or nothing does." The sections of *Track* are indeed numbered, but they are headed not by numbers themselves—1, 2, 3, etc.—but by the emptied-out sign of number: "#." (Larger divisions are headed "##.") Anti-gematria.

Duncan, late in his life, arrived in a similar neighborhood when he began to leave the poems of "Passages" unnumbered. They would no longer be a sequence—from Latin *sequor*, "follow"—but a cluster, a constellation of poems that could be entered at any point, read in any order. The "order" of "Passages," then, is something like that described in a sentence of Emerson's Finkelstein paraphrases: "The center is everywhere / and the circumference nowhere" (85). But Finkelstein—no Transcendentalist he—has fashioned in *Track* an order both looser and more vexed than Duncan's. To renounce number and sequence altogether, as Duncan did, bespeaks a homespun, very American antinomianism. To renounce number and sequence, but simultaneously to cling to the *sign of number*—for every "#" that appears in *Track* (and they are on almost every page of the book) can only remind the reader of the ordering principle the poet has renounced—is an act of troubling responsibility. In an era of textual freeplay, of bacchanalian indeterminacy, we would have our poets sever their bonds completely. Perhaps Finkelstein himself desires such freedom—freedom from titles, from numbering—but part of the pact in which his poetry engages is precisely to acknowledge the ultimate incoherence of pure freedom. Pythagoras found a divine order in number. For Finkelstein, the trace of number, the doubled crucifix of the #, is the fingerprint of a *deus absconditus*.

Perhaps I make too much of typography; multiplying commentary, however, is very much in the mode of the Talmudic ruminations to which *Track* repeatedly alludes, and which in part provide the poem a model:

In some versions
there are many versions
and in some versions only one

around which the commentators
weave endless versions
as if to explain. (21)

A single event-text, about which weave endless commentaries ("Eden gives way to forest")? Or endless initiatory moments ("forest gives way to Eden" [22])? Is there an ur-text on which these fragments of verse comment, or do they gesture toward Eden (a moment in which God would walk in company with his human creations), only to deny that moment any historicity? Of course they do—there is no ur-text to *Track*, but Finkelstein is fascinated with the myth of originary wholeness precisely *because* it is myth. We have no Acropolis, we latter-day Romantics, but the ruins of the Parthenon enthrall us as no whole Parthenon could. Like the Wailing Wall, they take on holiness in part through their very dilapidation:

> The ruins were holy
> wholly ruins
>
> The fathers came and went
> fathers found there
>
> We had come this far
> entering the present
>
> Only holy ruins
> wholly in the present. (64)

The Talmud is an echo chamber of voices, arguing over millennia. *Track* is as well haunted by voices, fragments of others' words that enter the poem and unsettle its surface. There are dying words: Jack Spicer's—"My vocabulary / did this to me"—and Emily Dickinson's—"Little Cousins, / Called back" (56). There is T. S. Eliot's claustrophobic description of history—"the contrived corridors / the cunning passages"—and Paul Celan's *faux naïf* description of his own poetics—"*Ganz und gar nicht / hermetisch*" (95). There is Genesis: "And the seven lean ones / ate up the seven fat ones" (70). And, in a bizarre moment—

> all the combinations
> all the coincidences
> take on a spooky radiance
>
> caled the bright light of shipwreck
> called the gentle flame of his story
> strong light of the canonical (71)

—George Oppen finds himself where he would never be in life, in company with Harold Bloom. Unlike the rabbis of Edmond Jabès's *Book of Questions* (and its many sequels), who argue, speculate, and parabolize at a hyper-

Talmudic rate, such outside voices enter *Track* only in bits and pieces, broken sentences picked up on a late-night channel-surf, foundation stones stumbled upon in a weedy meadow or beside an overgrown forest trail.

They are, that is, bits of ruins. But ruins are perhaps the fundamental condition of our knowledge, or at least of the ways that would lead us to knowledge:

Sightseers should note
the grandeur of the architecture
though much is in ruin

on the road to K
also called Gnosis
in some texts. (15)

Dante's ultimate moment of knowledge—we ought not to venture to call it a *gnostic* moment—came in a vision of the godhead, "the Love that moves the sun and the other stars." Finkelstein's *Track*, if it can be said to "arrive" anywhere, arrives at a rapprochement with ruination that recalls Ferdinand's joyful cry in *The Tempest*—"Let me live here ever!" (4.1.122):

Only in the present
entering the ruins
fathers found there
came and never left

I want to live
here forever
what you have given me
came and never left. (64)

In our present wandering condition—textual wandering, mid-life wandering—there is still the opportunity for perhaps the nearest experience to *gnosis* we can reach: human love.

Say in this sentence
two people are in love

Say love come quietly
at the end of the sentence

which has no ending

This bed they center is,
these walls thy sphere . . .

So that in the space evacuated
by a retreating deity

Two lovers embrace. (84–85)

It would be disingenuous, and untrue to the complexities of Finkelstein's poem, to claim that love settles all uncertainties, or serves as the panaceic human consolation in an uncertain world, as if *Track* were a postmodern rewriting of Arnold's "Dover Beach." The passage I have quoted is far from the last in the book, which ends on a far more unsettled note. But this arrival at love is for me one of the most luminous moments in *Track*, and its "spooky radiance" consoles one in the "cunning passages" and "contrived corridors" of the poem's darker movements.

The darkness is indeed all around us here—in the vibrating, buzzing confusion of a media society, in the still jarring echoes of the Holocaust, and in the chilly "space evacuated / by a retreating deity." But *Track*, with its impressive array of forms, tones, and voices, excavates an exhilarating variety of paths through that darkness. Only a fool would deny love its enlightening—perhaps preëminent—place in the poem. MFA programs and creative writing manuals, the favorite whipping-boys of the avant-garde, have made suspect the notion of a poet's achieving his "voice": who wants to find a voice, only to sound like everyone else? The voices of Finkelstein's *Track*, however, as various as they may be, speak to the heart of an unsettled time. Following them, we may not see precisely where the paths are leading, but we know we're getting *somewhere*.

Notes

1. Norman Finkelstein, *Track: A Poem* (Bristol, Eng.: Shearsman, 2012) 22; hereafter cited parenthetically in text. While this essay deals only with the first installment of this long poem—*Track* (New York: Spuyten Duyvil, 1999)—*Track: A Poem* collects that volume along with its sequels, *Columns: Track, Volume Two* (New York: Spuyten Duyvil, 2002) and *Powers: Track, Volume Three* (New York: Spuyten Duyvil, 2005).

2. Jerome Rothenberg, *Gematria* (Los Angeles: Sun & Moon, 1994) 165.

A New Negative Capability

Michael Heller

Every poem worth the reading clears its own space in the imagination of the reader, its own verbally constructed *mise-en-scène*—whether the "lone and level sands" of Shelley's "Ozymandias," the nightmare seascapes of Coleridge's Mariner, or the alas rather claustrophobic seventeenth-century dumbshows in which I've always mentally staged George Herbert's spiritual dialogues. Some poems, however, are more closely bound to particular places, particular terrestrial landscapes: Yeats's evocations of Ireland, Bunting's "Briggflatts," Rukeyser's *Book of the Dead*. Michael Heller's poems, now available in their imposing entirety in *This Constellation Is a Name*, more often than not take *place* in both a figurative and a literal sense, for Heller brings a traveller's—not a tourist's, mind you—keen observing sensibility to bear on everything around him.[1]

There are a lot of poems of literal travel here—Spain, France, England, the Far East—and there are a number of "vacation poems" (the Hamptons, Colorado), but Heller's most familiar stomping grounds as poet are the streets and neighborhoods of New York City, where he has lived his entire adult life, and the subtropical surrealism of Miami Beach, where he lived as a child (as recalled in his affecting memoir *Living Root*[2]). These cityscapes—"builded places," to echo the title of Heller's 1989 collection, *In the Builded Place*—are rich sites both of present experience and of layered memory, personal and historical.

Heller's early experiences of poetry were in the company of friends trained like him as scientists and working as technical writers in New York, and through them (Hugh Seidman, in particular), he came to know the work of Louis Zukofsky and the other "Objectivist" poets: those laureates of observation left him "convinced of a common / / clarity" (C 14). Zukofsky's spare, angular lines leave their mark on Heller's language, but far more lasting has been his meditation on the works of George Oppen, whose own difficult idiom is at the service of a fundamentally *ethical* vision of the poem. For Heller, as for Oppen (and for that matter, Paul Celan, who said "I cannot see any basic difference between a handshake and a poem"[3]), the poem is always a matter of communication, of one's person reaching out to another. "I suspect," Heller writes in "At Albert's Landing," "That mine is a poetry of clouds," perhaps no more than a notation of the passing phenomena of the world. The woods through which he and his son walk is "no paradise," "Just the real," but:

> Things lean and lean, and sometimes
> Words find common centers in us
> Resonating and filling speech.
> Let me know a little of you. (C 160–61)

The tension underlying all of Heller's poetry is that between the poem as communication, as spoken address, and the poem as autonomous artifact, sonorous but self-referential verbal object (perhaps, in Mallarmé's words, "Aboli bibelot d'inanité sonore"—*abolished tchotchke of sonorous emptiness*[4]). In "Fifty-three Rue Notre-Dame de Nazareth," Heller admits to being "another legatee of Mallarmé," having "played with the exclusionary pun," "strained against the tongue / Until the word displaced / The world's foreign body" (C 264). And in "To Postmodernity," he observes how "Some of the poets"—Mallarmé's more intransigent avant-garde heirs—are "anxious to disconnect / the dots and words," to expose "by luxuriant asides" "our non-being / and the certain emptiness of death, / the passivity needed to survive / the modern . . ." All very well, Heller grants—

> And yet love's obliquity
> is still a language,
> a tutory mastery of desires
> and hurts, leaps and kneelings
> at the utterance of a name. (C 358)

Like a self-assured Philippe Petit, Heller's poetry walks (and often dances) a tightrope suspended between linguistic play and felt experience. "Experience," however, is for Heller far more than just the individual's ongoing narrative (though he writes very affectingly indeed of his love for his wife and his memories of his family): it includes the rich cultural humus of every place he visits, the resounding historical echoes inhabiting the most seemingly insignificant made object. If Heller's New York is the New York of his uncle Nat and grandfather Zalman, it is also the New York of Walt Whitman and Edgar Allan Poe; his Paris is stalked by the presences of Baudelaire and Walter Benjamin, among whom he is a kindred flâneur.

I've always thought of Heller as a thrifty poet, chary both of his words and of his publications: a poem here, a poem there, a substantial collection every decade or so. But behold!, with *This Constellation Is a Name* one suddenly realizes that Heller has over the last forty-five years been building a more than impressive life's work—an *oeuvre*, as it were. To the central collections *Accidental Center* (1972), *Knowledge* (1979), *In the Builded Place* (1989), and *Eschaton* (2009), *This Constellation* adds gatherings of poems from the very beginning of Heller's career, "new" poems included in his two earlier selected volumes, and poems accreted over the past half-decade. It all adds up to some 550 pages of cunningly crafted, impressively varied, always assured, and very often deeply moving verse, a shining testament to the vocation Heller recalls in "Logobiography":

Letter will lead to letter.

This you knew when first
you spelled a word.
. . . .
This you knew.

Hearing a poem,
you knew this.

Those days—casting words about
until a line promised

to echo nothing
that you'd heard

And then, this you felt:

to make such a life
had been required of you

when first you heard a word. (C 511–12)

* * *

The prose works collected in Heller's *Uncertain Poetries: Essays on Poets, Poetry and Poetics* span some two decades, from the early 1980s to the first years of the new millennium.[5] They take various forms: theoretical essays, book reviews, lectures, examinations of individual poems. Some of their most telling pages are in the autobiographical mode of *Living Root*: parts of "Poetry

Without Credentials," much of "Encountering Oppen." But through all of these writings runs a ground bass most clearly adumbrated in the 1995 essay "The Uncertainty of the Poet." "What the literary artist experiences," writes Heller, "is a recognition that he or she has been drawn down a corridor made of words, pulled or birthed into and surrounded by language in all its manifestations. Our entrapment, our sentencing to language, terminates, as the poet Paul Celan punned, only in the parole of death" (U 3). Such immersion, even entrapment, in language is a historical event, a condition that has only come to light with the rise of twentieth-century philosophies of language, from Saussure and Wittgenstein to the poststructuralists.

But as we are entrapped in language, as we swim in it as a medium, are unable to see any outside to it (Wittgenstein: "*The limits of my language* mean the limits of my world"[6]), that very entrapment presents the contemporary poet with a paradox, an "uncertainty" manifested as the collision of two "nearly incompatible" yet "unavoidably interdependent" (U 4) views of language. The one is post-Saussurean, formalist—best exemplified in the poststructuralists—and holds that language is a "labyrinth" of self-referential "patterns, prestructurations, language games, self-contained linguistic envelopes." The word is "governed not by its relation to the objects it might name but by a design, authorial, cultural, musical." (The primary figure of such a vision of language, though Heller does not name him such, is of course Mallarmé; Heller sensitively reviews Henry Weinfield's translation of Mallarmé's poems in *Uncertain Poetries*.)

The other view of language, a "Romantic or traditional" view, takes language as a system of referential signs: "language, although it is patterned and has form, is yet endlessly combinatory, not because it is self-referential and manipulable, but because signs are constantly trying to pattern the flux of what exists beyond language" (U 4). It is in his attitude toward this older, commonsensical conception of language that Heller's scientific training shows itself. The death of a Cartesian linguistic vision, in which "clear and distinct" formulations stood in a relationship of self-evidently *true* correspondence to the world which they modelled, does not mean that language has been entirely cut loose from its moorings in the world. As any scientist knows, and especially in the wake of Einstein and Heisenberg, the languages and sign-systems of the sciences cannot provide absolute truths about the world: but that does not lessen the validity of progressive, constantly revised attempts to "pattern the flux of what exists beyond language." Such attempts are all that language has ever really aspired to, has ever really been able to achieve. Those attempts, in the end, are our linguistic way of being-in-the-world.

Heller is a poet of no illusions concerning the dream of a perfectly adequate language; at the same time, however, he is unwilling to cut himself adrift on the free play of unmoored signifiers. Such free play, he argues, is the end-product of the Language Poets' more radical experimentations, which he thinks about in "Avant-garde Propellants of the Machine Made of Words": "Once we try to claim for a work that it is non-expressive or non-referential, that its resonances as language no longer matter (a claim which by any test must fail), we have trivialized it out of existence. For what happens in some 'language-centered' writing is not so much that we are freed but that we are *severed* from even considering the social meaning of freedom by being delivered into the polymorphous pleasures of the non-referential—*plaisirs du texte* indeed, but privatized and unavailable for the social agenda which many of the language poets claim lies at the base of their work" (U 217). There has been a longstanding, once lively but by now very old argument about the "social agenda" of Language Poetry, and the degree to which its more "non-referential" exemplars serve that agenda. Heller does not *solve* that argument—which is like all deep literary disputes on some level irresolvable—but his is one of the clearest statements of what's at stake.

For Heller, Language Writing is ultimately a sort of formalism, obsessed with language as a self-coherent rather than referential system. Conversely, the limp, personal poetry of the workshops takes language's referential function—its correspondence to a world of emotions and events—too much for granted. To Heller, what makes poetry compelling, ultimately, is the way it suspends itself between the old "referentiality" and the new-old "formalism." This is the paradoxical and enabling "uncertainty" of the poet.

"Uncertainty"—for certainty short-circuits the process of thought. George W. Bush and Osama Bin Laden were quite certain of the rightness of their beliefs. Philosphical certainty, Heller quotes Gillian Rose in "Aspects of Poetics," "does not empower, it subjugates—for only thinking which has the ability to tolerate uncertainty is powerful, that is, non-violent" (U 230). "Aspects of Poetics" is perhaps the most searching essay in *Uncertain Poetries*, and in it Heller—usually quite chary of theoretical jargon—introduces a pair of terms that serves something of the same function "sincerity" and "objectification" did in Zukofsky's Objectivist writings: "precision" and "uncertainty." I quote at length, because it seems to me that here Heller presents a remarkably thought-through explanation and defense of his own post- or second-generation-Objectivist poetics:

> Precision in this sense becomes a pressure on the object-world, something like a phenomenological reduction or even an electron microscope uncovering the seed-syllable of poetry in thing and event. It may reveal

> how much interpretation (substitute the word mind-phantoms) comprises our so-called objectivities. In this interrogative mode, through its powers of representation and figuration, through its capacity to isolate and disjoin and to suggest recombination, precision becomes correlative with the possibilities of the poetic medium . . . .
>
> Uncertainty produced by such precision, far from consuming one in doubt, becomes a registration, even an acceptance of one's phantom-like existence. I'm not referring here to the indeterminacy or undecideability induced in some contemporary practice by chance operations or by the prepared effects of textual manipulation. Rather, I'm thinking of a condition induced by knowledge of our unreliability, our deference if you will, before the limitations and understanding of language and of otherness. Uncertainty, in effect, is already an aspect of an utterance, of saying and affirming. It advocates a kind of lightening up about our purported certainties and the hopes and fears in which most of those certainties are lodged. (U 231)

Uncertainty, then: a negative capability for our own time.

Uncertain Poetries pursues these themes in a number of guises, through the works of a rich variety of poets: Lorca and the *duende*, Pound, Rilke, Marianne Moore, Niedecker, David Ignatow, and Wallace Stevens. Particularly insightful are Heller's essays on Robert Duncan's "Poem Beginning with a Line from Pindar," on William Bronk, on Armand Schwerner, and on Oppen—the last intertwined with reflections on Heller's own growth as a poet. Throughout, Heller reads with a sensitive, patient, and reflective eye, never pursuing an agenda, always allowing the work at hand to reveal its own governing consonances and contradictions. These are subtle and often brilliant essays, and they stand well beside the poems of *This Constellation*—together confirming Heller's status as one of the most articulate and valuable poet-critics of our own turn of the century.

Notes

1. Michael Heller, *This Constellation Is a Name: Collected Poems 1965–2010* (Callicoon, NY: Nightboat Books, 2012); hereafter cited parenthetically in text as C.

2. Michael Heller, *Living Root: A Memoir* (Albany, NY: State U of New York P, 2000).

3. Paul Celan, "Letter to Hans Bender," *Collected Prose*, ed. Rosmarie Waldrop (Manchester: Carcanet, 1986) 26.

4. Stéphane Mallarmé, "Ses purs ongles très haut dédiant leur onyx," *Œuvres complètes I*, ed. Bertrand Marshal (Paris: Pléiade, 1998) 37.

5. Michael Heller, *Uncertain Poetries: Selected Essays on Poets, Poetry and Poetics* (Cambridge: Salt, 2005); hereafter cited parenthetically in text as U. For the full range of Heller's critical prose, *Uncertain Poetries* should be supplemented with *Conviction's Net of Branches: Essays on the Objectivist Poets and Poetry* (Carbondale: Southern Illinois UP, 1985) and *Speaking the Estranged: Essays on the Work of George Oppen* (Cambridge, Eng.: Salt, 2008).

6. Ludwig Wittgenstein, *Tractatus Logico-Philosophicus*, trans. C. K. Ogden (1922; London: Routledge & Kegan Paul, 1981) 149.

“The Lighthouses”

George Oppen

“The Lighthouses,” which appears in the final *Myth of the Blaze* section of George Oppen’s 1975 *Collected Poems,* was almost certainly written in the first half of the 1970s.[1] It shares a phrase, “neither Roman / nor Barbarian,” with “Semite,” which Peter Nicholls dates to the period of the Yom Kippur War (October 1973), and the second half of its dedication—“*(for L Z in time of the breaking of nations)*”—indicates a period of military strife.[2] “The breaking of nations” is from Jeremiah 51.20: “Thou art my battle-axe and weapons of war: for with thee will I break in pieces the nations”; but more proximately the phrase is from a haunting little poem by Thomas Hardy, written in the second year of the Great War:

In Time of “the Breaking of Nations”

I.

Only a man harrowing clods
In a slow silent walk
With an old horse that stumbles and nods
Half asleep as they stalk.

II.

Only thin smoke without flame
From the heaps of couch-grass;
Yet this will go onward the same
Though Dynasties pass.

III.

Yonder a maid and her wight
Come whispering by;
War’s annals will cloud into night
Ere their story die.[3]

The persistence of the quotidian in the midst of the Dynasts' wars; the cycles of agrarian labor, the ever-renewed "story" of adolescent love and desire, these are the "low" epos—Hardy implies—that will outlast the annals of nations and world-historical figures (like Napoleon, whose career Hardy had dramatized the decade before in his massive *The Dynasts*). In the time of "the breaking of nations," perhaps the poet should reserve some of his attention for the human experiences that escape the history books.

"if you want to say no say / no if you want to say yes say yes," Oppen begins "The Lighthouses," and it is here that the significance of the poem's dedication becomes clear. The words are more or less Louis Zukofsky's, from a May 1968 interview with L. S. Dembo. Dembo had asked him, "What do you mean, you got rid of epistemology in *Bottom* [*: on Shakespeare*]? The work seems to me to be all epistemology." To which Zukofsky replied, (mis)quoting his own "The Old Poet Moves to a New Apartment 14 Times": "'The questions are their own answers.' You want to say 'yes,' say 'yes'; you want to say 'no,' say 'no.'"[4]

Zukofsky's words may seem delivered *ex cathedra*; indeed, they rephrase the Sermon on the Mount, Jesus's condemnation of the verbal display of extravagant oaths: "But let your communication be, 'Yea, yea'; 'Nay, nay': for whatsoever is more than these cometh of evil" (Matthew 5.37). (The version of this admonition in the Epistle of James 5.12 is also close to Zukofsky's formulation: "But above all things, my brethren, swear not, neither by heaven, neither by the earth, neither by any other oath: but let your yea be yea, and your nay, nay: lest ye fall into condemnation.") The Dembo interview is frankly a comedy of crossed wires, Zukofsky insisting again and again on the fundamental straightforwardness of his writing, Dembo constantly puzzled and tangled in the obliquities of Zukofsky's poetry.

By the time of the composition of "The Lighthouses," Zukofsky and Oppen's friendship—the intense exchange of ideas of the late 1920s, the collaboration on To, Publishers and The Objectivist Press, the whole Objectivist "moment" of shared artistic endeavor of the early 1930s—was long in the past. The two men were no longer speaking—or at least, Zukofsky was no longer speaking to Oppen. Dembo had hoped to arrange a conference of the four original Objectivists (Zukofsky, Oppen, Carl Rakosi, Charles Reznikoff) at Madison in 1968; Zukofsky would not appear with the other three. In 1964, he had refused to read on a double bill with Oppen at the Guggenheim Museum.[5]

It is abundantly clear that Zukofsky resented Oppen's return to poetry after his nine-year exile in Mexico; more precisely, that he resented his immediate return to publication with 1962's *The Materials.* While Oppen had taken a quarter-century sabbatical from poetry after 1934's *Discrete Series,* Zukofsky had continued steadily to write in the face of scant public encouragement; by the time he and Oppen reestablished their friendship in 1958, Zukofsky had become considerably embittered, not least at the difficulties he encountered in seeing his poetry published. He deeply resented that New Directions (in collaboration with the *San Francisco Review,* published by Oppen's sister June Oppen Degnan), who were printing Oppen, Reznikoff, and Rakosi, would not publish his collected short poems. It is this resentment—what one might class among the vicissitudes, ultimately, of "pobiz"—that lay at the root of Zukofsky's break with Oppen.

Oppen was personally saddened by Zukofsky's rejection; but his differences with his older contemporary were ultimately deeper than arguments over publication. After his hiatus, Oppen had returned to writing a poetry that had little in common with the corruscating complexities of Zukofsky's work, early and late. The watchword was "clarity," "a substantial language / Of clarity, and of respect" ("A Narrative," 156). In "Route" Oppen wrote, "Clarity, clarity, sure clarity is the most beautiful thing in the world, / A limited, limiting clarity // I have not and never did have any motive of poetry / But to achieve clarity" (193). Such clarity, he felt, had little part in Zukofsky's poetry. "I stripped myself," he wrote in a Daybook, "while you, Louis, have hung on yourself every fancy rag you could find."[6] And it was more than a matter of ornamentation; on some level, Oppen believed that Zukofsky "used incomprehensibility and obscurity as a tactic" (Mary Oppen's words), a purposeful obfuscation.[7]

One can only imagine with what emotions (scorn? disgust?) Oppen would have read "A"-22 and -23, those two 1,000-line, intensely compacted, relentlessly quotational, relentlessly obscure capstones to Zukofsky's "A", which Zukofsky had completed around the same time he was writing "The Lighthouses." I suspect the two men were no longer reading one another at all.

But not quite at all: for "The Lighthouses" records a moment when Oppen, rereading the interviews Dembo had published in *Contemporary Literature* in 1969 as "The 'Objectivist' Poet: Four Interviews," found Zukofsky enunciating his own principles of "clarity," his own vision of the poet whose "yes" is "yes" and whose "no" is "no," whose probity of speech serves as "lights // of safety for the coasts // are danger . . ." (256). Despite their estrangement, the two men share at least two essentials: their Jewish heritage, their status as "*neither Roman // nor barbarian*" (in Oppen's paraphrase of Decimius Magnus Ausonius), and their sense of the valuable musicality of the poem—"the turn the cadence the verse / and the music . . ." And more important than these, and in memory of the most important friendship of his youth ("He taught me everything," Mary Oppen quotes her husband on Zukofsky[8]), Oppen celebrates a moment in which Zukofsky looks past the "fancy rags" of his late modernist poetics and agrees with Oppen in an assertion of "essential // clarity plain glass ray / of darkness ray of light" (257).

Notes

1. George Oppen, *New Collected Poems*, ed. Michael Davidson (New York: New Directions, 2002) 256–57; hereafter cited parenthetically in text. Davidson's note on the poem is on 406.

2. Peter Nicholls, *George Oppen and the Fate of Modernism* (Oxford: Oxford UP, 2007) 181.

3. Thomas Hardy, *Collected Poems* (1925; New York: Macmillan, 1953) 511.

4. Louis Zukofsky, *Prepositions+: The Collected Critical Essays* (Hanover, NH: Wesleyan UP, 2000) 243.

5. Mark Scroggins, *The Poem of a Life: A Biography of Louis Zukofsky* (Emeryville, CA: Shoemaker & Hoard, 2007) 407, 358.

6. Qtd. in Nicholls, *George Oppen* 151n.46.

7. Mary Oppen, *Meaning a Life: An Autobiography* (Santa Barbara: Black Sparrow, 1978) 209.

8. Mary Oppen, *Meaning a Life* 208.

Sound and Vision

John Taggart

[From a little over a decade ago, a meditation on what now—it seems clear—is to be considered "mid-period" Taggart: the poetics of Standing Wave, Crosses, When the Saints, *and above all that various and monumental collection* Loop, *a book which in my mind looms over American poetry of the 1980s and 1990s like the black monolith of Kubrick's* 2001*—or, more often, beckons like an enclave of vast, multilayered, shimmering Rothkos. The remarkable shift and efflorescence of Taggart's post-Crosses writing—*Pastorelles *and* There Are Birds*—is another loop entirely.]*

1. Sounds

"The act of reading," John Taggart writes in his book on Edward Hopper, *Remaining in Light*, "is akin to the ceaseless motion of an ant on a moebius strip."[1] For "reading," read listening, and looking, as well—the "gift," if you will, of sound and vision. A Möbius strip, of course, is a loop of paper—you can make one yourself—with a twist in it; it's that twist that makes the loop's face endless: a three-dimensional object with only one surface. Where *does* that highway go to? *Loop* is the title of Taggart's largest collection of poems; it was published in 1991, after, as Robert Fripp says somewhere about one of his records, "delays by dinosaurs." Eleven years before, the pop band Talking Heads released its fourth album, *Remain in Light*. It was a controversial record, the product in part of bandleader David Byrne's and producer Brian Eno's intense, schoolboy-crush-like collaboration. (The first product of their woodshedding was the Eno/Byrne *My Life in the Bush of Ghosts*, an odd and hyper-intellectual reimagining of the Parliament-Funkadelic sound, crossed with various African beats and more than a touch of mid-seventies Miles.) *Remain in Light* expanded the band—formerly a trim four-piece—with extra percussionists, backing vocalists, and guitars; it moved them from the taut, witty New York new wave into a more expansive, funky, polyrhythmic territory. Eno, Byrne, and the rest of the band collaborated on the compositions, and Eno's fingerprints were all over the vocal arrangements, more often than not odd workouts on the call-and-response pattern, Eno's baritone choruses responding to Byrne's edgy, faux-evangelist sprechstimme. And the songs—at least the longer ones—were built on loops, taped rhythm section passages over which guest musicians like Adrian Belew could wail to their hearts' delight.

The loop, whether actual or conceptual, was central to the early development of what came to be known as "minimalist" music. Steve Reich's early pieces "It's Gonna Rain" (1965) and "Come Out" (1966) were built out of tape loops; his "Violin Phase" pitted a taped violin part against a real-time violinist. Around the same time, Terry Riley was developing keyboard performance techniques that relied on loops and tape delays, most expansively showcased in his *Rainbow in Curved Air* album. The English composer Gavin Bryars's "Sinking of the Titanic" was a fully scored imitation of a vast, slowed-down tape loop; his "Jesus' Blood Never Failed Me Yet" (1971) was built—famously or infamously—around a tape loop of an old tramp's singing. Both of these Bryars works—not incidentally—were recorded and released in 1975 on Brian Eno's Obscure Records label, which also released the first recordings of another English minimalist, Michael Nyman—this, of course, long before Nyman became a soundtrack machine and minor celebrity.

Five years later, Eno produced Talking Heads's *Remain in Light*, and it was almost certainly at Eno's suggestion that Memphis trumpeter Jon Hassell was brought in to lend a breathy, multitracked horn part to the song "Houses in Motion." That part is vintage Hassell—pure r&b riffs through the verses and chorus, then, when it comes time for him to solo, Hassell's leaping up into the microtones and raga scales taught to him by his mentor, the great Kirana singer Pandit Pran Nath. Hassell, whose *Aka-Dabari-Java/Magic Realism* is one of the great unremembered records of the 1980s, has never quite settled down generically to any record company's liking. He contributed hip hop–styled opening music to the TV series *The Practice*, has played Duke Ellington standards and classical Indian ragas with guitarist Ry Cooder, has collaborated with the Burkina Fasan ensemble Farafina. And Hassell, of course, was present at the beginning of minimalism: he played on the 1968 large ensemble first recording of Terry Riley's groundbreaking piece *In C*.

In C is a composition for any number of musicians, playing any instruments capable of meeting the pitch requirements of the score. The score consists of fifty-three melodic figures, through which each musician progresses, determining for him- or herself how many times to repeat each figure and how to align it with what's being played by the other members of the ensemble. The music coheres, both through the individual musicians' sensitivity—their *lis-*

tening to their fellows—and through an underlying "pulse." Not the pulse of a metronome or drum machine, nor the pulse of a tape loop—but an organic pulse, carried and passed along by the members of the collective. "Large definitions commit one to a long line," Taggart writes. "The line is prevented from falling in on itself by a recurrent, but never exactly repeating, cadence. This cadence undergoes a continuous motion (transformation)."[2] And the poem—like the score of *In C*—cannot be an experience only of vision, but must be a *performed* thing: "As I came to discover, such a poem would have to be read aloud to make sense. The reader would have to break the silence of the cold page. There could be a liberation of participation, an ending of the silence and solitude."[3] More tersely: "'Peace On Earth' is meant to be more than one person's private response to the war in Vietnam."[4]

"A recurrent, but never exactly repeating, cadence." The mechanical loop repeats precisely, inexorably, with the sterility of Ford's assembly line; the "exactly repeating cadence" is the Taylorization of the poet, the talented sophomore's iambic pentameter. The mechanical loop's contents, even when human-generated—Tina Weymouth and Chris Frantz's rhythms, the old tramp Gavin Bryars recorded one day in London—come back to us again and again, "same as it ever was." The only thing that can be of interest about such loops is the human reaction to them. Bryars's tramp's singing is remarkably in tune, but, like a solo bluesman's, his sense of time is elastic: his melodic fragment ends on a fermata, and the first bar of the thirteen (the song is in 3/4 time) is ever so slightly shortened. The tramp, long dead but interred upon a tape loop, sings the song in precisely the same (irregular) way every time (approximately 170 iterations on the most recent recording of the piece); the accompanying musicians, however, seem always—over and over again—slightly taken aback by his irregularities. It is in their momentary awkwardnesss that the piece's pathos resides.

Gertrude Stein, in 1934:

> every time one of the hundreds of times a newspaper man makes fun of my writing and of my repetition he always has the same theme, always having the same theme, that is, if you like, repetition, that is if you like repeating that is the same thing, but once started expressing this thing, expressing any thing there can be no repetition because the essence of that expression is insistence, and if you insist you must each time use emphasis and if you use emphasis it is not possible while anybody is alive that they should use exactly the same emphasis. . . . insistence that in its emphasis can never be repeating, because insistence is always alive and if

> it is alive it is never saying anything in the same way because emphasis can never be the same not even when it is most the same.[5]

By itself, the tape loop goes nowhere, is pure repetition. When the voice enters—the voice that "invades," that "lays," that "eats the face away," that "turns the face of the listener, member among the members, into its excrement"—when the voice enters, the tape loop becomes the Möbius strip.

2. Reading: Vision and Revisions

One loop from *Remain in Light* to the first flowering of minimalism, then back again. This isn't playing degrees of separation, by the way—maybe instead something one might rudely miscall "songs of degrees." No one wants to be Greil Marcus here, and dig out the underground connections between Johnny Rotten and the seventeenth-century antinomians—at least not in this piece of writing. There is, however, an aesthetic continuity that flows underneath the more interesting developments in late twentieth-century pop music, "serious" music, and jazz, a continuity that one wouldn't want to reduce to the term "minimalism." An interest in repetition, in stasis, in movement through suspended movement.

"It occurs to me," says Taggart, "that all my work, before and since ["Slow Song for Mark Rothko"], involves translation or, more accurately, transformation to make the poem a 'sound object.'"[6] *Transformation* rather than *translation*: transformation is "the detail, not mirage, of seeing, of thinking with the things as they exist, and of directing them along a line of melody" (Zukofsky); translation is the poetics of August Kleinzahler's meager creative writing professors, "paunchy with drink": "If there is a mallard in the reeds / they will take it. / They will take it and make it their own, / something both more than a duck / and less."[7] But why need the poet *look*, at a mallard, or Edward Hopper's "A Woman in the Sun," or the panels of the Rothko Chapel, in order to write? Why not simply effuse, let the cords of sensibility vibrate like an Aeolian harp to the winds of inspiration? "What is at stake," writes Taggart, "is need. You find what you need, among the entire past and present universe, to get the job done. Your search in that universe of human objects and natural objects is guided by need."[8]

The basis of all of Taggart's poetry is looking—or listening, or reading—a repetitive, accretive, circling motion guided by need. "The poet, who is first a reader, makes no original discovery in reading. Instead, the poet becomes only more aware of the spider-web connectedness of his or her sources and of the innumerable ghostly speakers still beyond them."[9] "The world," Guy Davenport once said to me, "was invented and arranged for James Joyce's convenience." Every detail within Joyce's works, that is, connects to every other detail; and those works constitute a monstrous machine that spurs on its ant-reader to find the labyrinthine, rhizomatic connections that bind together, with a vast "spider web" or echo chamber, the entire phenomenal world. Davenport argues that Ruskin's *Fors Clavigera* is a precursor to Joyce's as a "daedalian" work, searching out with passionate attention the multiple, even endless intertwinings of human culture: Joyce, Pound, Zukofsky, David Jones, Basil Bunting, Susan Howe, have made such daedalian reading one of the principal and most vibrant modes of twentieth-century writing. Taggart stands, in his own idiosyncratic manner—and how else can any true artist stand?—with them. "Can love," Zukofsky writes—and for "love," read "passionate attention," or "need"—"rouse a thing of the past / And not see it as present?"[10]

"I wonder," Wallace Stevens—old, perhaps depressed—wrote in 1947, "have I lived a skeleton's life, / As a questioner about reality, // A countryman of all the bones in the world?"[11] Seven years later, he would answer himself, looking back upon his own poems: "That poem about the pineapple, the one / About the mind as never satisfied, // The one about the credible hero, the one / About summer, are not what skeletons think about."[12] Even as one reads, one turns back and rereads, one subjects one's visions to the process of revision. That process of self-revision, like the revision of one's precursors, is of course not immune to the dangers of mere translation. In 1993, Philip Glass released his "'Low' Symphony," based on music from David Bowie's 1977 *Low* album, which Glass claimed (somewhat unconvincingly) had been of influence on his own work. Glass's is a rather unmoving piece, burying Bowie and Eno's spare and suggestive synthesizer motifs in a wash of post-Brahms orchestration. Soon after, Gavin Bryars released "new," expanded versions of his "Sinking of the Titanic" and "Jesus' Blood," spinning those works out, through fussy arrangements, sound effects, and guest vocalists, into distended parodies of themselves. Wordsworth's last, unfortunate version of *The Prelude* comes to mind. Perhaps one should look away from the accredited composers of minimalism, to Bill Laswell's *Panthalassa* remixes of early seventies Miles, or to the *Sacrilege* CD, multiple reworkings by an array of star producers from the British, American, and European "techno" scenes of tunes by the legendary German band Can.

You may ask yourself, as Stevens does, "well—how did I get here?" Taggart has returned to his own earlier visions, and without fail he has transformed them, made them into new visions. "The Game With Red" returns to "The Rothko Chapel Poem," boiling that latter work's expansive, complex meditation into a stark claustrophobia: "I cannot get outside the dark red doorway."[13] The poet, "rectangles of light" falling through the windows onto his floor, works back through his entire *oeuvre* in "Rereading." Has he lived a skeleton's life, letting the days go by, water flowing underground? Of course not, for the poems reread in "Rereading"—among them "Peace on Earth," "The Rothko Chapel Poem," "Saul and David"—have come out of too scarifyingly immediate roots, and have themselves taken too deep root, for the poet to rest satisfied. There is a weariness here, a sense of the unending process of reading, of writing, of rewriting what has been written; the voice of "Vaguely Harmless," as much as it implores, repeats, and emphasizes, cannot forget the "bones and whispy bits of hair / bones and bits of hair stuck in the memory" of "Black and White Close-Up."[14] All the poet can do is keep reading, keep rereading and revising—keep moving: "What I can do is move wandering movement / what I can do is move in a wandering movement"[15]: "there can be no hope of rest."[16] To live—as poet and human being—is, again and again, with greater or lesser degrees of failure, to try to see. "I can't go on, I'll go on." "Not seeing," Taggart concludes *Remaining in Light*, "means not being alive. Being alive means seeing and thus trying to stay alive. We have the possibility of staying alive so long as we stay in motion, keep moving."[17]

Is it unfair to say that all of Taggart's poems are "remixes" of earlier texts, whether those texts are poems, paintings, recordings, passages of philosophy, snatches of conversation? No more unfair, I suppose, than to see *Ulysses* as a remix of the *Odyssey*, the events of Joyce's own life, and a broad swatch of the whole of Western literature and thought. Or to see Picasso's *Demoiselles d'Avignon* as a remix of Cézanne, or Alfred Schnittke's First Symphony as a complex rethinking of Shostakovich's programmatic works, of the relationship between jazz and classical music, and of the entire nineteenth century of European music. The loop of sound and vision is endless. That's where David Bowie is wrong, or self-defeating, or solipsistic—"I will sit right down / Waiting for the gift of sound and vision." The gift will not come to one who only sits and waits; hearing and seeing are functions of movement, of the constant, labyrinthine, repetitive, nervous movements of the ear, eye, and mind. And—need one add?—of voice, which is the gift of Taggart's poetry.

Notes

1. John Taggart, *Remaining in Light: Ant Meditations on a Painting by Edward Hopper* (Albany, NY: State U of New York P, 1993) 47.

2. John Taggart, "The Poem as a Woven Scarf," *Songs of Degrees: Essays on Contemporary Poetry and Poetics* (U of Alabama P, 1994) 76.

3. Taggart, "A Preface," *Songs of Degrees* 73.

4. Taggart, "The Poem as a Woven Scarf," *Songs of Degrees* 77.

5. Gertrude Stein, *Lectures in America* (1935; Boston: Beacon P, 1985) 167.

6. Taggart, "A Preface," *Songs of Degrees* 72.

7. Louis Zukofsky, "An Objective," *Prepositions+: The Collected Critical Essays* (Hanover, NH: Wesleyan UP, 2000) 12; August Kleinzahler, "An Autumnal Sketch," *Storm Over Hackensack* (Mt. Kisco, NY: Moyer Bell Limited, 1985) 35.

8. Taggart, "A Preface," *Songs of Degrees* 73.

9. Taggart, "Of the Power of the Word," *Songs of Degrees* 127.

10. Louis Zukofsky, *"A"* (Berkeley: U of California P, 1978) 199.

11. Wallace Stevens, "First Warmth," *Opus Posthumous*, ed. Milton J. Bates (New York: Knopf, 1989) 117.

12. Stevens, "As You Leave the Room," *Opus Posthumous* 117.

13. John Taggart, "The Game With Red," *Loop* (Los Angeles: Sun & Moon, 1991) 233.

14. John Taggart, "Vaguely Harmless," *Standing Wave* (Providence: Lost Roads, 1993) 73.

15. Taggart, "The Game With Red," *Loop* 233.

16. Taggart, "Rereading," *Standing Wave* 72.

17. Taggart, *Remaining in Light* 137.

III

Poetics

Queen Victoria's Birthday Present

On Writing Biography

Once upon a time, I believed an essay wasn't a *real* essay unless its title was broken midway through with a colon: the colorful phrase, followed by the dry but intriguing descriptive bit. I've tried to shed that habit over the years, along with many of the other excrescences of academic writing. If you prefer, however, you can make believe that "Queen Victoria's Birthday Present" is what the early modern bibliographers call a "short title," and the full name of this essay is something like "Turner's Naughty Pictures, Queen Victoria's Birthday Present, and the House on Willow Street: Some Aporias of Literary Biography."

The genre of literary biography is, like Caliban, a strange and hybrid creature, half scholarship and half "creative nonfiction," and one of those genres that I'm convinced doesn't get nearly the respect it deserves in the academy. I've devoted a good deal of my scholarly and critical energies to the writing of Louis Zukofsky; I've been at it a while, and my Zukofsky work has come to encompass a number of the modes in which we encounter and process literary texts in the academy: I've written "straight" literary criticism on Zukofsky's poetry and prose; I've edited and annotated his work; and most recently, I've written a critical biography of him. That last book was the most complicated and difficult thing I've ever tackled, and not just because of its rather considerable size.

I can't imagine that anyone who begins writing his first biography has any idea of what they're getting into: not merely the endless, squirrelly, obsessive-compulsive thumbing through indices, grubbing through archives, and asking people, "Did you know X?"; nor the monumental, continually revised timelines and databases, the ever-expanding file folders, bursting with sometimes semilegible photocopies, and the geometrically multiplying PDFs, image captures, emails, and "notes to self" crowding the laptop; nor even the sifting of all this into a "story" and rendering it into something resembling readable narrative prose (that last a task for which *nothing* in my experience and training as either poet or literary scholar prepared me).

Louis Zukofsky was not a fan of biography. His *Autobiography* (1970) consists of a handful of brief paragraphs of factual prose, interspersed among musical settings of his short poems. At its beginning is a single sentence summarizing Zukofsky's views on biography: "As a poet I have always felt that the work says all there needs to be said of one's life."[1] Keep off the grass, in other words. Nor, for that matter, does Zukofsky seem on first glance a promising subject for biography: his life, that is—in contrast to that of, say, Shelley or Byron or Basil Bunting or Elizabeth Barrett Browning—is rather devoid of exciting or diverting extraliterary incident. The drama of his biography lies in the revolutionary achievements of his writing.

On the other hand, being entirely enamored of Zukofsky's poetry—as I still remain—I was fascinated by such statements as his comment, with regard to the long poem *"A"*, that "the words are my life."[2] Surely a close examination and careful presentation of the events and circumstances of Zukofsky's life might serve to cast light—much needed light, so far as I'm concerned—on his poetry. That was my initial and abiding motivation in writing *The Poem of a Life*, however many byways and divagations I might have strayed into along the way.

And it turns out that Zukofsky's poetics, as uninterested as the poet might have been in biographical discourse *per se*, are rather relevant to the biographical enterprise. Biography, that is, is a type of historical and occasionally critical writing that's bound not merely by the formal constraints of narrative but by a certain basic connection to something we might provisionally call *reality*, or *truth*. I can play with the formal expectations of biography—I may begin my biography of Emily Dickinson by narrating the circumstances of her death, or by writing about her sister's discovery of her poems in manuscript "fascicles"—but I cannot claim that she was born in Idaho, or had a whirlwind love affair with Ralph Waldo Emerson. I am constrained to *tell* only what the evidence will support, and to present what the evidence will not support as *speculation*—I am bound by what, back before poststructuralism, we used to call "facts."

Now whatever else they might do, the various statements of poetics Zukofsky wrote on behalf of the Objectivist "movement" in the early 1930s set a kind of standard for the writer's dealings with the phenomenal world, a standard which can be summed up in his phrase "thinking with the things as they exist."[3] Michael Heller encapsulates it rather nicely when he calls the Objectivists "a flying poetic truth squad."[4] "*No myths* might be the Objectivist motto," writes Hugh Kenner.[5] If, when I began work on Zukofsky's biography, I had at the very outset to ignore his own rejection of biography, when it came to the actual research, sifting, and writing of the biography I found myself returning again and again to Objectivist principles: "Thinking with the things as they exist," "*No myths.*"

The problem, of course, is pinning down those "things," distinguishing them from attractive "myths." Perhaps what began to occupy me most of all as the project progressed, and continued to do so after it was done and off to the press, was a complex of methodological problems—problems specifically of biographical *evidence*—that eventually shade into theoretical or epistemological problems: problems of biographical *truth*. A biography "sells" itself to a reader on the basis of the elegance of its prose, the degree to which its narrative grips or compels, and the extent to which it proves enlightening or revelatory about its subject. But as a reader and writer of biography, I find myself more and more interested in how biographers handle the evidence upon which their stories are built, and the ultimate, irreducible slipperiness of that evidence. In a nutshell: if the biographer always has Joe Friday whispering in one ear, "Just the facts, ma'am" (itself a cultural misremembering, as Jack Webb never actually uttered quite that line on *Dragnet*), in the other she or he hears the echo of Friedrich Nietzsche's notebooks: "Against positivism, which halts at phenomena—'There are only *facts*'—I would say: No, facts is precisely what there is not, only *interpretations*."[6]

So—three "takes" on the issue of biographical evidence:

Take One: Queen Victoria's Birthday Present

Richard Ellmann's *James Joyce* is widely considered (in Anthony Burgess's phrase) "the greatest literary biography of the century."[7] It is the only book not by Joyce himself to be given a standard abbreviation in the style sheet for the *James Joyce Quarterly*, which at least suggests that in some quarters it approaches the status of primary text, of "truth."[8] But I'd like to look at a moment in Ellmann. First, a passage from the first chapter of *A Portrait of the Artist as Young Man*, where the narrator describes Mr Casey, the friend of Stephen Dedalus's father, Simon, a man who has spent time in an English jail picking oakum on account of his nationalist activities: "Stephen smiled too for he knew now that it was not true that Mr Casey had a purse of silver in his throat. He smiled to think how the silvery noise which Mr Casey used to make had deceived him. And when he had tried to open Mr Casey's hand to see if the purse of silver was hidden there he had seen that the fingers could not be straightened out: and Mr Casey had told him that he had got those three cramped fingers making a birthday present for Queen Victoria."[9]

It is axiomatic that Joyce's writing is almost always to some degree autobiographical, and *Portrait of an Artist* is usually read as a minutely autobigraphical account—Stephen Dedalus is Joyce himself, Simon Dedalus is his father John, and so forth. Who then is Mr Casey in "real life"? He is, according to Ellmann's biography, one John Kelly: "Kelly was in prison several times for Land League agitation, and John Joyce regularly invited him to recuperate from imprisonment, at that time very rigorous, at the house in Bray. In jail three fingers of his left hand had become permanently cramped from picking oakum, and he would tell the children that they had become so while he was making a birthday present for Queen Victoria."[10] Ellmann's source for this identification, his notes tell us, is Joyce's brother Stanislaus's memoir, *My Brother's Keeper* (edited by Ellmann himself). There we read that John Kelly of Tralee "was pale and handsome, slow of speech and movement, with regular, clean-cut features and a mass of black hair. The fingers of his left hand were permanently cramped from making sacks and picking oakum in jail."[11]

Note the two particulars that Ellmann's account in *James Joyce* adds to Stanislaus Joyce's memoir: that it was *three* fingers of Kelly's hand that were disabled; and that Kelly used to tell the children they had gotten that way "making a present for Queen Victoria." Stanislaus says nothing about Queen Victoria, nor does he specify the number of Kelly's cramped fingers. These two details, it seems to me, make Ellmann's account of the business immeasurably more vivid than Stanislaus's. But where did Ellmann get *them*? The answer is obvious, of course: from *A Portrait of the Artist as a Young Man*.

The autobiographical *novel*, then, has become a documentary source for a *biography* of its author. And it's no exaggeration to note that Ellmann does this on a fairly regular basis, throughout his life of Joyce. A wonderful circularity: Ellmann tells the story of Joyce's life, the "truth" that lies behind the fictionalized scenes and characters of the novels—but in doing so he draws more or less directly on the novels themselves for details, and sometimes fundamental data, which are presented in his biography as *truth*.

Now a keen Joycean (or Ellmannian) might point out that Ellmann *knew* Stanislaus Joyce, interviewed him on a number of occasions, and may well have gotten the details about John Kelly's *three* cramped fingers and Queen Victoria's birthday present from the horse's mouth, as it were. But positing a direct, *viva voce* revelation from Stanislaus to Ellmann doesn't really get us any closer to knowing how many of Kelly's fingers were cramped, or whether he'd actually made that crack about Queen Victoria. For one thing, the scene in *Portrait* takes place when Stephen is about six years old; James's brother was almost three years younger than him—he would've just turned four at the time of the famous, devastating Christmas dinner scene in *Portrait*, taking his meals with the rest of the children in the nursery. Let's be honest: how much evidentiary credence do we give to things people remember from when they were four? And what are the chances, if Stanny had indeed told these details to Ellmann—for which, remember, we have no evidence—that his own "memories" of the *three* cramped fingers and Queen Victoria's present hadn't been calqued onto his own childhood recollections by his multiple readings of his brother James's autobiographical novel?

Take Two: The House on Willow Street

It's hard not to argue that a biographer is getting into treacherous waters when she or he uses autobiographical *fiction* as a source of evidence for writing a writer's *biography*. Even autobiography is suspect, as I well learned when comparing William Carlos Williams's account of the early 1930s in his 1951 *Autobiography* to contemporaneous letters and documents: the good doctor's memory, it became abundantly clear, just wasn't very good. He was continually jumbling chronologies, forgetting events, putting people where they weren't. Samuel Johnson, in *Idler* 84 (1759), describes an ideal autobiographer—"He that speaks of himself has no motive to falsehood or partiality except self-love, by which all have so often been betrayed, that all are on the watch against its artifices . . . he that sits down calmly and voluntarily to review his life for the admonition of posterity, or to amuse himself, and leaves this account unpublished, may be commonly presumed to tell truth, since falsehood cannot appease his own mind, and fame will not be heard beneath the tomb"[12]—but even if such a paragon of impartiality existed, he would no doubt get all sorts of dates and names wrong along the way. Every statement of memory, every memoir, much be checked by the autobiographer against contemporaneous documentation—letters, usually.

But even more or less contemporaneous first-person evidence, it turns out, has to be handled carefully. Take for instance a letter of August 1955 from Louis Zukofsky to his friend Edward Dahlberg: Zukofsky likes the idea of the little press that Dahlberg proposes—the "Untimely Press"—but he has no money to contribute to the project. Indeed, the Zukofskys' house at 30 Willow Street, Brooklyn, has become a source of both headaches and financial worry. While the Zukofskys rented out one floor of the three-story brownstone, Zukofsky was uncomfortable with the role of landlord; and when the ten-year mortgage had come up for renewal a month earlier, the bank's terms had put them "in debt head over heels."[13]

The Zukofskys bought 30 Willow Street, a handsome row house, shortly after the end of the war, in May 1946. Right after he wrote Dahlberg in 1955, they were to put it on the market (unsuccessfully at first); they eventually sold it in 1957 and moved to a smaller apartment down the street. Now when I first drafted my own account of Zukofsky in the mid-fifties, I wrote this paragraph: "The botheration attending the publication of *Some Time* could not have come at a worse time for the Zukofskys, for through much of 1956 they were considering giving up the 30 Willow Street house and were preparing for Paul's Carnegie Hall debut, scheduled for the end of November. Zukofsky had been promoted to associate professor at Poly in May 1955, but the mortgage on the house had come due for renewal that July, leaving the family 'in debt head over heels.' They put the house on the market later that year, unsuccessfully." It was Zukofsky's son Paul (born 1943) who set me straight, and in no uncertain terms: *The bank mortgage*, he said, *had been short-lived; it had been transferred to Becky Thaew, Zukofsky's mother-in-law, who presumably didn't expect interest payments. The Zukofskys were at no point after the war in serious debt.* Why did they then sell the house? *Because they had a bad conscience about being landlords (Zukofsky's old Marxism asserting itself), and—more importantly—they simply got greedy, seeing that the house's value had doubled since the war; it seemed best to sell now, given that the whole capitalist system might go belly-up at any moment.*[14]

Now all of this testimony had to be calibrated against Paul Zukofsky's rather extraordinary loyalty to his mother's memory, his sneering disdain for his father's gormlessness in practical and financial matters, and his own full-blooded William F. Buckley–style enthusiasm for the free market. While Paul Zukofsky was certainly in a position to know far more about his parents' financial and real estate affairs, his own account of the matter was both informed by personal knowledge and colored by sentiment. But the next thing he mentioned rang very true indeed to me: that I ought to consider the source of my quotation—a letter to Edward Dahlberg.

Dahlberg (1900–1977) met Zukofsky at Brooklyn Polytech in the late 1940s, when Zukofsky was a newly appointed assistant professor and Dahlberg was what we'd now call an "adjunct instructor." Dahlberg is one of the great forgotten men of American literature. He began his career in the late 1920s as one of the most promising practitioners of a kind of bare-knuckled, grimy social realist fiction; he reemerged in the 1940s with a series of nonfiction works and memoirs cast in an astonishingly ornate, moving, Biblical prose. He is one of America's great stylists. And, as is evident both in his autobiographical works and in his copious letters, he is one of the most monstrously self-centered and self-involved figures in literature (a profession in which being self-centered and self-involved is by no means uncommon). When Paul Zukofsky in his e-mail named Dahlberg a "CONSUM-

MATE SPONGE," it sent me back to Dahlberg's letters to Zukofsky, to his letters to a variety of other correspondents, and to Dahlberg's own biography. And all of those sources made clear that yes, throughout Dahlberg's correspondence there is a constant undercurrent or open note of financial need—a constant crying out for money, and a savage, sneering disdain for those who have somehow been blessed by the Whore Fortuna—more blessed, that is, than the long-suffering and deserving Edward Dahlberg.

It makes perfect sense, then, that Zukofsky, ill at ease with his own relative financial comfort, already uncomfortable with the insistence of his publisher, Jonathan Williams, that he hunt up subscribers for his forthcoming book *Some Time*, and weary of the constant nagging demands of the impecunious Dahlberg, would exaggerate his own fiscal worries, would claim he was "in debt head over heels." It makes perfect sense—but it is unclear whether it gets us closer to the *truth* of the Zukofskys' financial state in August 1955 (barring a careful examination of their bank statements of that period, which I wasn't about to embark upon). I knew, however, that citing Zukofsky's letter to Dahlberg as evidence, verbatim, without comment, would not stand consideration of that letter in relationship to its addressee. So I wrote the following: "The publication of *Some Time* came at a busy time for the Zukofskys. Zukofsky had been promoted to associate professor at Poly in May 1955; later that year they put the Willow Street house on the market, with no success."[15] To quote Ezra Pound (himself quoting Thomas Jefferson, Sigismundo Malatesta, and the Vulgate version of Ecclesiastes), *Tempus loquendi, tempus tacendi*—a time to speak, and a time to remain silent.

Take Three: Turner's Naughty Pictures

When Joseph Mallord William Turner died in 1851 after a long career, he was widely recognized as England's single most important contemporary painter, and the thirty-two year-old John Ruskin was universally recognized as his most important critic and disciple. Ruskin had already written two volumes of his *Modern Painters*, a work single-mindedly dedicated to demonstrating that no one, *ever*, had painted nature as *truly* and masterfully as Turner, and in the process he had laid the groundwork for a new profession in Western culture—that of art critic. So it was no surprise that Turner named Ruskin as one of the executors of his will, and that the task fell to Ruskin—once the dust of several years' worth of lawsuits challenging the will had settled—of sorting and cataloguing the tens of thousands of sketches, paintings, and drawings Turner had left to the British nation, the famous "Turner Bequest."

Imagine Ruskin's discomfiture, then, when he discovered among Turner's drawings a cache of pictures that could only be described as "obscene": not merely the familiar erotica of nude women, but detailed drawings of female genitalia, numerous depictions of couples—both male and female and woman with woman—entwined in sexual congress. This discovery must have been a severe blow to Ruskin's elevated conception of Turner—he had once called him "sent as a prophet of God to reveal to men the mysteries of His universe, standing, like the great angel of the Apocalypse, clothed with a cloud, and with a rainbow upon his head, and with the sun and stars given into his hand."[16] So, in consultation with Ralph Wornum, the Keeper of the National Gallery, Ruskin had the offending pictures burned.

The simplest explanation of Ruskin's actions here is to put them down to proverbial Victorian "prudery," an apotropaic recoiling from the representations of sexuality. (Queen Victoria, one remembers, marveled at Leonardo's notebooks—but only with bits of brown paper inserted to cover up anatomical details.) But in Ruskin's case, it's more than a matter of a culture-wide "repression" of sex; Ruskin's own sexual history, as biographers have unraveled it over the past sixty years, was a strange one indeed. He married Euphemia Gray in 1848, and their marriage was annulled six years later on the grounds of nonconsummation. In a statement he prepared for the annulment proceedings, Ruskin stoutly asserted that he could prove his own virility at any time—he was not, that is, impotent; indeed, he implied on later occasions, he was a habitual masturbator. The problem lay with Effie, whose "person was not formed to excite passion. On the contrary, there were certain circumstances in her person which completely checked it."[17] According to Effie, "he had imagined women were quite different to what he saw I was; and the reason he did not make me his wife was because he was disgusted with my person the first night."[18] Ruskin never remarried, and no evidence indicates that he ever had sex: instead, he indulged in a series of flirtations and (mostly epistolary) courtships with *very* young girls. As Tim Hilton comments flatly in his magisterial biography, Ruskin "was a pædophile."[19]

Now the details of Ruskin's marriage, needless to say, do not figure in his early, more or less hagiographic biographies; but the tale of the Bonfire of the Turner Naughties was widely circulating by the end of the century. Ruskin's friend the Pre-Raphaelite William Michael Rossetti mentions it in his diary in 1869—he apparently had it from Charles Augustus Howell, Ruskin's gossipy and unscrupulous secretary—and a suitably embroidered version—supposedly from Ruskin's own mouth—appears in Frank Harris's pornographic memoir, *My Life and Loves*.[20] The earliest reference to the episode I've encountered in the more or less constant stream of Ruskin biographies (though I'll admit to not having consulted *all* of them) is a tentative one in

Amabel Williams-Ellis's 1929 *The Exquisite Tragedy*: the story, says Williams-Ellis, is a "probable legend" of which there is "no confirmation."[21] In 1976, however, the National Gallery put on display an 1862 letter from Ruskin to Ralph Wornum that had been unearthed in its archives: "I am satisfied that you had no other course than to burn [the drawings], both for the sake of Turner's reputation (they having been assuredly drawn under a certain condition of insanity) and for your own peace," Ruskin wrote. "And I am glad to be able to bear witness to their destruction; and I hereby declare that the parcel of them was undone by me, and all the obscene drawings it contained burnt in my presence in the month of December, 1858."[22]

Ruskin's biographers have felt duty-bound to mention this incident, but what have they made of it? If anything, it simply serves to buttress the widespread view of Ruskin as a self-righteous Victorian scold. Most biographers pass over it rapidly, understandably embarrassed. (Perhaps they fear the Turner scholars and biographers, understandably enraged over the destruction of the only surviving evidence of a great artist's erotic life.) John Dixon Hunt, in his fine life of Ruskin, disapproves, calling the burning of the letters "an act of pietistic destruction," and Ruskin's working with Wornum "a disgraceful piece of collaboration."[23]

Ruskin's latest and best biographer, Tim Hilton, speculates carefully: though Ruskin never spoke publicly about this, the obscene drawings may have convinced him that Turner's mind had become "diseased" in his later years. "Many years later," Hilton writes, "when Ruskin's own mind was in pitiful disarray, we occasionally find warnings about a 'passionately sensual character' that would lead to 'a kind of delirium tremens. Turner had it fatally in his last years'; and Ruskin's work with Wornum, otherwise forgotten, is suddenly mentioned in his diary's passages of insane free association that were written in the days before his own delirium."[24] The relevant notebook passage is dated 20 February 1878, three days before Ruskin's first complete mental breakdown: "Then Worums and my first necromancy!"[25] *Necromancy*—the summoning of the dead, the raising of the dead (like Saul and the Witch of Endor) in order to hear their voices: but how does one read the *burning* of Turner's works as an act of "necromancy"?

Around the turn of the last century, Ian Warrell, a curator at the Tate Britain, found himself unwilling to take Ruskin's letter to Ralph Wornum, and the various second- and third-hand account of the Turner burnings, as definitive evidence. So he painstakingly collated the entire Turner Bequest—almost thirty thousand bits of paper, drawings, sketches, and watercolors that had been repeatedly catalogued and described, but which had not been examined specifically with an eye for their racier contents. And among them he found enough erotic drawings—well over a hundred—to account for the "parcel" that Ruskin describes burning. It's of course impossible, given the size of the collection, to know whether or not *every* erotic drawing survives: but Warrell was able to account for most of the pages missing from Turner's notebooks, and made a compelling argument that it is at least possible—if not probable—that Ruskin had not *destroyed* but at some point *dispersed* and *concealed* Turner's naughty bits. And examining Ralph Wornum's diary for 1858, Warrell found no evidence of a meeting with Ruskin in December 1858, to burn Turners or anything else.[26]

Why then did Ruskin write Wornum in 1862, recounting a bonfire of Turner erotica, if such a bonfire never occurred? Warrell speculates that he might have wanted to provide legal "cover" for himself and the Gallery Keeper: a new law of 1857 had made the possession of such "obscene" representations illegal, even for national museums. More interestingly (and more speculatively), Warrell wonders whether Ruskin might not have been *suggesting* to Wornum that he burn the offending material.[27]

It seems likely, then—or at least highly possible—that Ruskin never participated in a destruction of Turner's erotic remains; if anything, he had connived at preserving and concealing those remains, while—just possibly—but quite speculatively—suggesting that they be destroyed. But what weight then do we give that word "necromancy," written in at the edges of the whirlpool of madness? Is it the "necromancy" of raising a specter of destruction that had no reality? Of guilt over lying to the legal authorities about the disposition of Turner's obscenities? Or is it simply the necromancy of examining and raising up the specter of Turner's lawless and obscene passions? We cannot *know*.

* * *

Three takes, then: In the first, a biographer fills in a set of tiny, admittedly trivial, details in his subject's childhood by appropriating vivid details from his subject's own autobiographical fiction. In the process, I think, the biographer elides the distinction between fiction and autobiography, and implicitly undermines the role of imagination and sheer *invention* in the fiction-making process—but certainly violates what seem to me to be canons of documentary evidence. In the second, the biographer finds himself doubting the strict veracity of his subject's direct epistolary testimony, on the basis of the testimony of the subject's son and on consideration of to whom a given letter was addressed. And in the third, a widely repeated, even iconic, action of the subject's life—perfectly congruent with everything else we know of him, and testified to by the subject himself—is shown, by a process of documentary examination of mind-boggling intricacy, quite possibly never to have happened, forcing us to revise our conception of the subject. Richard Ellmann did not *know* how many of John Kelly's fingers were "cramped"; I do not *know* the precise financial situation of Louis and Celia Zukofsky in August 1955; and despite what they thought was incontrovertible proof, a whole shelf of Ruskin biographers did not *know* what became of Turner's erotica.

Every biographer, consciously or unconsciously, finds him- or herself at some point traversing such a region of unknowing. How different biographers navigate such a region is an index of their various stances toward their art, their stance toward the asymptotic limit of "truth." For William Shakespeare, the subject of perhaps more biographies than any other writer in the English-language canon, almost the whole of his life is such an evidentiary blank. Almost everything one says about Shakespeare's life is speculation. But there is speculation and speculation: speculation that announces itself as such, and speculation that moves stealthily into assertion. I can by no means gainsay the beautiful readability and overall charm of Stephen Greenblatt's multizillion-selling *Will in the World: How Shakespeare Became Shakespeare* (2004), but I find my forehead wrinkling alarmingly toward the beginning of the book when, as part of his argument that the Bard was a crypto-Catholic, he speculates that Shakespeare worked for some time in a northern Catholic household as a schoolmaster, and might even have met the Catholic missionary Edmund Campion. Throughout, Greenblatt is careful to deploy the language of speculation: "would have," "might have," "may have been," "it is at least possible," "it is altogether possible," and so forth. But then, after he finally adduces a document whose provenance is absolutely unchallenged—an anti-Papal diatribe in *King John*—Greenblatt slips out of the language of speculation into the language of certainty: "This coarsely explicit piece of Protestant pope-baiting is by no means the sum of Shakespeare's mature attitude toward the Catholicism in which he *had been* immersed as a young man."[28] The preceding twenty pages or so may indeed give the impression that Shakespeare "had been immersed" in Catholicism in his youth, but Greenblatt hasn't presented real evidence, but rather a chain of speculation and thin circumstantial coincidences. A whole stack of "maybes" doesn't add up to a single "had been," but rather a big "might have been."

In contrast, Stephen Gill's level-headed but lyrical *William Wordsworth: A Life* (1990) is almost painfully scrupulous about its "gray areas." Of Wordsworth's 1792 sojourn in France, which included an affair with Annette Vallon and the birth of an illegitimate child, Gill writes, "To declare, as Mary

Moorman does, that Wordsworth felt for Annette 'all the worship of a great first love, even if it is admitted that probably the attraction was felt at first more on her side than on his', or, as [F. M.] Todd does, that 'had he never met Annette, there is no reason to believe that his political or poetic development would have been materially different', is to erect foundations for the interpretation of the next, crucial years of Wordsworth's life on sand. If what follows seems timid, the reason is that caution seems best when we know so little."[29] Gill's evidentiary "caution" is by no means a universal byword among biographers. Compelling biographies have been written on highly speculative foundations—Cynthia Griffin Wolff's *Emily Dickinson*, for instance, or—to take a fictive example—Stephen Dedalus's rhapsody on Shakespeare's life in the "Scylla and Charybdis" chapter of *Ulysses*.[30] But as a reader and biographer on Zukofsky—myself perhaps a second or third generation "Objectivist"—I find myself compelled, again, to "think with the things as they exist." The trouble, as my three "takes" indicate, is how slippery the evidence for those "things" inevitably turns out to be.

The *New Yorker* writer Janet Malcolm is no fan of biography: in her book on the afterlife of Sylvia Plath, *The Silent Woman* (1994), she calls it an industry of "voyeurism" and "busybodyism," a fundamentally "transgressive" genre read for the most part in "a state of bovine equanimity."[31] Sometimes it takes a hostile witness, however, to state an uncomfortable truth in its baldest form: "The ideal of unmediated reporting is regularly achieved only in fiction, where the writer faithfully reports what is going on in his imagination," Malcolm writes: "*In a work of nonfiction we almost never know the* truth *of what happened.*"[32]

I would not be taken as an apologist for a kind of thorough-going "postmodern" skepticism—though I think the conscientious biographer, in her or his most self-reflexive moments, feels the force of the post-Nietzschean critique of certainty (*no facts, only interpretations*) as forcefully as it can be felt. But I find myself lingering on the inevitable bad faith of the biographical enterprise, the biographer's inevitable bad conscience. When we fudge a fact, when we slide over a moment of real uncertainty, when we tell an outright lie—we do so in the assurance that nine times out of ten no one will notice. And when we report what seems an unassailable *fact*, as rocklike a datum concerning our subject's life as we could ask, we know by our own experience with "facts," "data," and evidence that that fact always has the potential, however slight, to be revised in the light of new evidence.

And, finally, our (public) success comes precisely to the degree that we are able to raise up a life-like simulacrum of our subject, to—like Odysseus in Pound's first Canto—give "blood to the ghosts" and make them speak in a manner that strikes us, our readers, and reviewers, as convincingly similar to how they might speak were they still alive: to knit a fabric of words that entirely covers the holes in our knowledge, a tapestry that so entrances our readers that they forget they are reading our own imagination of our subject's life, and begin to believe that they have been given *facts*—when, in true fact, they have only *interpretations*.

Notes

1. Louis Zukofsky, *Autobiography* (New York: Grossman, 1970) 5.

2. Louis Zukofsky, dust-jacket statement, *"A" 1–12* (Garden City, NY: Doubleday, 1967).

3. Louis Zukofsky, "An Objective," *Prepositions+: The Collected Critical Essays* (Hanover, NH: Wesleyan UP, 2000) 12.

4. Michael Heller, *Conviction's Net of Branches: Essays on the Objectivist Poets and Poetry* (Carbondale: Southern Illinois UP, 1985) 7.

5. Hugh Kenner, *A Homemade World: The American Modernist Writers* (1975; Baltimore: Johns Hopkins UP, 1989) 187.

6. Friedrich Nietzsche, *The Will to Power*, trans. Walter Kaufmann and R. J. Hollingdale (New York: Random House, 1968) 267, second emphasis mine.

7. Anthony Burgess, back-cover copy to Richard Ellmann, *James Joyce: New and Revised Edition* (New York: Oxford UP, 1982).

8. Finn Fordham, "Biography," *James Joyce in Context*, ed. John McCourt (Cambridge: Cambridge UP, 2009) 17–26, registers the restiveness among Joyce scholars at Ellmann's continued dominance of the Joyce biographical sphere.

9. James Joyce, *A Portrait of the Artist as a Young Man: Text, Criticism, Notes*, ed. Chester G. Anderson (1964; Harmondsworth, Eng.: Penguin, 1977) 28.

10. Ellmann, *James Joyce* 24.

11. Stanislaus Joyce, *My Brother's Keeper: James Joyce's Early Years*, ed. Richard Ellmann (New York: Viking, 1958) 13.

12. Samuel Johnson, *Samuel Johnson (The Oxford Authors)*, ed. Donald Greene (Oxford: Oxford UP, 1984) 300.

13. Louis Zukofsky to Edward Dahlberg, 29 August 1955; this letter is in the Harry Ransom Humanities Research Center, University of Texas at Austin.

14. Paul Zukofsky, e-mail to author, 19 February 2007 (paraphrased).

15. Mark Scroggins, *The Poem of a Life: A Biography of Louis Zukofsky* (Emeryville, CA: Shoemaker & Hoard, 2007) 276.

16. John Ruskin, *Works*, 39 vols., ed. E. T. Cook and Alexander Wedderburn (London: George Allen, 1903–1912) 3.254.

17. Mary Lutyens, *Millais and the Ruskins* (New York: Vanguard, 1967) 191–92.

18. Lutyens, *Millais and the Ruskins* 156. There has been much (ultimately fruitless) speculation as to what "disgusted" Ruskin about his wife's body.

19. Tim Hilton, *John Ruskin* (single-volume ed.) (1985 and 2000; New Haven: Yale UP, 2002) 253.

20. Frank Harris, *My Life and Loves*, ed. John F. Gallagher (1925; New York: Grove P, 1963) 400.

21. Amabel Williams-Ellis, *The Exquisite Tragedy: An Intimate Life of John Ruskin* (Garden City, NY: Doubleday Doran, 1929) 166.

22. Ian Warrell, "Exploring the 'dark side': Ruskin and the Problem of Turner's Erotica," *Turner's Secret Sketches* (London: Tate, 2012) 22.

23. John Dixon Hunt, *The Wider Sea: A Life of John Ruskin* (New York: Viking, 1982) 260.

24. Hilton, *John Ruskin* 250–51.

25. *The Brantwood Diary of John Ruskin*, ed. Helen Gill Viljoen (New Haven: Yale UP, 1971) 98.

26. Warrell, "Exploring the 'dark side,'" 47.

27. Warrell, "Exploring the 'dark side'" 48.

28. Stephen Greenblatt, *Will in the World: How Shakespeare Became Shakespeare* (New York: Norton, 2004) 111.

29. Stephen Gill, *William Wordsworth: A Life* (Oxford: Oxford UP, 1990) 58–59.

30. Cynthia Griffin Wolff, *Emily Dickinson* (New York: Knopf, 1987).

31. Janet Malcolm, *The Silent Woman: Sylvia Plath and Ted Hughes* (New York: Knopf, 1994) 9, 175.

32. Malcolm, *The Silent Woman* 154, emphasis mine.

A Fragmentary Poetics

On Writing Poems

[My poems have grown denser, more airless, since I composed "wee song," the sample around which this aphoristic essay revolves, almost two decades ago; but my writing continues to rely on the fragment and the quotation, the elements in which it is most akin to the modernist works through which I first came to poetry.]

I am a slow learner. My education—and it is still ongoing—has consisted of missed opportunities, hasty readings, and misremembered lessons. I am as well a slow writer. I draft painfully, in widely spaced turns, and rewrite obsessively. I leave much unfinished, discontinued. Appropriately, my poetry is a poetry of unfinished surfaces and discontinuities, a poetry of fragments. Perhaps in compensation, I have evolved (or discovered, or adopted—or stolen) a poetics of fragments.

•

"We commonly do not remember that it is, after all, always the first person that is speaking. I should not talk so much about myself if there were any body else whom I knew as well. Unfortunately, I am confined to this theme by my narrowness of experience."[1] The advantage of the personal voice in an essay on poetics is precisely similar to what Thoreau adumbrates in the opening pages of *Walden*. The first person, that is, allows the expositor of poetics to avoid proscriptivity, to display her or his praxis not as a model for suitable or correct—whether politically, socially, or aesthetically—writing, but as one particular path, chosen out of a number of alternatives. The first person allows for a descriptive poetics, as opposed to a universalizing blueprint.

Thoreau writes, and writes that he *speaks*. Here I only write. A few readers might hear my voice, but I am not speaking—I am writing these words in a composition book (trademark "The Scholar"), with a bright blue plastic fountain pen (brand name "Lamy"), filled with shocking violet ink. And I'm thinking these words in my brain, sounding them out as I go (I can feel my vocal cords contracting as I write, even though I'm not speaking them aloud). And I'm typing them into a Macintosh PowerBook 5300, hoping that the system won't crash and lose fifteen hundred words of semideathless prose, like it did last week. Or a month ago, as I'm revising and adding to what I've earlier written, patching, reshaping, and veneering sentences that on the page or screen, somehow don't *sound* right.

•

When I was younger, I wanted to write long poems that would hang together, that could be admired for the deftness with which their heterogeneous materials were woven into single fabrics. I admired odd, out-of-the-way by-blows of high modernist practice: Guy Davenport's *Flowers and Leaves*, Ronald Johnson's *The Book of the Green Man*. I also admired unwieldy nineteenth-century long poems no one I knew had read—Melville's *Clarel*, for instance—and claimed to admire vast poems I had only dipped into: Hardy's *The Dynasts*, Charles Montagu Doughty's *The Dawn in Britain*, Michael Drayton's *Poly-Olbion*. But I could not write like that. Poe dismissed *Paradise Lost* as passages of fine poetry bound together by stretches of versified description. He could not find the intensity of the brief lyric sustained over the length of the long poem. And I concurred with Poe, not in rejecting *Paradise Lost* but in foreswearing the long narrative poem, if only because I didn't have the patience to write the low-intensity passages that would lead from one high point to the next. I looked to Davenport, to Johnson, and to their modernist forebears, Pound and Zukofsky, for poetries in which bright moments and curious jewels of language were set side-by-side without regard for the flabby, less energetic verbiage that would explain their juxtaposition.

•

I read French haltingly, but Mallarmé's *Un coup de dés* was, in its form, a revelation for me. Where I loved his sonnets, toasts, monologues, and occasional verses for their dense, concentrated metaphoricity, I was drawn to *Un coup* for that same dense opacity expressed in a fundamentally *spare*, almost empty form. The shipwreck the poem tells of is as much a shipwreck of language as of anything beyond language, and leaves in its wake, not a harmonious description in classical French alexandrines, but a series of fragments of various shapes and sizes—flotsam and jetsam.

My friend Ted Pearson describes his own works as "long poems of very few words." This, then, was another model for the long poem, one that would mobilize fragments of language within the desert white space of the page. Space as a score for the voice, yes—but more crucially, empty space as the phenomenological environment of the reader, for whom blankness looms, broods around words that seem to shrink almost to nothing in their nakedness.

•

The fragment entices. It speaks of something more, no longer present. Shelley read the fragmentary statue of Ozymandias both as a testimony to a lost whole—the pride and pomp of the Pharaoh Ramses II, the "wrinkled lip, and sneer of cold command" that commissioned an undying, eternal monument to themselves—and, despite the attritions of time, a testimony to the art and skill of the sculptor who, with sly subversion, "mocked" the Pharaoh in depicting him. Friedrich Schlegel, leader of the Jena *Athenaeum* group, and perhaps the preeminent Romantic theorist of the fragment, argued a different line. "Many of the works of the ancients," he wrote, the Venus de Milo and the Nike of Samothrace surely in mind, "have become fragments. Many modern works are fragments as soon as they are written." This bespeaks a sensibility distinct from Shelley's, one that seeks aesthetic wholeness, not in the imagined totality of which the fragment is the eroded remainder, but in the fragment itself, whole unto itself: "A fragment, like a miniature work of art, has to be entirely isolated from the surrounding world and be complete in itself like a porcupine."[2]

Rilke, his poet's eye nuzzling about the "Archaic Torso of Apollo," admits, "We cannot know his legendary head" [*Wir kannten nicht sein unerhörtes Haupt*]. Nonetheless, the inner light that still suffuses the fragmentary statue "from inside" has the power to impose a self-altering imperative: "You must change your life" [*Du mußt dein Leben ändern*].[3] Who is "you," called upon with the familiar "du"? It is not the poem: it can only be the poet, for the fragmentation of the statue goes no further than its description *in* the poem: the poem itself is whole, a perfect sonnet, all its rhymes in place.

•

In English, the renaissance of the fragmentary that Schlegel heralds came about only in the first decades of this century, when poets like Eliot and Pound (in large part inspired by European modernist visual artists) discovered the resonance and power of the fragmented utterance. (Do I want to write literary history? Here?) When I was younger, I read *The Waste Land* as the record of a spiritual journey from despair to something like complacent hope. Now, I can read it only as a virtuosic collage of fragments. After a first exhilarated immersion, I read *The Cantos* like a good scholar, tracking down the sources of the quotations, annotating my copy of the poem (in brown ink, with a fountain pen) from an array of reference books fanned out on the table around me. When I began Olson's *Maximus*, I had George Butterick's guide to the poem in one hand, a mechanical pencil in the other. But this time, I found that source-hunting was impeding the movement, slowing down and even arresting the "projectivist" thrust of Olson's language. What I realized was that *The Cantos* had drawn me in, not as a treasure-trove of Pound's reading, but as a glittering, unsystematic hoard of resonant fragments. It was wrong, I realized—or wrong at least for me—to begin my first sustained reading of Olson's epic with Baedeker in hand. Butterick replaced on the shelf, *Maximus* could pull me forward with an energy kindred to that of *The Cantos* or of Williams's *Paterson*, another great modernist fragment-poem.

•

I happily admit that my writing technologies are antiquated. I write by hand, usually with a fountain pen, in bound books (some lined, some unlined). I used to use gray, round-cornered composition books, but I haven't been able to find them for some years, so at present I use a heterogeneous array of different books, ranging from large leather-bound business ledgers to tiny paperbacks. My writing is careful, almost obsessive (which is not to imply uniformly legible). I date each entry, and sometimes begin the day's writing by lamenting how long it's been since last I wrote.

I begin drafting a poem on one page; when I've written a few lines, I rewrite them, either immediately under the first draft or on the facing page. Rather than copying from the recto to the verso of the same page—which means flipping back and forth and often miscopying words or spaces—I will write a new draft into another notebook. So tracing the composition of a given poem (not something I often do) is a process of tracking down the notebooks of a given period, toggling back and forth between them, and trying to make out which version of a given line or passage is prior to the other.

One poet friend of mine writes only on yellow legal pads, with a sharpened pencil. Another can only compose at the keyboard; before the advent of the personal computer, he wrote at the typewriter. There are strong affinities between both of their poetics and my own. Does this mean that the old question, "How do you write?" is really irrelevant? I don't know. Sometimes I think so, sometimes not. Like Louis Zukofsky's, my handwriting is tiny and, I'm told, hard to read. Unlike Guy Davenport, no teacher has ever told me,

"You have neat and attractive handwriting." Occasionally, my hand has been the source of useful mistakes: copying from one notebook to another, I have misread my own writing, replacing the wooden original with a more vigorous, less logical alternative.

My working notebooks, when they aren't taken up with prose ramblings or actual drafts of poems, contain large stretches of random verbal material: words, phrases, sentences, quotations. Unlike Davenport, whose multiple notebooks are rigidly and productively segregated among subjects and modes, my own notebooks are rigidly and productively random. I admire his orderliness; I haven't the discipline to do it like that. (The story of my life in nine words.)

•

Discipline. Louis Zukofsky's works have occupied me for better than a decade now, and the more I learn of them, the more the man's sheer dogged discipline, his rage to order his materials, strikes me. One way of reading *"A"* might be to see the poem beginning in a *Cantos*-like mode, only more complex, more highly structured. As the poem progresses, Zukofsky finds that way of going just too simple. And so, with an almost obsessive attention, he devises crueler and crueler formal straitjackets to fit his language into: why not write a section in which distribution of "n" and "r" sounds is determined by the formula for a conic section? Why not try to imitate the structure of a baroque partita (since he's already done the baroque fugue)? Why not translate a stretch of the book of *Job* into an English that *sounds* as much as possible like the Hebrew? Why not try to fit six thousand years of history into a thousand lines of poetry, sedulously avoiding proper names? Why not do that last one twice?

The twenty-four movements of *"A"* have God's plenty for the structure-hunter. A horse in every movement, the letter "A" thematized in every movement, Pythagorean number-lore, literary history, current events—and all wound in upon ever-shifting and ever more complex formal systems. My mind boggles, and admires. But I haven't the discipline to do it like that.

•

I've read a lot about the poetics of the fragment, the poetics of the ruin. Most of the work in English deals with the Romantics, who loved plopping themselves down among the overgrown, broken walls of some medieval abbey and whipping out their notebooks and quills. The poet Heather McHugh's *Broken English*, despite some promising sentences on Tom Phillips's monumental *A Humument*, is only suggestive.[4] The most interesting writing on the fragment is in the French poststructuralist tradition: Philippe Lacoue-Labarthe and Jean-Luc Nancy's *The Literary Absolute*, Maurice Blanchot's *The Writing of the Disaster*.[5] Such works have all the pleasures and frustrations of most contemporary French philosophy: a heady playfulness and a capacious suggestiveness, paired with an absolute unwillingness to settle on positive statements.

In "*Noli me frangere*," Nancy and Lacoue-Labarthe write, "It is a mistake, then, to write in fragments on the fragment." "But what else," they hastily add, "is there to do? Write about something else entirely—or about nothing—and let oneself be fragmented."[6] (Am I writing in fragments here? I don't think so—that is, I suspect a hypotactic logic operating from paragraph to paragraph, block of prose to block of prose. Does it add up to an argument? Perhaps—but I hope not.)

•

Here's a passage I've found myself returning to repeatedly of late. It's by the Cambridge poet J. H. Prynne, and I can't tell whether it's the third section of "Evening Walk" or a separate poem (there's no table of contents to his collection *Wound Response*):

As grazing the earth
the sun raises
its mouth to the night
rick, ox-eye'd
and burning, strewn over
the phase path

At the turning-places
of the sun the
head glistens, dew falls
from the apse line:

O lye still, thou
Little Musgrave, the
grass is wet
and streak'd with light[7]

I think this is an *alba*, a dawn song to a lover: "Little Musgrave" (or Musgrove) is a character in a British Isles folk song, another version of which is "Matty

Groves"; his failure to leave his lover's arms results in his untimely death at the hands of her husband. I like that reference, and I like Prynne's cheekiness in deploying his archaic punctuation ("streak'd") even where it doesn't belong—"ox-eye'd," after all, needs no apostrophe. I like the technical terms—"the phase path," "the apse line"—planted like mines in a poem whose diction is drawn straight from the eighteenth century. And I like how the parts of each sentence, though grammatical enough, don't quite *fit*. How can one head "glisten" at (several) "turning-places of the sun"? What does it mean to speak of dew falling "from the apse line"? Prynne's poem intrigues me as a concatenation of linguistic fragments, some of them from radically different realms of discourse, strung like beads onto a single syntactic thread.

(And mostly, of course, I love the way the poem *sounds*.)

•

Is one still allowed to talk about *tastes*? (I've been reading Hume's essays lately, so you'll have to pardon me if I slip into an eighteenth-century periwig here. Anyway—.) My tastes are catholic, and eclectic. I can't for the life of me dislike some poets whose work, I'm told, is diametrically opposed to everything I'm invested in. On the other hand, I'm absolutely unable to muster enthusiasm for some poetry that, from its dust-jacket descriptions and from the testimony of friends, ought to be "just the sort of stuff you'd like." I can't even say I write the sort of poems I like best—I write, in short, the kind of poems I *can*. A poetics of necessity.

•

Overwriting and crossing out are mirror-image routes to the poetry of the fragment. The English artist Tom Phillips paints over pages of W. H. Mallock's Victorian novel *A Human Document* to produce his *A Humument*.[8] Phillips's pages are shimmering with color, pictures, and designs. And on each page, a few words of Mallock's text have been preserved, floating like speech balloons in a Bill Sienkiewicz comic book. But the words are joined together by minute umbilici, so that the reader is led from one to the next as overtly as David Hume, with a most un-Scottish geniality, leads you from clause to clause, proposition to conclusion. Phillips claims that there's a narrative here, its protagonist a chap named "Toge" (he can only appear, of course, when Mallock has used the word "together" or "altogether"). I don't know—I'd rather attend to the interplay of word and design in *A Humument*. Blake rewrote Milton twice, once by illustrating him, and once by making him the protagonist of an illuminated poem in which the author of *Paradise Lost* appears (quite un-Puritanically) in the nude. Phillips has rewritten Mallock's *A Human Document* by making its forgotten narrative into a succession of dazzling poem-illustrations, kin to Blake's composite art.

Ronald Johnson's *Radi os* rewrites the first four books of *Paradise Lost* by simply erasing most of their words. They remain naked on the page, still in their 1892 typeface (what coincidence caused both Phillips and Johnson to choose books published in that year?), sprinkled like the sparagmatic words of Mallarmé's *Un coup de dès*. They are fragments in perhaps the purest sense, though Milton's high diction and lofty rhetoric, perforce the only vocabulary Johnson has allowed himself, impose a certain cohesiveness of "poetic" tone upon them, as well as allowing Johnson an ample word-hoard for his favored themes of light and cosmology. But in their scattering, they do not submit to the same hypotactic unity imposed on the words that escape Phillips's overpainting.

outspread,
on the vast

Illumine,
I
Say first—[9]

Our top-down habits of reading would render these lines "outspread, on the vast Illumine, I Say first—." But our left-to-right habits (by no means inevitable ones—Leonardo, like all writers of Hebrew, wrote right-to-left, and some scripts are written *boustrophedon*, reversing direction at the end of each line) render them "Illumine, on the vast outspread, I Say first—." Johnson has rewritten *Paradise Lost* into a Transcendentalist celebration of mind, eye, cosmos, and artistic power, in the process losing the whole narrative machinery of Satan, God, and their respective cohorts. But he has also opened Milton's text—or those fragments of Milton's text he has retained—to a fertile syntactic and semantic undecidability, an opportunity for words to interact with their neighbors in ways completely foreign to the seventeenth-century poet.

•

David Melnick's *Pcoet* is yet more radical. Melnick's raw material here is not words or phrases, but the smallest building-blocks of language. And not phonemes, *sounds*—that would imply a theory of language in which the spoken is prior or superior to the written word, in which the writing poet is merely transcriber of what she or he has already uttered, silently or aloud—but graphemes, letters, the fragments of the *written* word. *Radi os* can be read aloud (and I am told Johnson has done so, magnificently). *Pcoet* is, in that sense, unreadable.

> qquerl
>
> asd tpelogn
>
> seruasiet nsovv
> zhsdiz, aomsa
>
> csdpZ zsdui[10]

The reading mind craves meaning. It wants to *make* sense out of a text. Melnick, fragmenting and recombining the basic particles of the sense-bearing strings we call words, continually frustrates that desire. I'm not so interested in the technicalities of Melnick's compositional technique—sometimes he seems simply to be typing English words as fast and as badly as he can, other times he seems to be working over French or Greek templates—or the avant-garde precursors of *Pcoet*—Velimir Khlebnikov's invented *Zaum* language comes immediately to mind—as I am in the end-result: letters; clusters of letters that are almost words; clusters of almost-words that are almost phrases—an apocalypse of fragmentation that offers both too little meaning to hold onto and too much meaning to take in at once.

•

(This isn't the place to write literary history. I can hear someone saying, "What about X, what about Y, what about *me*?" I'm citing poems I know and have thought about, poems that have been important to my own poetics [such as it is]. Perhaps poems that haven't been talked about enough? But not, certainly not, all of the texts that make important use of fragmentation, even in our own half-century.)

•

I have bits and pieces of language continually floating in my ears, usually harnessed to tunes. (Did I mention that I listen to a lot of music?) Those bits and pieces—fragments—usually find their way into my notebooks, put down in great paratactic lists. Sometimes, often years later, they find their way into poems. The phrases I use often have great resonance for me. Whenever I read them, their original context is dragged into my mind—the tail of Proust's madeleine wagging the great shaggy dog of Proust's memory. Nothing magic about that. Does a reader share in that resonance?—of course not. But I hope, somehow, that traces of the resonance I feel in the phrases will cling to them in the poem, will somehow "haunt" the reader. Maybe that's magic.

•

The best poetics is applied poetics. Poe's "Philosophy of Composition," of course, is a travesty of the process, several thousand words of breathless and didactic prose demonstrating precisely how Poe *wished* he had written "The Raven." Far more compelling is Zukofsky's "*'Mantis,' An Interpretation*," a free-verse poem explaining the origins, sources, and formal decisions involved in the composition of Zukofsky's Depression-era sestina "'Mantis.'" There's some justice in writing one poem to explain another, but even in Zukofsky, you end up feeling he's expatiating too much.

Perhaps the best way to present a poetics of fragments would be to hold up a poem which that poetics has produced, then run down some of the bits and pieces that have gone into it. This poem is called "wee song," and was written in the latter part of 1996:[11]

    the LORD draws
no one

                                        picks its way
                                    across the bottom

                                                    the LORD draws no
                                                          one

a tiny wee buke
  a broken gangrel

flashing eyes

stag
    hound

. . .

take it
like
    a man

turn again
home

blackwater
  side

"the only food
she had

"never dance
again"

bread
& morphine"

strathspey

. . .

sprinkled skirling
words

voicelings

lips parting
under water

farewell
fareweel

take back
  your name,
    your shiver

John—your
  pillow

. . .

Madonna of
the Rocks
  footwash

Baptist

crystals on
  your sleeve

auld black
  bitch of a
    boat

neither coal
nor candle

scrape lichens
from the stone—or
  "Charlie is my darlin'"

•

Most of my poet friends listen to serious music: avant-garde jazz, twentieth-century "classical." So do I; but truth be told, I like certain forms of popular music as much as the average twelve-year-old likes manufactured corporate pop. I'm not rash enough to claim that most pop lyrics are poetry, as many did back in the heady sixties (though there's a chiasmus in this Wallflowers song that beats anything since Alexander Pope), but I can't deny that as many of the stanzas buzzing in my head got there through my stereo system as from the pages of books. British Isles folk music, and its electrified avatars, is my true Penelope. When I read a poem in ballad meter, whether it's "Because I could not stop for Death" or Johnson's "I put my hat upon my head," I'm liable to sing it to the melancholy tune of "Mary Hamilton."

The folk-rock songs whose fragments make it into "wee song"—Richard Thompson's "Devonside," Oysterband's "Fiddle or a Gun," among others[12]—are songs whose lyrics are both highly intelligent, literate, and—to the ear of my mind—highly affecting. These fragments are keys to points in the songs where melody, instrumentation, and singing come together in a way that almost inevitably puts a catch in my throat, whether I've had a drink or not. But beyond my personal predilections, it seems to me that Thompson and Oysterband's John Jones have captured something quite integral to the power of the traditional ballad. The ballad, that is, usually tells a story, narrates a series of events. It bears the same relation to the average pop lyric that a short story does to a Mallarméan prose poem. In the course of centuries-long transmission, however, the ballad becomes fragmented and reformed. Singers forget lines and stanzas, and substitute lines of their own invention, stanzas from other, similar songs. In compiling his monumental *Minstrelsy of the Scottish Border*, Sir Walter Scott tried to iron over these discontinuities, to make the ballads into shapely, complete stories. But it's those discontinuities, the absences, that make the ballads so compelling to me, and it's those elements that Thompson and Jones have managed to capture in their own songwriting. We're never told who the "she" and "he" of Thompson's "Devonside" are, nor why the only nourishment she can offer him is "bread and morphine," but the words themselves—inseparable in my mind from their melody, Thompson's raw singing, and the astonishingly intuitive ensemble playing that accompanies them—compel my interest, my emotional investment.

•

Over the past two years, picking up threads from old childhood interests, I've pursued the harebrained goal of mastering the entire corpus of Scottish literature. I'm presently running down the last three or four of Scott's novels. They're terrifically readable, once you get past the almost uniformly turgid beginnings, and Scott has yet to be surpassed, even by such contemporaries as James Kelman and Irvine Welsh, as a master of vernacular Scots dialogue. Words stick in one's mind—*gangrel*, a wanderer or vagabond; the slight shift of pronunciation that makes "book" *buke*; *skirling*, "screaming," often applied (approbriously) to the sound of the bagpipes. And phrases. In *The Antiquary*, Steenie Mucklebackit has no sooner been buried than old Mucklebackit, under the pressure of grinding poverty, goes back to mending the fishing vessel from which his only son has drowned—that "auld black bitch of a boat."[13] The indecisive Englishman Edward Waverley, in the novel that bears his name, first sees the extent of Scotland's political and emotional divisions when he witnesses a crazed Jacobite woman set upon by a Whig crowd, all the while singing a song to the Bonnie Prince: "Charlie is my darlin'."[14] (The scholar in me knows that this is a bald anachronism: the poem in question was written—accounts differ—by some combination of Robert Burns [born 1759], Carolina, Lady Nairne [born 1766], and James Hogg [born 1770], and therefore is unlikely to have been sung during the 1745 uprising of which Scott writes. It rings in my head, however, not as another "Burns song," but in its context in *Waverley*.)

That the emotional crises of Scott's novels rarely involve his major characters—pasteboard heroes and heroines all—does not make them any less moving; in fact, the minor characters of his great Scottish novels—lower-class, ill-educated, singing or speaking their minds in wonderfully redolent Scots—in the end have all the good lines: the lines, that is, that stick in the reader's mind as luminous moments amid a great unsystematic, unsorted mindful of linguistic fragments from all realms of experience.

And the dog? Sir Walter's great deerhound, Maida, grew so impatient of portraitists that he would leave the room "whenever he saw an artist unfurl his paper and handle his brushes."[15]

•

Most of the other bits and pieces that make up the poem are also quotation, though I couldn't tell you what I'm quoting much of the time. All language, after all, is quotation; poets knew that long before Derrida told the academy. The words, wherever they come from (and I've heard them before), move me. They have a talismanic significance in my own imaginary. Not a hermetic significance: they aren't to be "explained" or decoded, and were I to go through a poem word by word, phrases by phrase, talking about what each fragment means to me, that exercise (tedious to be sure) would serve as neither a key to the poem nor a descriptive poetics. I don't expect to convey that talismanic significance in the "finished" poem. All I can offer is the poem itself, out of which a reader is welcome to make as much as she will.

God knows this is an attenuated offering, appropriate perhaps for an attenuated poetics. But I spend far too much of my time, professionally and personally, trying to explain things I'm not sure I understand. (Perhaps, finally, a satisfactory definition of *poetics*: n., the act of explaining something one's not sure one understands.) But one last bit of language—Louis Zukofsky's—stuck in my mind can stand as last word:

Can love rouse a thing of the past
And not see it as present?[16]

Notes

1. Henry David Thoreau, *A Week on the Concord and Merrimack Rivers, Walden, The Maine Woods, Cape Cod*, ed. Robert F. Sayre (New York: Library of America, 1985) 325.

2. Friedrich Schlegel, *Philosophical Fragments*, trans. Peter Firchow (Minneapolis: U of Minnesota P, 1991) 21, 45 (Athenaeum Fragments #24 and #206).

3. Rainer Maria Rilke, *Selected Poetry*, trans. Stephen Mitchell (New York: Vintage, 1984) 60–61.

4. Heather McHugh, *Broken English: Poetry and Partiality* (Hanover, NH: Wesleyan UP, 1993).

5. Philippe Lacoue-Labarthe and Jean-Luc Nancy, *The Literary Absolute: The Theory of Literature in German Romanticism*, trans. Philip Barnard and Cheryl Lester (Albany: State U of New York P, 1988; Maurice Blanchot, *The Writing of the Disaster*, trans. Ann Smock (Lincoln: U of Nebraska P, 1986).

6. Jean-Luc Nancy and Philippe Lacoue-Labarthe, "*Noli me frangere,*" in Jean-Luc Nancy, *The Birth to Presence*, trans. Brian Holmes et al. (Stanford, CA: Stanford UP, 1993) 266.

7. J. H. Prynne, *Wound Response* (Cambridge: Street Editions, 1974) 19.

8. Tom Phillips, *A Humument: A Treated Victorian Novel.* 5th ed. (London: Thames & Hudson, 2012); see also www.humument.com.

9. Ronald Johnson, *Radi os* (1977; Chicago: Flood Editions, 2005) 4.

10. David Melnick, *Pcoet* (San Francisco: G.A.W.K., 1975) 26.

11. Mark Scroggins, *Anarchy* (New York: Spuyten Duyvil, 2003) 41–49.

12. Richard Thompson, "Devonside" (Richard Thompson), *Hand of Kindness* (Hannibal Records, HNCD 1313, 1983); Oysterband, "Fiddle or a Gun" (John Jones and Ian Telfer), *Deserters* (Ryko Records, RCD 10237, 1992).

13. Sir Walter Scott, *The Antiquary* (New York: Collier, n.d.) 348.

14. Sir Walter Scott, *Waverley; or, 'Tis Sixty Years Since* (New York: Collier, n.d.) 244.

15. *The Journal of Sir Walter Scott*, ed. W. E. K. Anderson (1972; Edinburgh: Canongate, 1998) 66.

16. Louis Zukofsky, "*A*" (1978; New York: New Directions, 2012) 199.

Works Cited

Abrams, M. H. *Natural Supernaturalism: Tradition and Revolution in Romantic Literature.* New York: Norton, 1971.

Abrioux, Yves. *Ian Hamilton Finlay: A Visual Primer.* Cambridge, MA: MIT P, 1992.

Ackroyd, Peter. *Blake: A Biography.* New York: Knopf, 1996.

Ahl, Frederick. "Ars Est Caelare Artem (Art in Puns and Anagrams Engraved)." *On Puns: The Foundation of Letters.* Ed. Jonathan Culler. Oxford: Blackwell, 1988. 17–43

———. *Metaformations: Wordplay and Soundplay in Ovid and Other Classical Poets.* Ithaca: Cornell UP, 1985.

Allen, Donald, ed. *The New American Poetry 1945–1960.* 1960; Berkeley: U of California P, 1999.

Alpert, Barry. "Ronald Johnson—An Interview (1974)." *Ronald Johnson: Life and Works.* Ed. Joel Bettridge and Eric Murphy Selinger. Orono, ME: National Poetry Foundation, 2008. 545-60.

Antheil, George. *Bad Boy of Music.* 1945; Hollywood: Samuel French, 1990.

Archambeau, Robert. *Laureates and Heretics: Six Careers in American Poetry.* Notre Dame, IN: U of Notre Dame P, 2010.

Armantrout, Rae. *Collected Prose.* San Diego: Singing Horse P, 2007.

———. *Next Life.* Middletown, CT: Wesleyan UP, 2007.

———. *Versed.* Middletown, CT: Wesleyan UP, 2009.

———, Carla Harryman, Kit Robinson, Tom Mandel, Barrett Watten, Ted Pearson, Lyn Hejinian, Bob Perelman, Ron Silliman, and Steve Benson. *The Grand Piano: An Experiment in Collective Autobiography, San Francisco 1975–1980, Part 4.* Detroit: Mode A, 2007.

Auden, W. H. *Selected Poems.* New Edition. Ed. Edward Mendelson. New York: Vintage, 1979.

Azzi, María Susana. Liner Notes. Yo-Yo Ma, *Soul of the Tango: The Music of Astor Piazolla*, Sony SK 63122, 1997.

Bentley, G. E., Jr. *The Stranger from Paradise: A Biography of William Blake.* New Haven: Yale UP, 2001.

Bernstein, Charles. *My Way: Speeches and Poems.* Chicago: U of Chicago P, 1999.

———. *The Sophist*. Los Angeles: Sun & Moon, 1987.

———, and Bruce Andrews, eds. *The L=A=N=G=U=A=G=E Book*. Carbondale: Southern Illinois UP, 1984.

Bernstein, Leonard and David Johnson. Liner Notes. *Symphony No. 2*. Charles Ives. New York Philharmonic. Leonard Bernstein, cond. Columbia Masterworks KL 5489, n. d.

Bettridge, Joel, and Eric Murphy Selinger, eds. *Ronald Johnson: Life and Works*. Orono, ME: National Poetry Foundation, 2008.

Blake, William. *The Complete Poetry and Prose*. Ed. David B. Erdman. New York: Anchor, 1982.

———. *The Marriage of Heaven and Hell*. Ed. Sir Geoffrey Keynes. Oxford: Oxford UP, 1975.

Blanchot, Maurice. *The Writing of the Disaster*. Trans. Ann Smock. Lincoln: U of Nebraska P, 1986.

Boswell, James. *Life of Johnson*. Ed. R. W. Chapman. London: Oxford UP, 1953.

Burkholder, J. Peter. *All Made of Tunes: Charles Ives and the Uses of Musical Borrowing*. New Haven: Yale UP, 1995.

———, ed. *Charles Ives and His World*. New York: Oxford UP, 1955.

———. "Ives and the Four Musical Traditions." *Charles Ives and His World*. Ed. Peter J. Burkholder. Princeton: Princeton UP, 1996. 3–34.

Butterick, George F. *A Guide to the Maximus Poems of Charles Olson*. Berkeley: U of California P, 1978.

Carson, Anne. *Autobiography of Red: A Novel in Verse*. New York, Knopf, 1998.

———. *The Beauty of the Husband: a fictional essay in 29 tangos*. New York: Knopf, 2001.

———. *Eros the Bittersweet: An Essay*. Princeton: Princeton UP, 1986.

———. *Glass, Irony and God*. New York: New Directions, 1995.

———. *Men in the Off Hours*. New York: Knopf, 2000.

Carter, Angela. *The Sadeian Woman and the Ideology of Pornography*. New York: Pantheon, 1979.

Catullus, Tibullus, Pervigilium Veneris. Loeb Classical Library. Trans. F. W. Cornish, J. P. Postgate, and J. W. Mackail. Cambridge: Harvard UP, 1962.

Celan, Paul. *Collected Prose*. Trans. Rosmarie Waldrop. Manchester: Carcanet, 1986.

Clark, Tom. *Charles Olson: The Allegory of a Poet's Life*. New York: Norton, 1991.

Cowell, Henry and Sidney, eds. *Charles Ives and His Music*. New York: Oxford UP, 1955.

Crane, Joan. *Guy Davenport: A Descriptive Bibliography 1947–1995*. Haverford, CT: Green Shade, 1996.

Creeley, Robert. *The Collected Poems of Robert Creeley, 1945–1975*. Berkeley: U of California P, 1982.

———. *The Collected Poems of Robert Creeley, 1975–2005*. Berkeley: U of California P, 2006.

———. *Pieces*. New York: Scribner's, 1969.

———. *Selected Poems, 1945–2005*. Ed. Benjamin Friedlander. Berkeley: U of California P, 2008.

Culler, Jonathan. *Ferdinand de Saussure*. Rev. ed. Ithaca: Cornell UP, 1986.

D'Agata, John. "A _________ With Anne Carson." *Iowa Review* 27.2 (1997): 1–22.

Davenport, Guy. *7 Greeks*. New York: New Directions, 1995.

———. *Apples and Pears*. San Francisco: North Point, 1984.

———. *Archilochus, Sappho, Alkman: Three Lyric Poets of the Seventh Century B.C.* Berkeley: U of California P, 1980.

———. *The Cardiff Team*. New York: New Directions, 1996.

———. *Da Vinci's Bicycle*. Baltimore: Johns Hopkins UP, 1979.

———. *The Death of Picasso: New and Selected Writing*. Washington, DC: Shoemaker & Hoard, 2003.

———. *The Drummer of the Eleventh North Devonshire Fusiliers*. San Francisco: North Point, 1990.

———. *Eclogues*. San Francisco: North Point, 1981.

———. *Every Force Evolves a Form: Twenty Essays*. San Francisco: North Point, 1987.

———. *Flowers and Leaves: Poema vel Sonata: Carmina Autumni Primaeque Veris Transformationum*. 1966; Flint, MI: Bamberger Books, 1991.

———. "Fragments from a Correspondence." Ed. Nicholas Kilmer. *Arion* 13.3 (Winter 2006): 89–130.

———. *The Geography of the Imagination: Forty Essays*. San Francisco: North Point, 1981.

———. *The Hunter Gracchus and Other Papers on Literature and Art*. Washington, DC: Counterpoint, 1996.

———. *The Jules Verne Steam Balloon*. San Francisco: North Point, 1987.

———. *A Table of Green Fields: Ten Stories*. New York: New Directions, 1993.

———. *Tatlin!* New York: Scribner's, 1974.

———. *Thasos and Ohio: Poems and Translations 1950–1980*. San Francisco: North Point, 1986.

———. *Twelve Stories*. Washington, DC: Counterpoint, 1997.

———, and James Laughlin. *Selected Letters*. Ed. W. C. Bamberger. New York: Norton, 2007.

———, and Jonathan Williams. *A Garden Carried in a Pocket: Letters 1964–1968*. Ed. Thomas Meyer. Haverford, CT: Green Shade, 2004.

Dickinson, Emily. *The Poems of Emily Dickinson: Reading Edition*. Ed. R. W. Franklin. Cambridge: Belknap P of Harvard UP, 1999.

Doerr, Joe Francis. "Interview with John Matthias." *The Salt Companion to John Matthias*. Ed. Joe Francis Doerr. Cromer, Eng.: Salt, 2011. 208–32.

Duberman, Martin. *Black Mountain: An Exploration in Community*. New York: Dutton, 1972.

Duncan, Robert. *The Collected Early Poems and Plays*. Ed. Peter Quartermain. Berkeley: U of California P, 2012.

———. *The Collected Later Poems and Plays*. Ed. Peter Quartermain. Berkeley: U of California P, 2013.
———. *Ground Work: Before the War*. New York: New Directions, 1984.
———. *The H. D. Book*. Ed. Michael Boughn and Victor Coleman. Berkeley: U of California P, 2011.
———. *Letters: Poems 1953–1956*. Ed. Robert J. Bertholf. Chicago: Flood Editions, 2003.
———. *Selected Poems (Revised and Enlarged)*. Ed. Robert J. Bertholf. New York: New Directions, 1997.
T. S. Eliot. *The Complete Poems and Plays, 1909–1950*. New York: Harcourt, Brace, 1971.
———. *On Poetry and Poets*. 1957; New York: Noonday P, 1961.
———. *The Sacred Wood: Essays on Poetry and Criticism*. 1920; London: Methuen, 1960.
Ellmann, Richard. *James Joyce: New and Revised Edition*. New York: Oxford UP, 1982.
Emerson, Ralph Waldo. *Essays and Lectures*. Ed. Joel Porte. New York: Library of America, 1983.
Empson, William. *Milton's God*. 1961; Cambridge: Cambridge UP, 1981.
Enslin, Theodore. *Carmina*. Dennis, MA: Salt-Works P, 1976.
———. *Re-Sounding: Selected Later Poems*. Jersey City, NJ: Talisman House, 1999.
———. *Then, and Now: Selected Poems 1943–1993*. Ed. Mark Nowak. Orono, ME: National Poetry Foundation, 1999.
Faas, Ekbert. *Towards a New American Poetics: Essays and Interviews*. Santa Barbara: Black Sparrow, 1978.
———. *Young Robert Duncan: Portrait of the Poet as Homosexual in Society*. Santa Barbara: Black Sparrow, 1983.
Feder, Stuart. *Charles Ives, "My Father's Song": A Psychoanalytic Biography*. New Haven: Yale UP, 1992.
Finkelstein, Norman. *Columns: Track, Volume Two*. New York: Spuyten Duyvil, 2002.
———. *Powers: Track, Volume Three*. New York: Spuyten Duyvil, 2005.
———. *Track*. New York: Spuyten Duyvil, 1999.
———. *Track: A Poem*. Bristol, Eng.: Shearsman, 2012.
Finlay, Alec, ed. *Wood Notes Wild: Essays on the Poetry and Art of Ian Hamilton Finlay*. Edinburgh: Polygon, 1995.
Finlay, Ian Hamilton. *Inter Artes et Naturam*. Paris: ARC, 1987.
———. *Selections*. Ed. Alec Finlay. Berkeley: U of California P, 2012.
Fordham, Finn. "Biography." *James Joyce in Context*. Ed. John McCourt. Cambridge: Cambridge UP, 2009. 17–26.
Frost, Robert. *Collected Poems, Prose, and Plays*. Ed. Richard Poirier and Mark Richardson. New York: Library of America, 1995.
Furlani, André. *Guy Davenport: Postmodern and After*. Evanston: Northwestern UP, 2007.
Gifford, Don, with Robert J. Seidman. *Ulysses Annotated: Notes for James Joyce's Ulysses*. Rev. and expanded ed. Berkeley: U of California P, 1988.

Gill, Stephen. *William Wordsworth: A Life*. Oxford: Oxford UP, 1990.

Gizzi, Peter. *The Outernationale*. Middletown, CT: Wesleyan UP, 2008.

———. *Some Values of Landscape and Weather*. Middletown, CT: Wesleyan UP, 2003.

Greenblatt, Stephen. *Will in the World: How Shakespeare Became Shakespeare*. New York: Norton, 2004.

Hall, Donald, Robert Pack, and Louis Simpson, eds. *New Poets of England and America*. New York: Meridian, 1957.

Hardy, Thomas. *Collected Poems*. 1925; New York: Macmillan, 1953.

Harris, Mary Emma. *The Arts at Black Mountain*. Cambridge: MIT P, 1987.

Harris, Frank. *My Life and Loves*. Ed. John F. Gallagher. 1925; New York: Grove P, 1963.

Harvey, David. *The Condition of Postmodernity: An Enquiry into the Origins of Cultural Change*. Oxford: Blackwell, 1990.

Hejinian, Lyn. *The Cell*. Los Angeles: Sun & Moon, 1992.

Heller, Michael. *Conviction's Net of Branches: Essays on the Objectivist Poets and Poetry*. Carbondale: Southern Illinois UP, 1985.

———. *Knowledge*. New York: Sun, 1979.

———. *Living Root: A Memoir*. Albany: State U of New York P, 2000.

———. *Speaking the Estranged: Essays on the Work of George Oppen*. Cambridge: Salt, 2008.

———. *This Constellation Is a Name: Collected Poems 1965–2010*. Callicoon, NY: Nightboat Books, 2012.

———. *Uncertain Poetries: Selected Essays on Poets, Poetry and Poetics*. Cambridge: Salt, 2005.

Hertz, David Michael. "Ives's *Concord Sonata* and the Texture of Music." *Charles Ives and His World*. Ed. Peter J. Burkholder. Princeton: Princeton UP, 1996. 74–117.

Hilton, Tim. *John Ruskin*. Single-volume ed. 1985 and 2000; New Haven: Yale UP, 2002.

Hunt, John Dixon. *Nature Over Again: The Garden Art of Ian Hamilton Finlay*. London: Reaktion, 2008.

———. *The Wider Sea: A Life of John Ruskin*. New York: Viking, 1982.

Ives, Charles. *Essays Before a Sonata, The Majority, and Other Writings*. Ed. Howard Boatwright. New York: Norton, 1962.

———. *Memos*. Ed. John Kirkpatrick. New York: Norton, 1972.

Jameson, Fredric. *Postmodernism; or, The Cultural Logic of Late Capitalism*. Durham, NC: Duke UP, 1991.

Jarnot, Lisa. *Robert Duncan, The Ambassador from Venus: A Biography*. Berkeley: U of California P, 2012.

Johnson, Ronald. *The American Table: More Than 400 Recipes That Make Accessible for the First Time the Full Richness of American Regional Cooking*. New York: William Morrow, 1984.

———. *ARK*. 1996; Chicago: Flood Editions, 2013.

———. *The Book of the Green Man*. New York: Norton, 1967.

———. "Charles Ives: Two Eyes, Two Ears." *Parnassus: Poetry in Review* 3.2 (1975): 345–49

———. "From the Notebooks." Ed. Peter O'Leary. *Facture* 1 (2000): 59–98.

———. "Hurrah for Euphony: Dedicated to Young Poets." *The Cultural Society*. <http://www.culturalsociety.org/texts/prose/hurrah-for-euphony-dedicated-to-young-poets/>.

———. *A Line of Poetry, a Row of Trees*. Highlands, NC: Jargon, 1964.

———. "Planting the Rod of Aaron." *Northern Lights: Studies in Creativity* 2 (1985–1986): 1–13.

———. *Radi os*. 1977; Chicago: Flood Editions, 2005.

———. *The Shrubberies*. Ed. Peter O'Leary. Chicago: Flood Editions, 2001.

———. *Sports and Divertissements*. Dunsyre, Scotland: Wild Hawthorn, 1965.

———. *To Do As Adam Did: Selected Poems*. Ed. Peter O'Leary. Jersey City, NJ: Talisman House, 2000.

———. *Valley of the Many-Colored Grasses*. New York: Norton, 1969.

Johnson, Samuel. *Samuel Johnson (The Oxford Authors)*. Ed. Donald Greene. Oxford: Oxford UP, 1984.

Jones, David. *Epoch and Artist: Selected Writings*. Ed. Harmon Grisewood. New York: Chilmark P, 1955.

Joyce, James. *A Portrait of the Artist as a Young Man: Text, Criticism, Notes*. Ed. Chester G. Anderson. 1964; Harmondsworth, Eng.: Penguin, 1977.

———. *Ulysses: The Corrected Text*. Ed. Hans Walter Gabler et al. New York: Random House, 1986.

Joyce, Stanislaus. *My Brother's Keeper: James Joyce's Early Years*. Ed. Richard Ellmann. New York: Viking, 1958.

Katz, Vincent. *Black Mountain: Experiment in Art*. 2003; Cambridge: MIT P, 2013.

Keats, John. *The Selected Letters of John Keats*. Ed. Lionel Trilling. Garden City, NY: Doubleday, 1956.

Kelly, Robert. *Axon Dendron Tree*. Annandale-on-Hudson, NY: Matter, 1967.

Kenner, Hugh. *A Homemade World: The American Modernist Writers*. 1975; Baltimore: Johns Hopkins UP, 1989.

———. *The Pound Era*. Berkeley: U of California P, 1971.

Kleinzhler, August. *Storm Over Hackensack*. Mt. Kisco: Moyer Bell Limited, 1985.

Lacoue-Labarthe, Philippe and Jean-Luc Nancy. *The Literary Absolute: The Theory of Literature in German Romanticism*. Trans. Philip Barnard and Cheryl Lester. Albany: State U of New York P, 1988.

Leeds, John. *Renaissance Syntax and Subjectivity: Ideological Contents of Latin and the Vernacular in Scottish Prose Chronicles*. Farnham, Eng.: Ashgate, 2010.

Lutyens, Mary. *Millais and the Ruskins*. New York: Vanguard, 1967.

MacDiarmid, Hugh. *Letters*. Ed. Alan Bold. Athens: U of Georgia P, 1984.

Mac Low, Jackson. *Representative Works: 1938–1985*. New York: Roof Books, 1986.

Malcolm, Janet. *The Silent Woman: Sylvia Plath and Ted Hughes*. New York: Knopf, 1994.

Mallarmé, Stéphane. *Œuvres complètes I*. Ed. Bertrand Marchal. Paris: Pléiade, 1998.

———. *Œuvres complètes II*. Ed. Bertrand Marchal. Paris: Pléiade, 2003.

———. *Selected Prose Poems, Essays, and Letters*. Trans. Bradford Cook. Baltimore: Johns Hopkins UP, 1956.

Marvell, Andrew. *The Complete Poems*. Ed. Elizabeth Story Donno. Harmondsworth, Eng.: Penguin, 1972.

Matthias, John. *Beltane at Aphelion: Longer Poems*. Athens, OH: Sparrow P/Ohio UP, 1995.

———. *Collected Longer Poems*. Bristol, Eng.: Shearsman, 2012.

———. *Collected Shorter Poems, Volume 2: 1995–2011*. Bristol, Eng.: Shearsman, 2011.

———. *New Selected Poems*. Cambridge, Eng.: Salt, 2004.

———. *Pages: New Poems and Cuttings*. Athens: Swallow P/Ohio UP, 2000.

———. *Swimming at Midnight: Selected Shorter Poems*. Athens: Swallow P/Ohio UP, 1995.

———. *Trigons*. Bristol: Shearsman, 2010.

———. *Working Progress, Working Title*. Cambridge, Eng.: Salt, 2002.

Maud, Ralph. *Charles Olson at the Harbor*. Vancouver: Talonbooks, 2008.

———. *Charles Olson's Reading: A Biography*. Carbondale: Southern Illinois UP, 1996.

———. *What Does Not Change: The Significance of Charles Olson's "The Kingfishers."* Madison, NJ: Fairleigh Dickinson UP, 1997.

McFarland, Thomas. *Romanticism and the Forms of Ruin: Wordsworth, Coleridge, and Modalities of Fragmentation*. Princeton: Princeton UP, 1981.

McGann, Jerome J. *Black Riders: The Visible Language of Modernism*. Princeton: Princeton UP, 1993.

———. *The Textual Condition*. Princeton: Princeton UP, 1991.

McHugh, Heather. *Broken English: Poetry and Partiality*. Hanover, NH: Wesleyan UP, 1993.

Melnick, David. *Men in Aida, Book One*. Berkeley: Tuumba, 1983.

———. *Pcoet*. San Francisco: G.A.W.K., 1975.

Milton, John. *The Riverside Milton*. Ed. Roy Flannagan. Boston: Houghton Mifflin, 1998.

Mullen, Harryette. *Blues Baby: Early Poems*. Lewisburg, PA: Bucknell UP, 2002.

———. *Muse & Drudge*. Philadelphia: Singing Horse, 1995.

———. *Recyclopedia: Trimmings, S*PeRM**K*T, and Muse & Drudge*. St. Paul, MN: Graywolf, 2006.

———. *S*PeRM**K*T*. Philadelphia: Singing Horse, 1992.

———. *Sleeping with the Dictionary*. Berkeley: U of California P, 2002.

———. "Telegraphs from a Distracted Sibyl." *American Book Review* 17.3 (February–March 1996).

———. *Tree Tall Woman*. Galveston, TX: Energy Earth Communications, 1980.

———. *Trimmings*. New York: Tender Buttons, 1991.

———. *Urban Tumbleweed: Notes from a Tanka Diary*. St. Paul, MN: Graywolf P, 2013.

Murray, Caitlin, and Tim Johnson, eds. *The Present Order: Writings on the Work of Ian Hamilton Finlay*. Marfa: Marfa Book, 2010.

Nancy, Jean-Luc. *The Birth to Presence*. Trans. Brian Holmes et al. Stanford: Stanford UP, 1993.

Nelson, Cary. *Repression and Recovery: Modern American Poetry and the Politics of Cultural Memory 1910–1945*. Madison: U of Wisconsin P, 1989.

Nicholls, Peter. *George Oppen and the Fate of Modernism*. Oxford: Oxford UP, 2007.

Nietzsche, Friedrich. *The Will to Power*. Trans. Walter Kaufmann and R. J. Hollingdale. New York: Random House, 1968.

O'Leary, Peter. "Gilding the Buddha: My Apprenticeship with Ronald Johnson." *Ronald Johnson: Life and Works*. Ed. Joel Bettridge and Eric Murphy Selinger. Orono, ME: National Poetry Foundation, 2008. 587–640.

———. "An Interview with Ronald Johnson (1995)." *Ronald Johnson: Life and Works*. Ed. Joel Bettridge and Eric Murphy Selinger. Orono, ME: National Poetry Foundation, 2008. 561–85.

Olson, Charles. *The Collected Poems of Charles Olson (Excluding the Maximus Poems)*. Ed. George F. Butterick. Berkeley: U of California P, 1987.

———. *Collected Prose*. Ed. Donald Allen and Benjamin Friedlander. Berkeley: U of California P, 1997.

———. *The Maximus Poems*. Ed. George F. Butterick. Berkeley: U of California P, 1985.

———. *Selected Writings*. Ed. Robert Creeley. New York: New Directions, 1966.

Oppen, George. *New Collected Poems*. Ed. Michael Davidson. New York: New Directions, 2002.

Oppen, Mary. *Meaning a Life: An Autobiography*. Santa Barbara: Black Sparrow, 1978.

Oysterband. *Deserters*. Ryko Records, RCD 10237, 1992.

Palmer, Michael. *The Lion Gate: Selected Poems 1972–1995*. New York: New Directions, 1998.

Panofsky, Erwin. *Three Essays on Style*. Ed. Irving Lavin. Cambridge: MIT P, 1995.

Penberthy, Jenny, ed. *Niedecker and the Correspondence with Zukofsky, 1931–1970*. Cambridge: Cambridge UP, 1993.

———. "A Posse of Two: Lorine Niedecker and Ian Hamilton Finlay." *Chapman 78–79* (1994): 17–22.

Perloff, Marjorie. *21st Century Modernism: The "New" Poetics*. Oxford: Blackwell, 2002.

Phillips, Tom. *A Humument: A Treated Victorian Novel*. 5th ed. London: Thames & Hudson, 2012.

Pound, Ezra. *ABC of Reading*. New York: New Directions, 1960.

———. *The Cantos*. New York: New Directions, 1995.

———. *Literary Essays*. Ed. T. S. Eliot. 1935; New York: New Directions, 1968.

———. *Poems and Translations*. Ed. Richard Sieburth. New York: Library of America, 2003.

———. *Selected Letters 1907–1941*. Ed. D. D. Paige. 1950; New York: New Directions, 1971.

———. *Selected Prose, 1909–1965*. Ed. William Cookson. New York: New Directions, 1973.

———. *The Spirit of Romance*. New York: New Directions, 1968.

Prunty, Wyatt. "Emaciated Poetry." *Sewanee Review* 93.1 (Winter 1985): 78–94.

Prynne, J. H. *Stars, Tigers and the Shape of Words*. London: Birkbeck College, 1993.

———. *Wound Response*. Cambridge, Eng.: Street Editions, 1974.

Puttenham, George. *The Arte of English Poesie*. 1589; facsimile repr., Kent, OH: Kent State UP, 1970.

Rainey, Lawrence. *Ezra Pound and the Monument of Culture: Text, History and the Malatesta Cantos*. Chicago: U of Chicago P, 1991.

Reece, Erik Anderson. *A Balance of Quinces: The Paintings and Drawings of Guy Davenport*. New York: New Directions, 1996

Rilke, Rainer Maria. *Selected Poetry*. Trans. Stephen Mitchell. New York: Vintage, 1984.

Rosenblum, Roger. *Transformations in Late Eighteenth Century Art*. Princeton: Princeton UP, 1967.

Rothenberg, Jerome. *Gematria*. Los Angeles: Sun & Moon, 1994.

Rumaker, Michael. *Black Mountain Days: A Memoir*. Black Mountain: Black Mountain College Museum and Arts Center, 2003

Ruskin, John. *The Brantwood Diary of John Ruskin*. Ed. Helen Gill Viljoen. New Haven: Yale UP, 1971.

———. *Works*. 39 vols.. Ed. E. T. Cook and Alexander Wedderburn. London: George Allen, 1903–1912.

Samperi, Frank. *Lumen Gloriae*. New York: Grossman, 1973.

———. *The Prefiguration*. New York: Grossman, 1971.

———. *Quadrifarium*. New York: Grossman, 1973.

Saussure, Ferdinand de. *Course in General Linguistics*. Ed. Charles Bally and Albert Schehaye. Trans. Roy Harris. La Salle, IL: Open Court, 1983.

Schlegel, Friedrich. *Philosophical Fragments*. Trans. Peter Firchow. Minneapolis: U of Minnesota P, 1991.

Schmidt, Michael. *Lives of the Poets*. London: Weidenfeld and Nicolson, 1998.

Scholem, Gershom. *Kabbalah*. 1974; New York: Dorset, 1987.

Scott, Sir Walter. *The Antiquary*. New York: Collier, n.d.

———. *The Journal of Sir Walter Scott*. Ed. W. E. K. Anderson. 1972; Edinburgh: Canongate, 1998.

———. *Waverley; or, 'Tis Sixty Years Since*. New York: Collier, n.d.

Scroggins, Mark. *Anarchy*. New York: Spuyten Duyvil, 2003.

———. *The Poem of a Life: A Biography of Louis Zukofsky*. Emeryville, CA: Shoemaker & Hoard, 2007.

Sedley, David. "Plato's *Cratylus*." Stanford Encyclopedia of Philosophy. <http://plato.stanford.edu/entries/plato-cratylus/>.

Seidman, Hugh. *Blood Lord*. New York: Doubleday, 1974.

———. *Collecting Evidence*. New Haven: Yale UP, 1970.
———. *Throne/Falcon/Eye*. New York: Random House, 1982.
Selinger, Eric Murphy. "*ARK* as a Garden of Revelation." *Ronald Johnson: Life and Works*. Ed. Joel Bettridge and Eric Murphy Selinger. Orono, ME: National Poetry Foundation, 2008. 323–42.
Sewell, Elizabeth. *The Orphic Voice: Poetry and Natural History*. 1960; New York: Harper, 1971.
Sheeler, Jessie. *Little Sparta: The Garden of Ian Hamilton Finlay*. Photographs by Andrew Lawson. London: Frances Lincoln, 2003.
Silliman, Ron. *The Alphabet*. Tuscaloosa: U of Alabama P, 2008.
———. *The New Sentence*. New York: Roof, 1987.
———, ed. *In the American Tree: Language, Realism, Poetry*. Orono, ME: National Poetry Foundation, 1986.
Spicer, Jack. *The House That Jack Built: The Collected Lectures of Jack Spicer*. Ed. Peter Gizzi. Hanover, NH: Wesleyan UP, 1998.
———. *My Vocabulary Did This to Me: The Collected Poetry of Jack Spicer*. Ed. Peter Gizzi and Kevin Killian. Middletown, CT: Wesleyan UP, 2008.
Starobinski, Jean. *1789: The Emblems of Reason*. Trans. Barbara Bray. Charlottesville: U of Virginia P, 1982.
———. *Words upon Words: The Anagrams of Ferdinand de Saussure*. New Haven: Yale UP, 1979.
Steele, Richard, and Joseph Addison. *Selections from the Tatler and the Spectator*. Ed. Angus Ross. Harmondsworth, Eng.: Penguin, 1982.
Stein, Gertrude. *Lectures in America*. 1935; Boston: Beacon P, 1985.
Stevens, Wallace. *Opus Posthumous*. Ed. Milton J. Bates. New York: Knopf, 1989.
Stratton, Dirk. *Ronald Johnson*. Western Writers Series 122. Boise, ID: Boise State UP, 1996.
Taggart, John. *Crosses: Poems 1992–1998*. London: Stop P, 2006.
———. *Dodeka*. Milwaukee: Membrane P, 1979.
———. *Loop*. Los Angeles: Sun & Moon, 1991.
———. *Peace on Earth*. Berkeley: Turtle Island Foundation, 1981.
———. *The Pyramid Is a Pure Crystal*. New Rochelle, NY: Elizabeth P, 1974.
———. *Remaining in Light: Ant Meditations on a Painting by Edward Hopper*. Albany, NY: State U of New York P, 1993.
———. *Songs of Degrees: Essays on Contemporary Poetry and Poetics*. Tuscaloosa: U of Alabama P, 1994.
———. *Standing Wave*. Providence, RI: Lost Roads, 1993.
Terrell, Carroll F. "Louis Zukofsky: An Eccentric Profile." *Louis Zukofsky: Man and Poet*. Ed. Carroll F. Terrell. Orono, ME: National Poetry Foundation, 1979. 31–74.
Thompson, Richard. *Hand of Kindness*. Hannibal Records, HNCD 1313, 1983.
Thoreau, Henry David. *The Journal of Henry David Thoreau*. 2 vols. Ed. Bradford Torrey and Francis H. Allen. 1906; New York: Dover, 1962.

———. *A Week on the Concord and Merrimack Rivers, Walden, The Maine Woods, Cape Cod*. Ed. Robert F. Sayre. New York: Library of America, 1985.

Von Hallberg, Robert. *American Poetry and Culture, 1945–1980*. Cambridge, MA: Harvard UP, 1985.

Watten, Barrett. *Bad History*. Berkeley: Atelos, 1998.

Whitman, Walt. *Complete Poetry and Collected Prose*. Ed. Justin Kaplan. New York: Library of America, 1982.

Williams, William Carlos. *Imaginations*. Ed. Webster Schott. New York: New Directions, 1970.

Williams-Ellis, Amabel. *The Exquisite Tragedy: An Intimate Life of John Ruskin*. Garden City, NY: Doubleday Doran, 1929.

Wittgenstein, Ludwig. *Philosophical Investigations*. 3rd ed. Trans. G. E. M. Anscombe. 1953; New York: Macmillan, 1968.

———. *Tractatus Logico-Philosophicus*. Trans. C. K. Ogden. 1922; London: Routledge & Kegan Paul, 1981.

Warrell, Ian. *Turner's Secret Sketches*. London: Tate, 2012.

Wolff, Cynthia Griffin. *Emily Dickinson*. New York: Knopf, 1987.

Wordsworth, William. *Poetical Works*. Ed. Thomas Hutchinson, rev. Ernest de Selincourt Oxford: Oxford UP, 1969.

Yates, Frances A. *The Art of Memory*. Chicago: U of Chicago P, 1966.

Zukofsky, Louis. *"A"*. 1978; New York: New Directions, 2011.

———. *"A" 1–12*. Garden City, NY: Doubleday, 1967.

———. *Anew: Complete Shorter Poetry*. New York: New Directions, 2011.

———. *Autobiography*. New York: Grossman, 1970.

———. *Prepositions+: The Collected Critical Essays*. Hanover, NH: Wesleyan UP, 2000.

Index